T0304604

STRATEGY AND RISK MANAGEMENT

Ron Rael, CPA, CGMA

13602-359

Powered by

Notice to Readers

Strategy and Risk Management: An Integrated Practical Approach does not represent an official position of the American Institute of Certified Public Accountants, and it is distributed with the understanding that the author and the publisher are not rendering legal, accounting, or other professional services in this publication. If legal advice or other expert assistance is required, the services of a competent professional should be sought.

1 2 3 4 5 6 7 8 9 0 PIP 1 9 8 7 6 5 4 3

ISBN: 978-1-94023-521-9

Dedication and Acknowledgements

I have met and known great examples of balanced risk takers. Each of them has a unique approach to managing this delicate balance between opportunity and risk and has taught me more about how to manage risk than any research material or expert.

I dedicate this work to Ann Rael, Ken Stouffer, Justin Rael and Martha Garcia. I also thank public role models such as Walt Disney, Steve Jobs, Rosa Parks, Justice Thurgood Marshall, Mother Teresa and many more whose lives demonstrate that one can be a fabulous dreamer.

I dedicate this work to the many people who take the high road when facing tough choices in their everyday lives.

"Life is being on the wire; everything else is just waiting." Karl Wallenda

Contents

Introduction

The New Opportunity

After completing a presentation in Phoenix, Arizona, and exchanging business cards with a few executives, I packed up while noticing that a few participants lingered. As I headed for the door, one of those participants, Justin, stood up when I passed his table in the ballroom of the hotel. "Can I buy you a cup of coffee, Mr. Rael?" he asked.

"Please, call me Ron. Thank you for attending. It's a pleasure to meet you." I shook his hand as he introduced himself. Justin led me to the dining area at the front of the hotel. The air around filled with the buzz of busy professionals and the aroma of freshly brewed coffee. We were silent until seated.

"I really appreciated your presentation today and was intrigued when you spoke about how vital enterprise risk management is to both profitability and longevity. I knew then that I needed your advice. I am in a quandary about what to do with an opportunity that recently arose for my company, but it's like riding a mule."

"A mule?" That was a metaphor about risk I had not heard before.

"See a mule can get me to where I want to go, yet she might throw me off in a split second and deliver a fatal kick to my head. With a mule you never know which one you might get."

"Ouch!" I winced at his rustic analogy. "That sounds more descriptive of risk taking than my taking a leap of faith." My frivolity kicked in. "What about riding a reliable horse, Justin?"

He chuckled, "If you can show me where I can find a reliable and steady steed, you are hired," he grinned back. Silently to myself I thought, "He gets my humour. That's a good sign."

After getting acquainted we set up a meeting date at my office three weeks hence. As we walked towards the conference centre's parking lot and got blasted by the 32° Celsius heat, Justin said that he would bring along his partner, Paul, and warned, "Paul may be resistant to my idea of asking for help, but I believe he will come around."

"That could be a warning or a challenge," I thought as I got into the rental car.

Three Weeks Later

The rain in Seattle, Washington, clicked against my window. Looking out I noticed the fog lifting. "It will be warmer today," I thought. My nose detected the clean scent of spring wafting in the partially open window. Ding! My Outlook calendar was reminding me about the 1.30pm meeting with our new client. I perused the file of research we conducted on Justin, Paul and their enterprise. "There has to be something that Justin didn't disclose to me." I soon found out what this meeting was really about.

Promptly 10 minutes later, Darcy ushered both men into my office. As I shook their hands and led them to my conference room, I did a quick profile. Justin, a native of New Mexico, the elder of the two, looked like he spent lots of time outdoors. He was lean, wiry, tanned and in great shape and dressed in crisp jeans, a cotton madras shirt, and new cowboy boots. Noticing his calm manner and short greying hair, I estimated his age to be over 45. Paul clearly was the dynamo of the pair and resembled a GQ model. A child of southern California he was elegantly clad in an expensive charcoal-coloured suit, matching tie and highly polished loafers without socks. Paul's tan was not from outdoors, but his light cocoa colouring matched his longish surfer-style blond hair. I guessed him to be in his mid-30s.

"We could use some of this rain in southern Arizona. Mind if I take some home with us?" Justin teased.

"Yes if we can have some of your sunshine and warm spring weather in exchange." I noticed that although Justin was playful, Paul stayed somewhat aloof. "I've got to get him to loosen up, or this could be a hard sell," I thought.

After the typical ice breaking self-introductions, exchanging of cards and discussing Seattle's wet weather, each of us relaxed.

"How can the High Road Institute (HRI) help you?" I wasn't sure how much Justin told Paul about our initial meeting in Phoenix, so I played it low key.

Paul went first. "We have been in partnership for eight and one-half years, and while I think we've accomplished a lot, I'm afraid we're at a crossroads. If Justin and I can't figure out how to see eye to eye on the future of PJ Investments (PJI), we'll have to dissolve, and ..."

Justin cut in, "It will be like a messy divorce! We'll have to liquidate most of our holdings, thus creating a lot of hurt feelings, while tarnishing our firm's reputation. I'll also take a bath on my net worth."

"I'll lose money too!" interjected Paul as he glared at Justin.

"Looks like Justin is the alpha male in this partnership, but Paul wants to be," I noted to myself.

Justin stayed quiet. Paul spoke up, "I believe that we should and can continue to work together, but ..."

Waiting a beat I asked, "But what, Paul?"

"We used to be in sync about the investments we made, but lately all we do is argue."

"What do you disagree about?"

"Where to put our investment dollars." Justin sat up in his chair as he said this. "Paul takes too many risks."

"I do not! You've become too complacent!" From this unwarranted emphasis I could tell Paul was hurting and a bit angry.

I sat on my chair's edge and took control of the conversation in order to prevent any more arguments. "You want us to help you define your risk appetite, I assume."

Paul took my hint and sat back, "If that's what you call it. Justin told me about your expertise when he returned from the executive briefing he attended. I watched your DVD, and two things really hit home for me. You spoke about balance and about the cost you cannot afford. I tried to look at this situation objectively and saw that we are missing both of them. I feel we are not in balance because Justin and I have different opinions on this unaffordable cost."

Facing Paul, Justin said, "What I believe that Ron's firm can do for us, Paul, is to add some structure to our approaches to the risks we choose. It struck me that we have been extremely lucky because most of our risky ventures paid off in the past, but the stakes are higher today, and I don't think we can afford to make any mistakes with future investments, especially with the one that fell into our lap last month. That's the one I told you about in Phoenix, Ron."

I turned to Paul, "You have an equal stake in this decision. Is that what you want?"

"Well... I only have information about your services from your website, but when I read your blogs regarding how managing risk requires a thoughtful, disciplined approach, I agreed with Justin that we should ask you to work with us."

"That is what we can do," I replied. We took a break to replenish our coffee, and I gave them a tour of HRI's facilities. We chatted as I introduced them to the HRI team. They asked many questions. As we headed back to my office I could tell Paul had cooled off.

I asked, "Do the two of you have time today, so that we can define the scope of this project?" We spent the next three hours and our lunch time going over the specifics of how HRI could assist them to do a better job of assessing, managing and mitigating risk. I explained that this work would require a shift in their firm's culture. At the time they didn't realise what this meant and why it is necessary.

We met numerous times over the next seven months, mostly in Phoenix where it averaged 38° Celsius. (I don't do heat well!) I introduced them to many of the tools that are available to successfully avoid worst case scenarios. In the end the two partners adopted the same risk appetite, and their firm grew by 30% that year. Despite the pain that comes with change, the culture of PJI and all the subsidiaries are now more risk savvy. In addition its ability to take more risks has improved. In risk management this is known as your risk appetite.

I am using the experiences we had with Justin, Paul and PJI as a case study to explain how you too can introduce proper disciplined risk management into your company or organisation. I will share with you the tools they employ. I will share with you the stories I use to illustrate the basic concepts of proper risk management and how your efforts will pay off in the areas of stronger leadership, profitability and flexibility.

Note: For the rest of the book the content approximately will be how I explain the concepts to Justin, Paul and the rest of our clients. All our client's names and information are altered for confidentiality purposes.

"Only those who will risk going too far can possibly find out how far one can go." T.S. Eliot

1

Introduction to Enterprise Risk Management

"Is there something wrong with me because I am scared to take a risk?" Lila K.

It is not just the large, complex or regulated organisation that needs proper risk management–every organisation needs it.

Unforeseen events take place every day and in many unexpected ways: the global economic meltdown; Hurricane Katrina; the tsunami in Southeast Asia; Japan's catastrophic earthquake; the September 11 attacks; or the uprising against the political leaders of Egypt, Tunisia and Libya. Each of those events was unexpected, but having a proper risk management plan in place will help any organisation survive such catastrophic occurrences.

Enterprise risk management (ERM) extends to your everyday business decisions because employees take actions and make decisions daily that could have a detrimental effect on your profits and business's longevity and future. Employees make dozens of decisions daily, and any one of them could come back to bite you, even when the decision does not seem to have hidden or unknown ramifications.

That is why your organisation must have a protocol in place for identifying and mitigating all major business risk long before it is needed.

This easy-to-understand and innovative book will help your organisation jump-start the process of establishing an enterprise wide risk management programme. The best news is that a programme is not expensive. Your major investment consists of expanding your firm's planning and communication processes and getting employees involved in the effort. The real price of ERM is a shift in your cultural norms that, sadly, is a "cost" some executives are reluctant to pay.

The tools and ideas in this ERM road map will make your organisation flexible, which allows you to capitalise on pleasant and unexpected opportunities and survive major threats. Practising formal disciplined risk management is like training to run a marathon. Even if you never enter a race you are already capable of doing so.

That is what true risk management is about: your organisation owning the capability to handle any aspect of Murphy's Law, the well-known saying, "If anything can go wrong, it will."

Who This Book Is for

This book is written for business owners and key decision makers because they are often the ones who decide if a risk or an opportunity is worth taking. This book is also a guidebook for both risk takers and risk avoiders. Even in the upside of risk taking, costs must be assessed and weighed. This is what risk management is about and why we will most often address the costs and downsides. The tools I provide will address both sides of the cost-benefit ratio for taking risks.

When you have completed this book, in addition to knowing how to control or tame risk, you will have learned about

- yourself.
- how you view risk.
- what you value.

As you travel the road to proper risk management described in this book, you will experience the following:

- *Risk management tools.* These 21 ready-to-use tools will enable you and those who work for you to put into action what you have learned. Appendix A, "Roadmap," summarises each tool and organises them according to the five and one-half enterprise risk management steps that are woven throughout the book.
- *Principles of risk management.* These 15 sound bite truths help you remember and teach key elements of proper risk management.
- *Action plans.* At the end of each chapter you will be asked to apply what you have read. The quicker you do each one the faster your organisation or team will be able to lower the price tag of your opportunities.
- *Murphy's laws.* These are bits of cynical humour designed to demonstrate that even well thought-out plans can and do go awry.
- *Rhetorical questions.* Along the road, you will encounter questions that are indented and set in boldface italics. They are designed to create a pause to get in touch with your hard-won wisdom (because I believe that you already know much about navigating potholes, which is something you regularly do).
- *Illustrations and graphics.* Some readers are visual learners; therefore, these are to be used to summarise broad messages about risk management.
- *Stories and case studies.* Stories about how and how not to deal with risks are tools to communicate, learn and teach others. Our brains retain pictures and stories for a long time.
- *Self-tests and pop quizzes.* These are designed to provide you lasting insights into aspects of risk management.

It is my hope that, after reading this material, you will make a commitment of employing an ERM-driven strategic approach in running your organisation. When you reach the end you will know how to create a simple yet powerful risk management plan for your company, team and family.

Success Requires Commitment to Risk Management

Before you delve too deeply into risk management and how it will enhance your ability to achieve your goals and dreams, answer this simple quiz.

You and Risk Management Pop Quiz

In my initial meeting with Justin and Paul, the partners at PJ Investments we met in the introduction, I gave them this test. I urge you to take it, so you can see if you truly understand risk management.

When you hear or read the term risk management what do you automatically think of?

- ☐ Insurance
- ☐ Investments
- ☐ Gambling
- ☐ Opportunity
- ☐ Loss
- ☐ Danger or harm
- ☐ Profits
- ☐ (Other) ____________

Justin responded with insurance, gambling, loss and danger. Paul's choices were investments, opportunity and profits. This told me they had polar opposite views of risk.

If, like Justin and Paul, you checked at least one of the boxes for insurance, investments, gambling, loss, danger or harm, or profits, you really need to keep reading this book.

If you checked opportunity you have some understanding of risk management and probably want or need more.

Risk Management Defined

Real-world risk management is having a comfort level that whatever risks come your way, you have the ability to deal with them. This confidence comes from these three factors:

1. Murphy's law (if anything can go wrong, it will) is a reality. Risk management requires having a system or methodology in place to examine risks before you take them, and I stress the word *before*. All too often the business owner or manager worries about the impact of a major risk after the risk has been taken. This is why and when opportunities are frequently mishandled.
2. Your employees have tools to examine and measure the impact of a risk. They know how to use and apply them in their everyday decision making efforts.
3. Leaders or decision makers all across your organisation use insightful information to confidently (as opposed to rashly) step into the unknown.

As you journey through this book you will discover how to be a wise risk taker, even if, like Lila, who subsequently will be discussed, you do not see yourself as one right now. If you are a person like Paul who frequently jumps into the unknown, you will learn how to better size up your risks.

Stewardship and Risk Management

If you are a business owner, manager, supervisor, member of a board or leader of a team, one responsibility you have is to ensure everyone you lead is simultaneously on the watch for opportunities and risks. Doing so demonstrates that you are taking your stewardship responsibility seriously.

Risk management is a vital responsibility to show good stewardship when running and operating any organisation, such as

- a military unit,
- a small business,

- a government agency,
- an investment club or
- a family land and buildings venture.

It is even a primary responsibility for those who manage large publicly traded and international companies. Many organisations are choosing to implement an ERM process to ensure that a uniform approach to risk identification, measurement and treatment gets utilised in the organisation.

Cost and Risk Management

Risk management is a necessary aspect of stewardship because of this first truism:

First Principle of Risk Management

Every opportunity has a cost. Every opportunity carries a risk or downside.

Your cost or price in both a business and personal risk could be monetary or something intangible, such as your ego.

To explain the truism of the first management principle that every opportunity has a cost, let's look at the dilemma faced by High Road Institute client Lila.

Lila K. is a smart and talented woman who has a gift for innovative thinking and problem solving when working for someone else, but things changed when she became an entrepreneur. Lila was at a loss to determine why she suddenly became scared to take risks.

During a coaching session she told me, "I really could kick myself. Over the last four years I had several ideas for products that did not exist, but each time, less than a year later, someone else saw the same solution that I did and made a fortune from their idea. I'm angry because if I had been able to get even one of my ideas into the marketplace, I could very well be wealthy today. Ron, is there something wrong with me?"

This was my advice. "Lila, there is nothing wrong with you. Your view of risk, as with most business professionals, is a bit skewed because several times you saw an opportunity but did not feel comfortable taking the risk that is inherent in the opportunity."

Lila's cost was the potential profits she missed out on because she was unwilling to face the fear that someone else with a different risk appetite was willing to face. This other person with a similar idea was willing to take the risk, whereas Lila was not.

Lila asked another question. "Why do some people take a risk when others do not?"

The simple answer to this important question boils down to the price you must pay to take a risk or seize an opportunity.

When I say the word *cost* I am not referring to the concept of the price of something you buy, as in how much I pay for a loaf of bread. In risk management cost is the value that you place on something that you hold dearly yet could sacrifice or give up if you try to seize that opportunity.

In Lila's case her risk was putting money, time, reputation or something else on the line in order to turn her ideas into products. Her willingness or ability to seize the opportunity was superseded by the cost, which usually is based upon fear or something else that is considered too steep to pay. I gave Lila a copy of a favourite quotation from the author Win Borden, whose advice she could memorise and follow.

"If you wait to do everything until you're sure it's right,
you'll probably never do much of anything."

The Cost of Success

Success in both life and business requires taking risks. As the first principle of risk management will tell you, the "cost" or price when you strive for success is taking risks. Humankind's history is littered with tales about four sorts of people:

1. Unsuccessful people who never took risks, the vast majority of whom were unwilling to pay the price
2. Unsuccessful people who took rash risks and unconsciously paid the price
3. Successful people who took wise risks and unconsciously paid the price
4. Successful people who took wise risks and consciously paid the price

Justin and Paul were in the third group, and my job was to move them into the fourth group, which is where you also want to be. This book shows you how to become one of this fourth group who take wise risks and know the costs.

Sceptics Exist

According to a survey by the American Institute of Certified Public Accountants and the Chartered Institute of Management Accountants, 45% of companies with a median revenue of $50m lack an ERM programme and do not plan to implement one.

Source: http://www.aicpa.org/InterestAreas/BusinessIndustryAndGovernment/Resources/ERM/DownloadableDocuments/Enterprise%20Risk%20v3.pdf

The Cost of Failure

An example of an ultimate risk taker is Paul Allen, cofounder of Microsoft. Allen is amongst the richest people in the world. He was featured in the May 3, 2004, *Business Week* article "The $12 Billion Education of Paul Allen." Allen has lost $12 billion of his net worth while developing as a manager and an entrepreneur. Twelve billion dollars! He invested money in different ideas and enterprises for many years and lost money on each one. He took (and still does take) tremendous risks with his money.

Think about these questions:

- How many companies can afford to lose $12 billion to learn how to take risks?
- How many companies can afford to lose $1m to learn how to take risks?
- How much can you afford to lose when your next opportunity fails to materialise?
- Can you afford to undertake an expensive education on how to take safe risks?

That is the rationale for this book's theme: conditioning yourself and those around you to regularly ask, "Are we able to pay the cost for that particular risk?"

Managing everyday risk in business and life boils down to asking yourself, "What is the cost I cannot afford?"

You should ask yourself this question before you do something that you define as risky.

Summary of Risk Management– Watching for the Potholes

Murphy's Law of Business Mishaps

Anything that can go wrong in a business setting will take place when you are out of the office or on vacation. The longer you are away the bigger the problem.

Risks are like a pothole in the road of life. They are not easy to spot when travelling at the speed of business. When you hit one and feel your car shake you wish you had seen it sooner, so that you could have avoided that awful frame-jarring sensation to your car and body.

A risk is also like the mule Justin described. You can hope for the best—a peaceful ride—while simultaneously planning for the worst—rejection or a kick to the head.

This is proper risk management in a nutshell: a systematic and holistic way for your organisation to view and define risk taking, so that you understand the costs you can and cannot afford well in advance. Then when you hit a pothole or encounter the capricious Mr Murphy, you will know how to handle the situation, so that what you put at risk is not so costly to you or your organisation.

"One of life's joys is crashing into the unknown. One of life's miseries is when the unknown crashes into you." Ron Rael

Your Action Plan

Step One

Complete the "You and Risk Management" pop quiz. How do you currently define risk management? Think about why you define it that way. How is your definition affected by the chances you take?

Step Two

Make a list of costs that you cannot afford. This could be harm to your family, damage to your reputation or loss of your job. Think about why these are important to you, other than their financial value.

Step Three

How do you plan on using the information you take away from this book? In other words what problems or issues do you hope this information will address?

2

The WHAT of Risk Management

"I wish I had looked before I leapt. If I had, I might not be so deep in debt and unemployed!" Peter G.

I travelled to Phoenix, Arizona, to meet with the entire team of 67 talented people who managed PJ Investments' (PJI's) diverse business portfolio. In an air-conditioned, recently remodelled conference room, I spent the better part of a day explaining to them what risk management was all about for their organisation.

I briefly discussed the definition of *risk management* in the previous chapter, but now I will go more in depth.

What Risk Management Is

Risk management is the process of identifying, prioritising and mitigating the impact of unforeseen events. It is a form of proactive contingency planning designed to avoid difficult situations or to prepare your organisation for undesirable consequences. It is a process for lessening the negative impact of choices you make while acknowledging Murphy's Law.

Daily you face innumerable risks, and the function of risk management is to address the most critical ones that can disrupt your organisation, harm its business model or negatively impact any of your numerous stakeholders. Risk management encompasses both financial risks and everyday business risks. Critical risks are those that are integral to conducting business or that threaten your business's continuity. Their potential costly impact requires that they receive special attention and that you devote resources to managing them.

Risk management is about assessing what level of risk appetite you are willing to accept and what level is appropriate for the near future. Your risk appetite will frequently change. When you proactively manage risk you must ask and answer the following questions:

- Are my organisation's critical risks being managed to minimise the likelihood that events would adversely affect the achievement of my business objectives?
- Do we have a formal risk assessment process in existence now?

Let us understand why we even need to discuss the formal management of perceived risk in a business organisation. A story about one of my clients, Peter, illustrates the main reason.

The Born (Entrepreneur) Incident

Infected with entrepreneuritis at an early age, Peter is a born risk taker who loves to reach for the brass ring, but whenever he does he rarely sweats the details. Seven years ago Peter envisioned himself as an entrepreneur but lacked the money and wherewithal to start from scratch. While reading an issue of *Success* magazine Peter noticed an ad for people who want to control their own destiny. This had been a dream as long as he could remember.

Peter followed up and discovered that he could purchase a pizza franchise for only $75,000 down. At that time he only had $40,000, but he was determined to become his own boss and scraped together the rest of the money, mostly by convincing his father-in-law, Jon Smithers, to lend him $25,000.

After six years of hard work and long hours, Peter's pizzeria had a steady customer base and started to turn a profit. Due to his blind devotion to this business and other personal reasons, Peter's wife (the former Miss Smithers) filed for divorce. Her father immediately demanded that Peter repay his debt. Short of cash Peter approached a regional bank for a line of credit, telling the bank that he needed more capital to grow the business. Although this was factual he intentionally omitted the real purpose for the money.

As he signed the lengthy loan documents, Peter failed to notice that there was a provision in this line of credit that could potentially place it into default if any of the facts he provided were misrepresented.

Less than one year later a lending officer discovered that Peter used most of the loan proceeds to pay off Mr Smithers. Peter failed to disclose this liability on the loan application form. His bank was very risk averse due to its big losses in subprime lending. The wary banker, fearing that Peter may have omitted other facts, convinced his loan committee to declare Peter's line of credit in default. Once that happened the bank cleaned out the pizzeria's current account.

Peter was left without the cash he needed to buy supplies, pay employees or make interest payments to the franchisor, which then declared the franchisee agreement in default and forced the closing of Peter's pizza parlour. Because he had signed a personal guarantee for his business's many debts, which at the time he felt were of no consequence, Peter found himself alone; without a business; in debt to the tune of $600,000; and without any source of income.

In our coaching session soon after this took place, Peter sighed and told me, "I guess I should have paid more attention to the details of what I was getting myself into. I always seem to jump into the deep end of the pool before testing the waters. Is that a bad thing, Ron?"

I responded, "Entrepreneurs, investors and innovators love to charge ahead when an opportunity arises. This is not your problem. What is reckless is you failed to do adequate planning before you decided to chase that dream."

Peter, prior to meeting with us, did not practise any risk management, yet his appetite for risk was voracious, which placed him in peril. Because he failed to dispassionately think about what could go wrong, he mismanaged an opportunity, and the personal and professional cost to him was steep. It never entered into his thought process that there could be potholes on the road to success.

What Risk Management Is Not

Whenever I am introduced as someone who consults and speaks on risk management, I am usually asked one of two questions: "Do you sell insurance?" or "Do you sell investments?" The reason for these questions has to do with people's skewed view of risk management. People generally associate it with a specific effort, such as deciding how much insurance coverage they need or managing their investment portfolio.

Having adequate insurance coverage is only one infinitesimal piece of risk management, which you will soon discover. In fact, in this entire book, only one small section is devoted to insurance coverage.

Risk Taking Versus Risk Management

Many managers and executives fail to see the difference between risk taking and risk management. Quite often seasoned managers and executives tell me, "Risk management prevents risk taking."

Nothing could be further from the truth. You will be a smarter risk taker when you practise risk management. You take risks every day but may not practise risk management.

First, risk management is more than just worrying about tomorrow. In today's world so many things can go wrong to keep you from staying in business. Second, if your company is not innovating or growing, it will not survive. These two realities mean that every organisation must have a clearly defined risk management programme that equips employees with tools to anticipate the cost or downside of each risk faced.

Risk management assists you and other decision makers in making informed choices, prioritising actions and distinguishing among alternative courses of action.

> **Murphy's Law of Risk's Urgency**
>
> The more urgent the problem the more people will demand that it be allowed to run its natural course.

Risk Taking Is Necessary for Survival

Each time you take a risk you are undertaking an exercise in being creative. Risk taking is a willingness to face your fears and a choice to differently do or see something. You use your natural curiosity and creativity to try something new, unique or untested. As a species we would not have survived if man did not take risks. Things we now take for granted, such as the following, would never have taken place if some person had not been a risk taker:

- *Eating certain foods.* Some human had to be the first to eat a bird's egg, blue cheese or a kumquat.
- *Flying and driving.* We once thought these as impossible.
- *Using electricity.* Its initial use was by the state to execute convicts.
- *Creating high rise buildings.* Living 136 stories off the ground.
- *Crossing dangerous, wide bodies of water with bridges.*
- *Sailing far away or around the world.* Remember Magellan?
- *Changing the course of nature.*
- *Running for office.*

Risk Management Is Necessary for Success and Growth

Risk management does not prevent you from taking risks. Instead it makes you aware that Mr Murphy could pop up when you least expect him, and when he does you will know how to protect yourself and your organisation.

Another way to examine the relationship is as follows. Risk is a given, and you rarely have a choice in the matter and outcome. You never know where the potholes are located, but you don't have to place yourself or your treasures in peril. Risk management is a voluntary activity that you do have a choice in, and you influence the outcome. You look for the potholes and do your best to avoid them or at least not let them disrupt your plans.

The successful and sustainable business must take calculated risks in order to achieve its specific objectives and carry out its defined strategies. Your organisation must measure its risks, try to minimise them, and if possible use the risk to its advantage. Risk management must be an integral part of all your organisational processes.Risk management is an attitude and a skill that will ensure your organisation is around for a long time. It directly affects your profitability and indirectly affects budgeting, employee morale, reputation, insurance costs, internal controls and disaster planning.

The importance of conducting regular risk assessments grows each day because uncertainty, volatility and catastrophic risks are here to stay. The world has transformed from a series of loosely connected, reasonably predictable economies to a complex web of relationships in which the global impact of local events is almost simultaneously felt.

Another reason why risk management is not a flavour of the month topic is the following truism:

> **Second Principle of Risk Management**
>
> The past is not a good predictor of the future.

Many organisations, and yours may be one, must take on more and more risks to survive through growth, innovation, technology or global expansion. Each time you do this your risk exposure grows. By seeing the relationship between risk and risk taking, you will fully understand why this is a requirement for longevity in business and life in general.

Relationship of Risk and Risk Taking

As shown in this graphic (Figure 2-1) there is a direct correlation between risk taking and the amount of the risks undertaken. In other words, when your organisation increases its risk taking as it moves into the unknown future, it will be exposed to a greater number of risks with potential positive or negative consequences. Unfortunately, like Peter, many entrepreneurs and owners of small to mid-sized businesses do not find out about this one-to-one relationship until it is too late. The people who suffer from this expensive wisdom are the firm's employees and its investors and creditors and, often, their families.

Figure 2-1
Relationship between Opportunity and Risks Faced

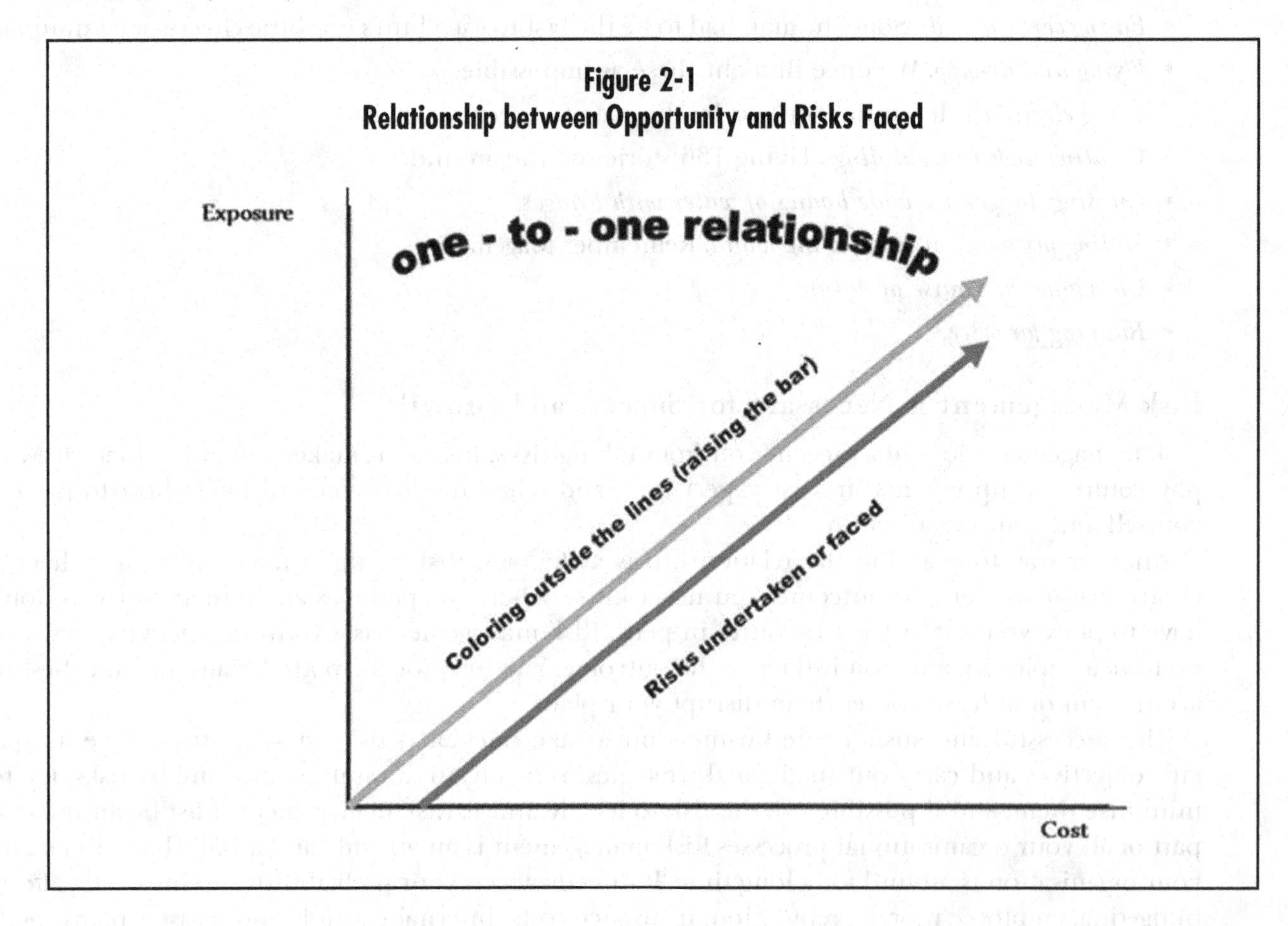

Peter chased an opportunity to become his own boss, a laudable risk, but he failed to realise that his exposure or vulnerability drastically grew. Because he ignored some basic fundamentals of running his own show, the risk was greater than the opportunity. Peter's "cost" was more than he could afford because his risk appetite was low, but the exposure was high.

Risk management is not an isolated or a stand-alone activity that is separate from the main work your business performs. Risk mismanagement is a major stewardship responsibility of the entire management team and an integral part of all your organisational processes, especially strategic planning and change management.

Other Viewpoints

Christopher Grose, a consultant with the firm Risk Controls Group, very succinctly articulates what risk management is all about. Grose was quoted in *Business 2.0* magazine stating, "Risk management is all about helping you to take the risks..not to avoid them but take them in the knowledge that you can handle them" (Volume 3, 2002).

Jeff Burchill, a knowledgeable expert in the insurance field,is quoted in *Treasury &Risk* as saying that all loss is preventable (http://www.treasuryandrisk.com/2008/12/01/cfos-to-watch). He is the CFO of FM Global, a 175-year-old commercial property insurer. Burchill is not saying that risk management is the same as buying insurance; rather, you purchase coverage to help you recover when you hit an unexpected and costly pothole.

Both experts remind us that confidence and foresight are the ways to lower the negative impact of your risks, which is a major intention of formalised risk management.

What Risk Is

I now turn your attention to what risk looks like and why it is not, as some people believe, gambling or bad outcomes.

Risk Can Be Seen from Two Views

An organisation whose corporate culture fosters smart and innovative behaviours and decisions must have two major components of dealing with risk in its risk management programme. One is a global view (10,000-metre view) on the strategic level. The second is a localised (100-metre view) analysis of risk on the individual level. If any of your employees cannot adequately define the risk undertaken before they act, the resulting high costs could damage your firm's reputation and future. Both views are important and support each other.

Every company must address the potential impact of unexpected events that could have major financial consequences. Sadly not all organisations have a culture that is prepared for the deep analysis, agile detection and quick response required for risk management.

The 10,000-Metre View of Risk

Pilots who fly jets rely on sophisticated instruments to "see" their destination and all obstacles because they cannot adequately do this with their eyes. Similarly, because you cannot be everywhere at once, your corporate culture norms and risk management system allow you to detect costly or painful hazards and obstacles in the hullabaloo of daily business.

The 100-Metre View of Risk

Employees see risk in their daily work because they are the ones who touch the product, deliver the service, make the sale and interact with the customer. They are not aware of huge risks, yet they know of the small and mid-sized ones that can turn ugly fast. As their leader you must have an open and unfiltered channel with them, so they can advise you about these looming obstacles and potholes. Employees are your eyes and ears into the sources of many localised business risks.

In risk management you want your employees to be both risk takers and risk managers. To serve this vital role all your employees must think for themselves while being accountable for each and every risk they accidentally or intentionally undertake.

Risk Can Be Unpredictable

Predictable Risk

Each decision made and every action taken in a business setting involves humans. By extension every risk is entered into by a person. In business there are two classes of risks: predictable and unpredictable. Risks in the predictable category are those in which we can fairly predict a probable outcome in advance. Whenever you toss a coin to decide something, you can expect that the coin will land heads up 50% of the time. There is still a risk that the coin will not show the side you want or need, but statistics prove the 50% odds. According to Justin, no two mules act alike, and one that seems calm can unexpectedly kick you off.

People want all their risks to be predictable, but Murphy's Law and Justin's mule do not work that way.

Unpredictable Risk

You invest $500,000 in technology tools, but you gain no improvements in productivity or cost savings. This risk you took, despite your best efforts, is the category of risk we face most often: unpredictable risk. It is hard to predict the outcome and even harder to manage. When you add the reality that we all see risks differently, you can understand why proper risk management must include assessing the human factor when assessing or gauging risks.

People do not want their risks to be unpredictable, yet every road to success and profitability has unseen potholes. Nearly all the risks that have a steep cost or fatal downside are unpredictable.

Your Personal Risk Appetite

There is little difference between risk taking in the contexts of your job and personal life. In both venues you face known and unknown perils, and you strive each day to deal with each one as it crops up.

Because risk management is a human endeavour, it will always be affected by the individuals involved. Despite intensive research on the specific risk, whether it is a reasonable one like the decision to grow or an unreasonable one like establishing your business in a crime zone, how you decide to act (or not) will be decided by personal factors, such as the size, cost, payoff and other considerations.

Risk Management Tool One– Personal Risk Spectrum

There are many different flavours in the spectrum of individual risk taking. As a leader who is trying to build a culture that balances innovation with control and to develop employees who think for themselves, you must examine a risk through the eyes of your employees. The "Personal Risk Spectrum Tool," as shown in Figure 2-2, enables you to do that:

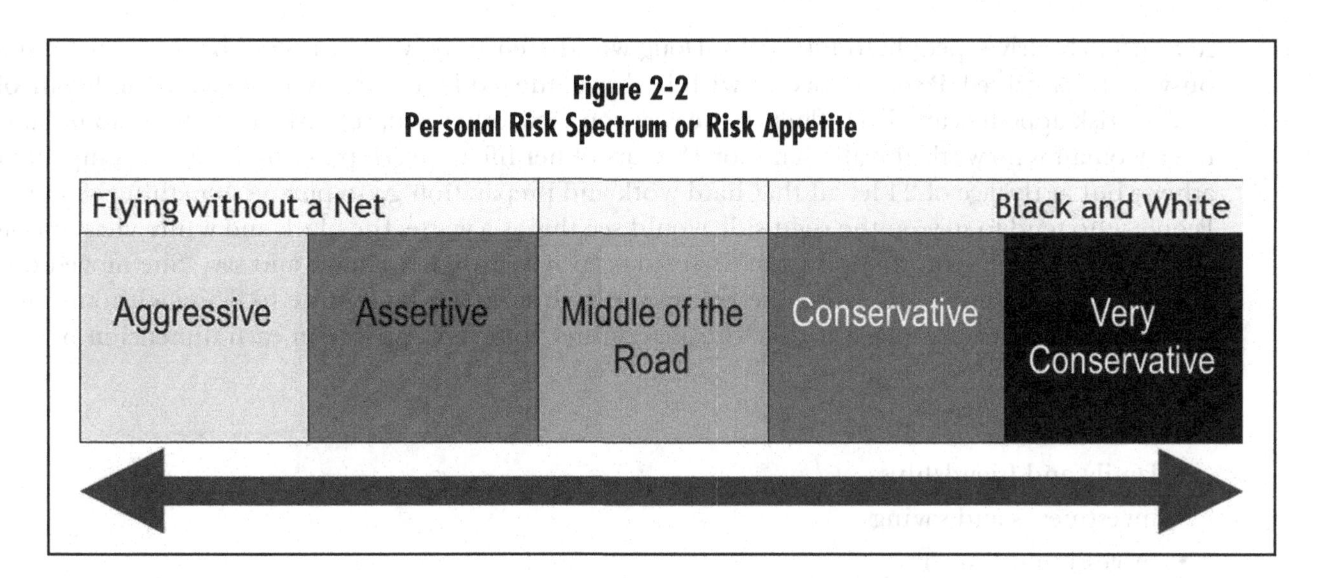

Each human being defines risk along this broad spectrum, depending on what we have at risk and the value we place upon it. I look at risk taking on the individual level as a range across a spectrum going from "flying without a net" on one end to "black and white" on the other. This tool demonstrates the wide diversity of the phenomenon referred to as risk appetite. Those who tend to stay on the right have a small appetite, and in comparison people who stay on the left have a larger appetite.

Think about your friends and colleagues and how they would fall across the risk spectrum. Maybe you socialise and work only with people who have the same risk-taking preferences as you. Maybe you have friends from all walks of life who, if you put them all in the same room, would find very little in common.

In addition to sliding across the spectrum, depending on what we hold as risky, people alter their views over time. I know many entrepreneurs who, in the early days, took all kinds of risks to get their businesses started. Then as they grew more successful and matured in their decision making, these risk takers became more cautious, conservative and even risk averse.

When the time was right I told the management team about Doug, an entrepreneur I worked for, as a way of illustrating how the personal risk spectrum tool works.

Doug and the 40-Year Itch

Doug is an example of the person who unknowingly had an itch to control his own destiny. He retired from a large national organisation after 40 years of managing his career and family finances on the black and white, or right side, of the risk spectrum. Doug was restless in retirement, so he withdrew some of his retirement funds and started a business. In this act he shifted away from his black and white view of risk regarding career and finances. Doug found a demand that was not being filled in the industry he knew and loved. His business was quasi-successful until he recognised an even greater need going unmet. Doug's new freight forwarding business grew very fast, and when he needed help he brought his two daughters into the business. In just five years, his business went from zero to grossing over ten million dollars in revenue. Soon Doug was flying without a net. Because of his willingness to take a risk, Doug built up a financial legacy for himself and rewarding careers for his daughters.

Shifting Across the Spectrum

What risk looks like to you all boils down to your individual values and what you define as precious. You use these personal intangibles in your cost-benefit ratio of looking at risk. Monetary reward rarely drives people to take risks. Doug was driven to fly without a net by the need to stay busy and feel valued. Peter jumped in with both feet fuelled by the desire for freedom and control.

Your risk appetite can also influence the way you view other people's risk-taking behaviour. Imagine a woman who worked really hard for 18 years of her life to develop her body into a competitive athlete but at the age of 24 let all that hard work and preparation go to pursue something less risky. People who tend to stay on the right side would see this as a waste: the black and white view. People who are comfortable on the spectrum's left side can recognise her choice and say, "She moved on."

Like Doug you may shift across the risk spectrum from black and white to flying without a net, depending on what you place at risk. This determines your risk appetite in each dimension of your life, such as

- relationships.
- family and friendships.
- investments and savings.
- profession or career.
- education and personal development.
- income.

What a Risk Management Programme Is

Risk management is part of decision making, yet some people do not always view it that way. They see risk management as something separate from everyday decision making.

Yes managing risk is common sense, and habitually doing it pays off in many ways. When you practise risk management you are simply protecting the firm's bottom line and top line (turnover) and assets, people and reputation.

You Already Manage Risk

Here are three examples of how you practise risk management but may not realise it.

Case Study: Opportunity to Fill a Position

"Assume you are attempting to fill a high level management position, and you get wind of a candidate who may be qualified, but it is someone you have never met. Raise your hand if you would do research on the candidate." Everyone raises a hand.

"Why," I asked pointing to Paula.

"I might make a mistake and hire someone who is unqualified or doesn't fit in," she responded.

I asked her, "If you hired this person, and he or she did not work out, would it be a waste of precious company resources?"

"Yes," Paula answer back.

"To prevent a waste of time, money and maybe embarrassment, you would conduct an assessment in the form of a background check and numerous interviews to reduce your risk of making a hiring mistake."

Case Study: Risk in Construction of a Building

"Assume you need a new warehouse that costs about $2.5m to build from the ground up. As you plan you decide to defray some of this cost by making part of it available for lease to another company. Assume it will take 24 months to get this building built, equipped and ready for use. Raise your hand if you believe it would be a wise investment to spend time planning this out to ensure the building accommodates your current and future needs, as well as the needs of potential tenants."

Everyone raises a hand."Tracy, why is this investment of time necessary?"

She replied, "That is a lot of time and money that could be better spent if we make a wrong decision. Since there are so many unknowns, we must take the time to find realistic assumptions about the future and confirm them."

"Exactly. This intense and drawn-out planning is a risk assessment designed to make a smart decision. Since you do this often, Tracy, do you agree that is what you are really doing?"

Tracy nodded her head in agreement.

Case Study: Doing Business Abroad

"Assume that you are considering the acquisition of another oil and gas company with mineral rights in Columbia. You are told that you must pay a transfer tax of $200,000 to acquire those rights, money paid directly to a government agency. Raise your hand if, before you paid this money, you would consult with legal experts here and in Columbia to ensure that this was an up-and-up deal."

Every hand goes up. Looking in his direction, I queried, "Paul, since this is your area of expertise, why are you willing to pay large sums of money to various attorneys."

He said, "This deal could turn ugly fast. Since the government there is known to be corrupt, we might pay the money and not get what is promised, or we could be accused of bribery. We cannot afford either of those scenarios."

"You would ask the attorneys to help you define the possibility that there are unforeseen potholes in this deal. From what I have explained today, does this qualify as a formal risk assessment, Paul?" I purposely directed this to him because I could tell he was still sceptical about the value of risk management.

His face reflected that a light bulb turned on. "Up until today I would have said, 'No that is standard procedure,' but it is dawning on me that all along we have been doing a form of risk assessment on every company we acquired and sold. You win Ron."

My playful internal voice said, "I didn't know we were in a contest!"

If you have a brain you are already performing risk assessments as an element of your jobs as managers and executives. I am encouraging you to stop doing it in a seat-of-the-pants or ad-hoc manner and make it part of your organisation's standard operating procedure.

By having one company standard and adhering to it, your company will be more attractive to investors, lenders and maybe even buyers. When an organisation demonstrates that it has identified and analysed risks according to a best practice standard, such as enterprise risk management, it gains an advantage over a competitor that does not strategically or holistically manage risk.

Preview of a Risk Management Structure

The process of formal risk management takes many forms. In a later chapter you will be given a detailed step-by-step process for developing a formal risk management programme. For now here is a simple summary of what one looks like.

High Road Institute's Process for Implementing an Effective Risk Management Programme

Step One: Define risk.

Step Two: Examine your attitude towards risk.

Step Three: Analyse the ability of the organisation to handle risk.

Step Four: Minimise each risk's exposure or downside.

Step Five: Quickly recover from the negative impacts of the risk.

Step Five and One-Half: Learn something, so you can accept even greater risk with confidence.

There at this first manager meeting in Phoenix, I briefly explained each step of our methodology for implementing a risk management protocol in their organisation. By this time everyone, including Paul, was ready to know what they would be doing at future meetings, but I had one more bit of background to give them.

Different Approaches or Frameworks

Table 2-1 shows a comparison from five different sources on how others suggest formal risk management could be implemented or structured.

Table 2-1 Risk Management Implementation Road Maps

Source →	The Center for Strategy, Execution, and Valuation (1)	Ernst & Young CPAs (2)	Arthur Anderson CPAs (3)	The American Institute of Certified Public Accountants (4)	International Organisation for Standardization (5)
Steps					
1	Assess the maturity of the organisation to achieve a deep understanding of the strategy of the organisation and the related risks.	Research and define what shareholders value about your company.	Establish a risk management (RM) infrastructure.	Establish context for what risk looks like and understand risk	Communicate and consult about potential risks.
2	Gather views and data on strategic risks via a strategic risk assessment (SRA).	Determine strategy to handle risks: avoiding, managing, insuring or hedging.	Assess overall business risk.	Identify situations that can affect business objectives	Establish the context for the risk.
3	Prepare a preliminary strategic risk profile (SRP) while reviewing the process for identifying risks in the strategy-setting process.	Identify risks surrounding your key shareholder value drivers.	Develop business RM strategies.	Analyse and assess the risks	Conduct risk assessments in three substeps: identify, analyse and evaluate.
4	Validate and finalise the SRP, and review the process for measuring and monitoring the organisation's performance.	Communicate to shareholders what you will do about the risks.	Develop and implement RM techniques.	Design strategies for managing risks	Treat the risk.
5	Develop an SRA action plan.	N/A	Measure and monitor RM process performance.	Implement and integrate processes	Monitor and review the risk and outcomes.

Table 2-1 Risk Management Implementation Road Maps (continued)

Source →	The Center for Strategy, Execution, and Valuation (1)	Ernst & Young CPAs (2)	Arthur Anderson CPAs (3)	The American Institute of Certified Public Accountants (4)	International Organisation for Standardization (5)
Steps					
6	Communicate the SRP and SRA action plan.	N/A	Improve business RM process.	Measure and monitor the business's efficiency, profitability, and vulnerability	N/A
7	Implement the SRA action plan.	N/A	N/A	Report data to the executives in charge	N/A
8	Develop an ongoing process to periodically update the assessments of strategic risks.	N/A	N/A	N/A	N/A

Road Maps Source Notes:

(1) DePaul University Kellstadt Graduate School of Management, published in *Strategic Finance* December 2009.

(2) Information provided to clients by the public accounting firm Ernst & Young.

(3) Information provided to clients by the (now defunct) public accounting firm Arthur Anderson.

(4) A *Framework for Risk Management* issued by the AICPA's risk advisory services task force.

(5) *ISO 31000:2009 Risk Management—Principles and Guidelines* issued by the International Organisation for Standardization.

What did you notice that was similar in the different frameworks?
What did you notice that was different or unique in each approach?

One Example

The International Organisation for Standardization defines risk management as "coordinated activities to direct and control an organisation with regard to risk" when risk is defined as the "effects of uncertainty on objectives." Risk management is an integral part of all organisational processes and a vital aspect of decision making by everyone in the organisation.

Cost of a Risk Management Programme

Just because a smaller firm cannot afford to devote the entire amount of resources that must be dedicated to a formalised risk management programme, it does not mean that it doesn't need one. Sometimes smaller firms are more severely hurt by unforeseen circumstances than larger ones. Having a disciplined repeatable approach to risk taking is not expensive, but it can be costly due to the structural improvements that are necessary. Your real yet intangible costs of having this programme include

- awareness.
- balance.

- measuring.
- goals.
- willingness.
- change.

Cost– Awareness That Risk Exists

To be effective in managing risk at the personal and business level, you must stay aware. This is hard for many people because so much distracts their focus and attention, including technology, noise and constant interruptions.

In risk management everyone from the CEO on down must believe that risk exists and address it as soon as the peril is identified. The price to pay is the willingness of everyone involved to pause, look, listen, pay attention and question. In other words everyone in your organisation must stop running on autopilot.

This deep awareness is not only about the risk event itself but also the events before and the repercussions after. Think of throwing a rock in a deep lake. You might believe the risk is only in the throw. Risk could be in your environment (forest fire coming at you), the rock (radioactive) and where you got the rock (polluted waste). Risk management is a huge responsibility, as shown in Figure 2-3:

Figure 2-3
Risk Awareness Scope

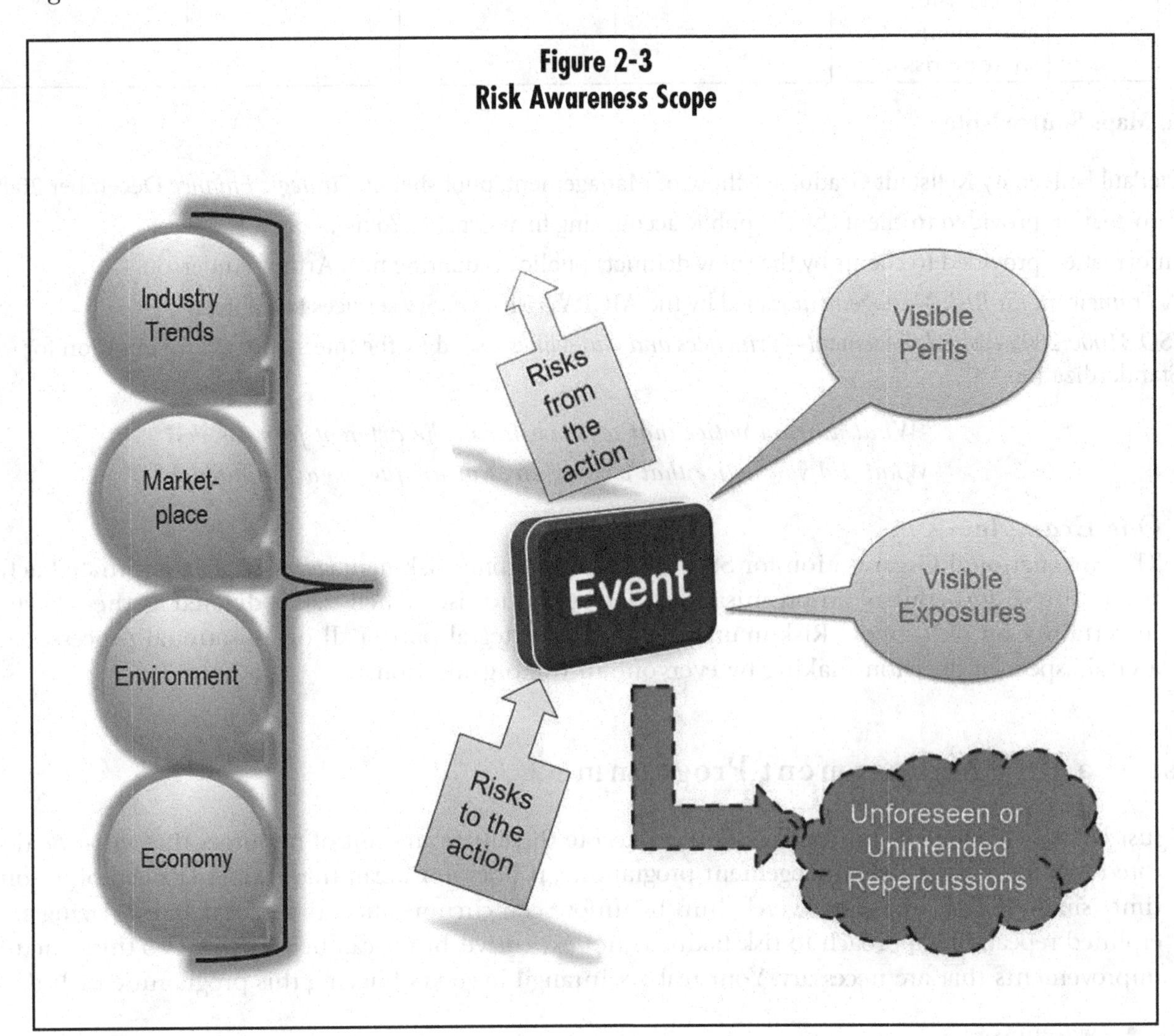

The zone to the left in Figure 2-3 represents the context in which your organisation exists. The event represents what we normally clue in to as the problem. Proper risk management requires that you also make yourself aware of

- risk from your actions.
- risks you bring with you before your actions.
- visible perils after the event take place.
- visible exposures or weaknesses that result from the event.
- unforeseen or unintended negative repercussions from the event.

That is one wide, broad and deep scope of awareness!

Cost– Finding Appropriate Balance

In business it is so easy to get too thinly spread or take on too many things you define as important. You cannot be everything to everyone. Success comes from staying focused on what you do best and making that priority number one. The price you pay is a willingness to find the right, not perfect, balance. In the short term this is easy, but in the long run you will get out of balance often.

A valuable exercise in managing risk is for you and your team to pause regularly and pose these questions to yourselves:

- What is most important right now?
- What have we done well in the past that worked?
- What are we trying to become best at in the future?

Cost– Measuring Your Exposure

A vital part of managing risk is to measure each one, which goes hand-in-hand with awareness. Failure to measure risk is like finding a hole in the floor of your car and then ignoring it. It could be a small problem, or it could be huge. If you fail to take the time to determine which it is, you will never know

- if it is a real problem,
- the best way to react,
- the urgency of the problem or
- the cost to fix the problem.

When you stop to fix the hole or take your car to an expert, you have valuable knowledge that will save you time, money and energy. The notable cost of measuring risk is the establishment of a reliable and consistent reporting protocol.

However good risk measurement has two types of payoffs in the form of a return on investment (ROI1) and a return on innovation (ROI2). There are many different ways to measure these returns, but make sure, at regular points in time, you know where you are as it relates to the risk you undertake.

Another valuable risk management activity is for your team to pause and conduct a self-analysis about its approaches to seeking opportunity. Use these questions to prime the team's thought process:

- Why are we undertaking this risk, and why do we believe the payoff exceeds the cost of the risk?
- How will we measure this risk to know when to pull the plug?
- Who will take responsibility for objectively measuring the risk, and what is that person expected to do with the data?

Cost– Setting Appropriate Goals

The real yet intangible price of performing risk management is the discipline of setting realistic goals. Far too often some people will set a goal that is impossible or improbable. The more off the charts your goal regarding reasonableness, the greater risk you accept. This frequently occurs when an organisation establishes stretch goals without first ensuring that the capability exists to achieve them.

Cost– Willingness to Alter Your Plans

Today you cannot have just one set of plans for anything you strive to achieve. A huge price to pay for managing risk is to let go of your ego. The size of this cost is directly related to the size of your ego. If you are like most people actively chasing success, it is easy to keep moving forward even when the tea leaves say to stop. Once you commit to formally managing risks, you must be willing to change if the risk exceeds the payoff, or the cost is too dear.

For many people, especially driven entrepreneurs and investors, altering plans or giving up can seem like a defeat. As Tacitus once said, "He that fights and runs away, may turn and fight another day." I suggest you adopt this motto: "If you have a hard time changing your plans, it is better to back off a costly risk today, so you can afford the cost of a better one tomorrow."

Cost– Embracing the Pains of Change

A painful price you face is the need to shift your culture. If you implement a risk programme without doing this well, it is the equivalent of randomly dropping seeds on unprepared soil. The seeds probably will not survive. Similarly if your culture is not adjusted to support the risk management efforts, it will fail to deliver the bottom line results that are possible.

> **Murphy's Law of Risk Consultants**
>
> Simple problems attract complex solutions. Big problems attract simple solutions. Complex problems attract experts who know nothing.

The Catch-22 Syndrome of Risk Management

You may by now see a clear indication of a catch-22 inherent in risk management. In case you missed it, here it is more explicitly, with you as the focal point:

> Catch-22 comes from the title of a book written by Joseph Heller. He described it as a situation in which a desired outcome or solution is impossible to attain because of a set of inherently illogical rules or conditions. The rules or conditions create a situation or predicament characterised by absurdity or senselessness. It also means a contradictory or self-defeating course of action, like the phrase, "Damned if you do, and damned if you don't."

Catch 1

You see an opportunity to do something new that contains a cost you might not be able to afford. You believe that doing a formal risk assessment will take too long and may not give you the answer you want, so you take the leap anyway and end up flat on your face. You will have wasted your time, energy and (probably) financial resources, and it will take you time to recover.

Versus

You see an opportunity to do something new that contains a cost you might not be able to afford. You believe that doing a formal risk assessment is worth it, and it indicates that you should go for the brass ring. You take the leap but end up flat on your face. You will have wasted your time, energy and (probably) financial resources, and it will take time to recover.

Are you better off by doing the formal risk assessment?

Catch 2

You see an opportunity to do something new that contains a cost you might not be able to afford. You believe that doing a formal risk assessment will take too long and may not give you the answer you want. However you get on the horse anyway and end up with your brass ring. You are happy.

Versus

You see an opportunity to do something new that contains a cost you might not be able to afford. You believe that doing a formal risk assessment is worth the effort and discover that you should go for the brass ring, which you obtain. You are happy.

What difference did performing a risk assessment make?

Managing risk does not mean that you won't end up in the same position, regardless of whether you end up with a win, loss or draw. Managing risk is adopting the discipline of going into the unknown with a plan and an indication of what you may have to pay should Mr Murphy make his appearance or if the pothole is larger and deeper than expected.

Although a formal risk assessment may not pay off in a singular or specific risk, it will improve your organisation's and employees' ability to measure and predict likely outcomes. It also assists in faster recovery when you find yourself flat on your face in a pothole.

Because people who live to take risks, such as investors, inventors, enterprisers and entrepreneurs, generally are perceptive and intuitive, they (and you) sense this catch-22. This is why many of you do not practise risk management or believe that formal risk management is a waste of your valuable time.

Risk Taking Is a Paradox

I hear you; however, let's debunk your illusion that you or your company will not benefit by doing a formal risk assessment. The answer is in the four paradoxes of risk taking.

> A paradox is two true positions or statements that, at face value, seem to be diametrically opposed. Upon further examination both positions are accurate because the two opposing forces are connected.

First Paradox of Risk Taking

Mistakes are an inevitable part of learning, and mistakes waste money and resources.

Second Paradox of Risk Taking
A business is not growing if it is not risking, and business failures often result from the negative impact of risks taken.

Third Paradox of Risk Taking
The culture of the organisation must be risk tolerant, and the culture must be able to expose areas sensitive to risks.

Fourth Paradox of Risk Taking
Taking risks is facing uncertainty, and leaders exist to reduce uncertainty.

Back to PJI

I posed this question to the managers of PJI: "What are these four paradoxes saying to you?" Their responses were similar to the most common answers I receive:

- They are saying damned if we do, damned if we don't.
- They are saying risk is inevitable.
- They tell me that, as managers, we must be concerned about both sides of risk.
- The downside, as well as the upside, of any opportunity is equally important.
- These paradoxes say that risk is inevitable, but we can do things to plan for them.

For me James Dean, the actor, summed up these four paradoxes of risk taking very well:

"Dream as if you'll live forever. Live as if you'll die today."

In a nutshell what these paradoxes, taken together, tell us is that we cannot know everything, so we must be able to handle whatever risk occurs, especially those that we cannot foresee.

My next question was directed to both Justin and Paul. "How do these four paradoxes particularly affect the owner of a business?"

At first neither one could answer the question. Then Justin stood up and addressed his team. "Ron is subtly telling us that we cannot assume that any risk we take won't be costly. Being risk aware is simply good management and part of my responsibility as the CEO."

Paul, not wanting to be outdone by his partner, provided us with this gem. "I guess in the past we assumed that each investment we made was focused on the positive, and we are lucky that we never got badly burned. Now I see why we need to be cautious but with a bottom line reason to be."

Later I will provide you statistics that show that doing the formal risk assessment is worth the effort, despite the outcome—good or bad—of your pursuit of the brass ring.

Not There Yet

A recent survey of 125 CFOs showed that risk management still has a long way toward becoming a discipline to be taken for granted in many organisations. In the survey, 82% of these finance executives blame the financial crisis of 2007–08 on "risk management's inability to understand complex financial instruments." Nearly three-fourths of the CFOs said "risk management now outranks in importance on such issues as long-term and short-term debt financing, relationships with financial institutions, pension plan asset allocation, and the ability to secure equity financing." [*CFO* magazine January 2009]

Onward

We ended the session and enjoyed some scrumptious desserts. The paint smell was no longer noticeable. After I answered all their questions, and we set the agenda for the next meeting, I shared with these curious and committed managers a quote that sums up why risk taking and risk management are copartners in your drive for business success.

> *"Living at risk is jumping off the cliff and building your wings on the way down." Ray Bradbury*

Your Action Plan

Step One
Where do you generally fit on the personal risk spectrum? In other words where would the people you know best place you on this scale? Why do they have that opinion of you?

Step Two
Where in your business or personal life do you believe that taking more risks would be beneficial? Where in your business or personal life do you believe that you need to be more aware of the risks taken?

Step Three
Make a list of the ordinary risks your organisation takes. What makes them ordinary?

Make a list of unusual or extraordinary risks that your organisation takes. What is the intent or purpose behind those risks? For example

- We need to grow.
- The owner is generally aggressive.
- We have a history of taking big leaps of faith.

3

WHY Is Risk Management Important to Us?

Reasons Why Formal Risk Management Is Vital to Success

"I take smart risks! That's why we are successful." Dana P.

New parents quickly discover that their child masters a one-word sentence that tests the parents' wisdom: "Why?" No matter what you tell a child under the age of three, the response you get is, "Why?" The question itself is forceful because you are challenged to come up with a reasonable answer (other than, "Because I said so!"), and doing this keeps your brain synapses functioning.

It was a 41° Celsius May morning when I next met with PJ Investment's (PJI's) management team. I knew the managers of PJI were eager for me to answer the HOW question: "How do we practise risk management?" However this does not logically follow the WHAT question. You must accept the two reasons why formal risk management is vital to your business's success before you learn the process and tools.

Reason 1

You already understand a generic reason using the mental image of a pitfall and the analogy of Murphy's Law, but to correctly implement this strategy for longevity in business, you need more context or grounding. Children are always asking "why" questions because they know nothing about life as you the adult know it. So they ask you to provide them with an understanding (context) of the crazy, dynamic world they are encountering. Because you know very little about enterprise risk management (ERM), you too need a deep understanding of this perilous world you work in.

Reason 2

In an ERM system, every workday, you send all your employees on a search and destroy mission. You will empower and make them responsible to seek, assess and then eradicate the risks they encounter as they do their job. As soon as you "volunteer" them for this important assignment, guess what you will hear?

Why do I have to?

If you lack a sufficient understanding of why this responsibility is in their job description, you will be tempted to respond, "Because I said so!" That comment will sound professional (sarcasm intentional).

Reasons to Care about Formal Risk Management

> **Murphy's Law of Risk Expansion**
>
> Catastrophe is a risk that was ignored by everyone.

My next assignment for nine PJI managers was to lead a small group brainstorming session on reasons why the entire leadership team needed to care more about formal risk management.

Here is why you and other managers in your organisation need to be concerned about implementing a risk management programme:

- Protecting your profits
- Protecting your assets
- Protecting your employees
- Protecting your investors
- Protecting your stakeholders (bankers, vendors, customers and so on)
- Protecting your reputation or brand
- Ensuring the longevity or future of your organisation
- Avoiding taking a bad or costly risk

Not Just Risk Avoidance

Some managers believe that one way to manage risk is to avoid it. This is impossible because a business cannot avoid taking a risks. Life is full of risk. Owning, leading or managing a business means you face risk every day.

I continued the meeting with a story about another client, Dana, who swiftly went from success to near failure because of unforeseen risks.

It's a Small (Appliance) World

Dana started her growing enterprise Smaller is Better 17 years ago and, until last year, was running a distribution business with $39m in turnover and employing 50 people. Dana describes herself this way: "I like to take risks, but I am smart about it. Before I make a critical decision I do research and ask other people's opinion before acting."

Space is precious in Japan, so many of the appliances in Japanese residences are smaller than those we see in American homes. Dana saw the possibility of importing these products. To get started she established a relationship with a major Japanese appliance manufacturer. Together they designed an American version of a few products and jointly recruited appliance retailers in seven western states. With Dana's permission the manufacturer made similar arrangements with other distributors, so they had outlets all across the United States.

As she built her company, Dana would do exhaustive research for each new product idea. She then travelled to Asia to find a manufacturer who was willing to work with her to add a new line of small appliances for the fickle American market. With each product line she added she became less dependent on the original Japanese manufacturer. Yet up until one year ago 55% of Smaller and Better's sales came from those products.

Last year Dana nearly lost her business because of some hidden pitfalls she never saw as she travelled the road to success. Despite hearing rumours that the giant discount retailer Walmart was attempting to make inroads with her Japanese manufacturer, Dana ignored them as idle gossip. Then on June 1 of last year, this supplier announced to Dana and the other distributors that carried the American products that they would be dropped from its supply chain. Walmart would be the supplier's exclusive retailer and distributor. Dana and her management team were devastated and felt betrayed. They knew they would have to quickly replace the business, or the company would have to drastically downsize.

A few weeks later, after putting in an exhausting schedule of nonstop meetings, Dana collapsed in her office. After numerous tests Dana learned she had contacted a rare deadly virus localised to southern Japan, probably during one of her frequent visits there. She required an immediate liver transplant and surgery. Because few Westerners contracted the disease, her medical team could not estimate how quickly she could recover or even if she could.

Because the surgery was risky, and she would be in quarantine for several weeks before the surgery, Dana was urged to give someone in her company a power of attorney regarding key business decisions. Believing he would do right by her she assigned it to her younger brother, Perry, who worked for her as a senior product manager.

Unfortunately Dana did not know that Perry, jealous of her financial success, believed he could run the business better than her and believed the Walmart problem was her fault. During his first ten days as temporary CEO, he had constant arguments with her management team and ended up firing several of them for insubordination. Because of his meddling and micromanaging, several key employees resigned.

After ten days of quarantine and a successful surgery and transplant, Dana was told about this mess. Ignoring her doctors' warning Dana left the hospital in an attempt to repair the damage and revoke the power of attorney. She fired Perry, who threatened to sue, and quickly rehired key employees who quit or were fired. She appointed a trustworthy warehouse manager to act as CEO until she was able to fulfil that role again. These two stressful events caused a severe relapse, leaving Dana bedridden for four months.

Back at work today Dana and her management team are tirelessly working to repair the damage and replace the lost sales. The survival of Smaller is Better is still in question but not as perilous as it was. During a coaching session Dana admitted to me with tears in her eyes, "I guess I really goofed up and turned a blind eye to things I took for granted. It was a mistake to ignore the warning signs about Walmart and Perry. My brother's recklessness hurts far worse than the surgery. In your opinion what should I have done differently?"

I responded, "Dana you are a good risk manager because you only took on the appropriate amount of risk that you felt you could handle with the successful track you were on. There were other risks outside of your immediate vision. These areas probably contained warnings, but since every key decision requires your input, you lack the bandwidth to see them. You neglected to heed these truisms of successfully surviving risks."

Third, Fourth, and Fifth Principles of Risk Management

When it comes to proper risk management, expect the best and plan for the worst.

Each risk usually provides indicators of its existence. If these go unnoticed their negative impact exponentially increases.

The more people who are involved in monitoring a risk, the less likely its impact will be detrimental.

As a leader and business professional, Dana did a proper job of expecting the best from her people and suppliers. She failed to realise that she needed to plan for the unexpected. She did not foresee that carrying the company on her back blinded her to a holistic view of risk.

> **Murphy's Law of Risk Awareness**
>
> A neglected risk goes from bad to worse. An addressed risk goes from bad to terrible.

Why Peril Awareness Is a Group Effort

I asked the nine senior managers of JPI to join me at the front of the ballroom where I had placed nine flipcharts. As I handed each person a marker this was my instruction "In the next three minutes write down all the risks you faced on your trip from your home to this hotel."

They each rapidly wrote while I timed them. As I expected no one got past seven items. A few had only two or three written. They listed

- being involved in an accident (nine responses).
- getting a speeding ticket (nine responses).
- arriving late (nine responses).
- running out of gas (four responses).
- forgetting to bring a notebook (three responses).
- getting lost (two responses).
- being here too early (one response).

You all did a great job, but there are some perils you missed. What about the risk of

- assuming you carpooled here, the designated driver failing to pick you up?
- backing your car over a toy left in the driveway?
- hitting a pedestrian with your car?
- having a heart attack or epileptic fit while driving?
- having your car stolen from this parking lot?
- your engine overheating or failing?
- forgetting your cell phone?
- spilling hot coffee on your lap while driving?
- getting a flat tire and not having a spare?
- experiencing mechanical difficulties?
- having your insurance cancelled today?
- failing to kiss your spouse or children goodbye?
- getting carjacked?
- being kidnapped?
- finding out too late that this meeting was moved to another site, and you are not informed?

While going through my list I read their faces. Some rolled their eyes, and others giggled as my risks got a little more ridiculous. Kerry, a general manager, couldn't take it any longer. "Mr. Rael, some of those aren't risks. Why would someone want to take my car on the freeway, and why would I even consider driving without insurance? I fail to see your point."

My point was that risks exist that you may not be aware of or that seem improbable from your point of view.

"You all listed only the low-hanging fruit or most obvious perils. Yet each of mine is an actual risk you faced. Each one has its own probability and surrounding assumptions. For example, if you were a billionaire, your risk of getting kidnapped is higher than someone in your income bracket. The risk of your insurance being cancelled is very low, assuming you pay your premiums on time. A risk of going to the wrong location depends upon whether or not you are in the communication link. So each risk has a degree, a probability and a context for it, but you cannot exclude or ignore them, even when they do not appear on your leadership radar.

"As senior leaders, you generally have a focus. Tracy looks at risk through the CFO's point of view. Kerry, you look at risk through a business unit perspective. Shauna, as human resource director, sees risk through the employee context.

"There is an infinitesimal number of risks that PJI faces, but you might miss them because of your singular or limited focus. Consider the PJI employee who, because of their specific job, will only perceive what might be risky through that window. Kerry, what happens if all of you combined fail to pay attention to costly risk?"

He responded, "We would look like we were clueless."

"Do any of you sometimes feel clueless or out of the loop when it comes to executive decisions made by Justin or Paul?" Several of them nodded their heads. "Please don't take my question as a criticism," I said, noting that Paul was about to object. "In risk management, synergy, cooperation and interdependence are vital to the success of the programme."

I turned towards Justin and inquired, "Justin are these traits—synergy, cooperation and interdependence—somethingyou want from this team?" I pointed to the nine people standing by the flipcharts.

"Yes," he responded.

I continued."Therefore managing risk is an important management responsibility. Do you agree Justin?"

Pausing to consider this, he replied, "Yes, I see that it is."

Why Risk Management Is a Leadership Responsibility

Assume I gave you the custody of my very precious 6-year old granddaughter to watch over while I was out of the country for an emergency. In asking you to do this favour, I take a major risk and assume several things, such as

- you are trustworthy.
- you will know how to protect my granddaughter while she is in your care.
- you have adequate protection measures (a secure house, the wherewithal to watch her and meet her needs, and so on).
- you won't take advantage of her or me.

When you run or manage an organisation, those who place their trust in you—employees,investors, lenders, creditors and customers—have similar assumptions about you. They believe and demand assurances that you and your fellow managers

- are trustworthy.

- will know how to protect and look out for their interests.
- will have adequate protection measures.
- will not take advantage of them.

For these reasons, especially the third, you are obligated as the leader and manager to protect yourself and others from the repercussions of unwanted, unwarranted or unforeseen risks. Because of these next items your obligation does not stop there. As a manager your responsibility is to protect and foster the growth of your organisation. The following are areas where a formal risk management programme will support your obligations as a leader.

Desire for Innovation and Creativity

Organisations undertake four sources of risks when they believe themselves to be innovative and desire a culture where employees think for themselves. In an organisation that desires innovation and creativity, the four sources of innovation risk are as follows:

1. *Your strategy risk.* This requires clear direction setting and involvement to help your entire organisation know where you are going and the ability to measure your progress.
2. *Out of the loop risk.* This is the fear that you fail to be in touch with your customer's needs and demands. To lessen the risk you must stay in constant contact with past and present customers.
3. *Your capability risk.* This is a fear that you will not be able to execute your carefully designed plans and use the innovation to generate income. Mitigating this risk requires an independent evaluation of your plans before they are implemented.
4. *Unclear expectations risk.* All too often senior leader's expectations for new products or services go largely unspoken. They are in someone's mind but frequently not communicated well enough to others. Most importantly of all, there is no way to measure innovation and creativity. Managing this risk requires the need to develop and explicitly publish agreed-upon expectations for all your innovations.

Defining your innovation risks up front will allow you to take the critical first step towards successfully managing them.

Need for Fraud Prevention and Detection or Proper Governance

Almost every business leader believes that only people with high ethical standards work for them, yet the latest research shows that 30% of today's workers are always looking for ways to steal from their employers, and another 30% will steal if given the opportunity. Fraud is most likely to occur when an employee serves as the sole contact with a particular vendor or when one person performs several incompatible functions. Once fraud schemes begin they are hard to detect and even harder to stop.

Detecting fraud is difficult even for professional investigators. Your best option is to mostly concentrate on prevention. Therefore having a risk management structure in place forces you and other leaders to seek out areas that are at risk and areas vulnerable to fraudulent activity. Then threats easily will be uncovered.

Need Adequate Checks and Balances

A comprehensive system of controls will not prevent fraud, but one will increase the likelihood of both the deterrence and detection of fraudulent activities.

If someone is trying to cheat you, there is clear evidence of fraud right in front of you, but you need to know where to look. In managing your perils, awareness begins in simple actions that are powerful internal controls, such as

- analysing patterns.
- looking for photocopied or altered forms.
- analysing credit invoices for excessive activity or unusual patterns.
- checking that the vendor was properly approved.
- looking for complaints from outsiders and employees.
- conducting address checks and site visits more often.

Desire to Maximise Profits

Firmwide risk management allows you to examine all the risks that you potentially face, allows you to measure the impact of those risks on the organisation and helps you identify appropriate steps to manage or mitigate those risks. The range of risks that businesses face includes hazard risks, such as property damage and theft; financial risks, such as interest rate and foreign currency exchange; operational risks, such as supply chain problems or cost mismanagement; and strategic risks, such as misaligned products or overly aggressive strategies. The key to your programme is to address all those risks in an integrated fashion because each challenge can cause profits to disappear

One reason that an ERM programme protects profits is due to the process of identifying, quantifying, and prioritising risks, making them more real and visible to leaders who normally fail to give risk management the attention it deserves. Another reason is that a firm-wide awareness requires a holistic approach to risk management beyond the traditional parameters of things that are insurable. This cultural discipline greatly expands your company's definition of risk to include anything that threatens its continuity. A company-wide approach helps you to sort risks into those that can help the company grow and those that will only lead to loss. In the rush of every growing competition, sometimes this differentiation is not easy to spot.

Need for Good Stewardship of Corporate Assets

When I put my granddaughter in your care, I believed you would know how to practise good stewardship and that you would treat my very precious darling as if she were your own child by taking special care of her and her welfare.

Whether you own or manage a company or serve on an organisation's leadership team, you are watching over and protecting a wide spectrum of assets. Proper formal risk management is simply living up to your stewardship obligation.

> Stewardship entails the act of serving as a guardian, protector or person legally responsible for someone's entrusted assets or affairs.

Ten Ways ERM Can Make an Impact

Notice how this list mirrors the reasons why you and others need to care about risk management. When you invest in a structured firmwide risk management programme, you will automatically enhance

1. governance and leadership over the entire entity.
2. sustainability or continuance into the future.

3. the firm's mission or purpose.
4. shareholders' investment in you.
5. the trust that various stakeholders place in you.
6. financial operations or check and balances known as internal controls.
7. your firm's reputation and brand.
8. the ability to simultaneously stay focused and be flexible.
9. the bottom line, however your organisation defines that.
10. firm integrity.

Murphy's Law of Opportunity Impact

Just as you expect the unexpected, everything turns upside down.

Onward

To sum up the day this is what I shared with PJI's leaders:

"Global perils can come from any place within your business model, your strategy or your marketplace. Each one can deeply affect this firm's

- profits.
- creativity.
- continuity.
- brand or reputation.
- leadership team's integrity.
- employees' ethical conduct.
- internal capabilities.
- goal execution and completion.

"This is why the firmwide plan for anticipating and dealing with suspected perils must become part of your everyday managing and leading.

"I know you are anxious to get to the HOW of risk management. In order to prepare you, this is your assignment. You must spend time over the next two days listing all the potential risks that this company or your department faces. After your own list is complete, sit down with at least two non-management employees, and ask them to describe specific risks or obstacles that they experience within the scope of their job. Please go deep and wide just as we did on the exercise regarding your risks of arriving here today. List each and every one no matter how ridiculous or far-fetched the risk or obstacle might be. I will award a prize to the person with the longest list of possible risks.

"The rest of our meetings will be devoted to the process of managing risk."

I closed the session by sharing another favourite quotation because it also summed up the day.

"Risk varies inversely with knowledge." Irving Fisher

Your Action Plan

Step One

Spend time over the week listing all the potential risks that your organisation, business unit or department faces.

Step Two

After your own list is complete, sit down with at least several non-management employees, and ask them to describe specific risks or obstacles that they see within the scope of their job. Please go deep and wide, meaning look beyond the obvious big risks.

List each and every one no matter how ridiculous or far-fetched the risk or obstacle.

Step Three

Cite at least five specific and personal reasons why you and other managers in your organisation need to be very concerned about implementing a risk management programme.

4

WHICH Risks Do We Need to Be Concerned About?

"I feel like I am king of the world, or at least I am on top, and want to go out that way." Allison P.

It was a 41° Celsius May morning when I next met with PJ Investment's (PJI's) management team. As I led them into our room they noticed numerous flipchart sheets taped to the left and right side walls, but the sheets were folded in half, so they could not see what was on them. Their curiosity was high, which is what I desired, but they would have to wait to satisfy their curiosity. I needed to ease them into what I knew would be an exhausting session.

There is a saying that goes, "It is not the same to talk of bulls as to be in the bullring." Therefore, today, we will grab the bull by the horns and face the situation. This, in essence, is the first step in managing risk.

"The last time we were together I asked each of you to make a list of the possible risks or obstacles that both you and your employees felt this organisation faced. The 21 sheets on the left side of this room show what you came up with." (My assistant opened the sheets, so that participants could see the data.) "There are 169 unique risks that employees in this organisation are concerned about."

Selecting one of the newer additions to the management team, Sondra, I asked her, "What does this long list of risks tell you?"

She replied, "It tells me several things. My company faces a lot of issues each day, many that could undermine our success. It also helps me to understand why we are going through this training with you, but suddenly I'm worried about our future. Should I be?"

I said, "Before I answer your question, Sondra, would all of you please turn your attention to the information on this chart?" I pointed it out. "As you are aware we surveyed your employees and asked them to describe this company's readiness to deal with surprises or unexpected challenges. We gave them six categories to choose from."

I am confident that we are ready.	8%
I believe we can handle unexpected surprises.	11%
I think we can in some areas but not all areas.	27%
I do not have a lot of confidence that we can handle unexpected surprises.	44%
I believe we are not ready for surprises.	7%
I have no opinion or do not know.	3%

"We received 291 anonymous responses to the survey, which means 72% of your employees responded. Notice in the percentages that the rule of 80/20 applies. Only 20% of your employees have confidence that this organisation has the ability to handle risk, and 80% do not share this confidence. This tells me most employees are not sure that you are capable of dealing with these identified risks.

"Sondra, you asked if you should be worried. As an important decision maker in this company, based on the statistics, should you be concerned?"

Sondra answered, "I think I should be."

Immediately Paul raised a hand, looked at me sternly and said, "Ron I disagree with your conclusion to the survey. I concede there are certain parts of the organisation that employees perceive as not managed well." I noticed that he glanced over at Justin as he said that. "But I know there are many business units that manage their risks well. Maybe the employees in those safe areas did not answer the survey." I sensed that Paul was provoking a fight.

The normally relaxed Justin stirred in his seat, and before he could defend himself I said, "I agree with Paul that there is a difference in how risk is managed in this diverse organisation, but rather than trying to justify or dismiss your employees' opinions, we will complete an exercise that explains the employees' responses."

Enterprise Risk Management Step One– Obtain Consensus on Allowable Risk

Risk Management Tool Two: Process for Gaining Consensus on What Risk Looks Like

These were my instructions to each small group:

- Individually, write out the phrases or terminology you would use to define the word *risk*. In other words complete this sentence, "Risk is…"
- Read your definition out loud to the other members of your group.
- As a group please boil the essence of your individual responses into one combined definition you all can agree on. This will take time and patience. Your final product must be one that the six of you will support.

This exercise demonstrates that there are a wide variety of ways for people of your organisation to see and define risk. The outcome of your hard work will jump-start the process of gaining a consensus on a commonly acceptable definition of what is risky and what is the cost you cannot afford.

All humans want to be successful, but most do not take the risks that are necessary to achieve success. Why? The answer lies in how people view risk: something desirable or something to avoid.

When it comes to understanding how we humans look at risk in two very different ways, the "Uncertainty Domino" helps. If you have never played traditional dominos, I assure you it is a fun game. Every domino tile contains two numbers, either of which can be an option for play. Similarly people can look at risk in either of two ways: as a problem or an opportunity.

Figure 4-1
The Uncertainty Domino

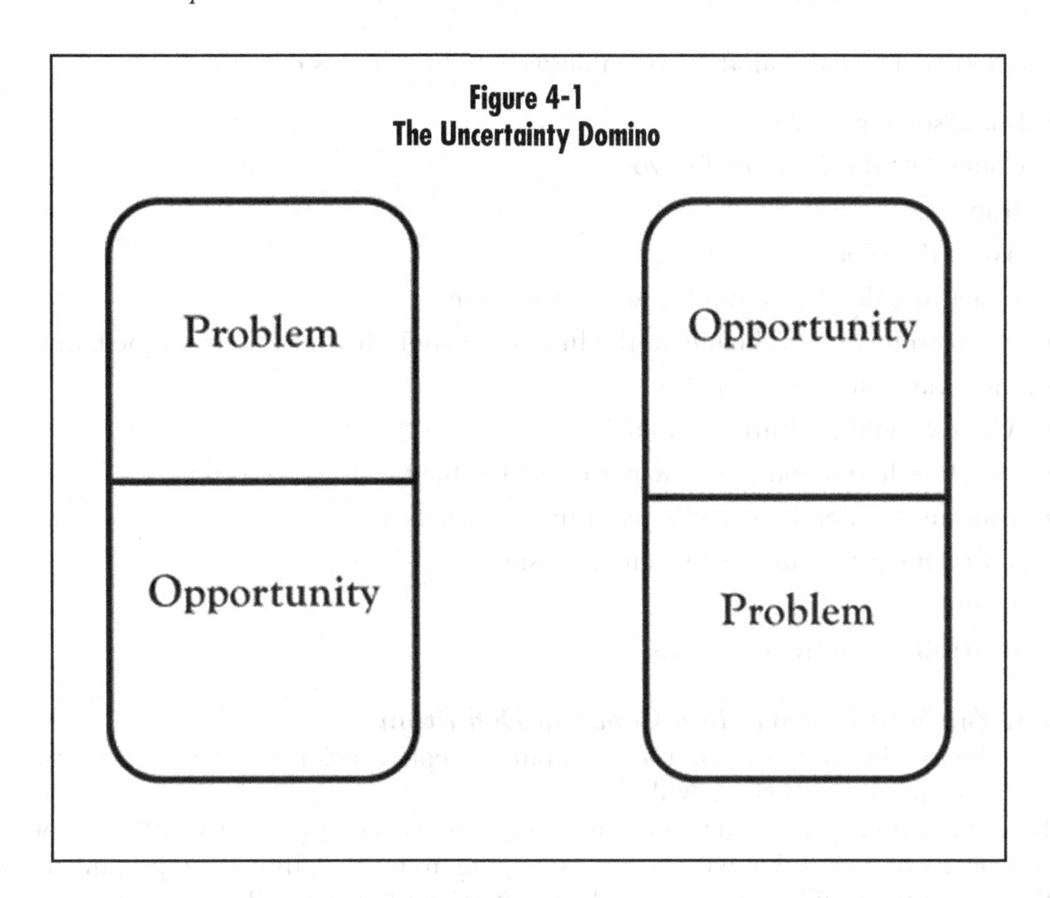

Some of your internal employees will see risk as a problem because they focus on the problem, know the dire implications of risk failure and let their fears come into play. Many employees see risk as a problem because that little voice in their brain says, "I don't think I should be doing this."

An equal number of people see risk taking as a great opportunity and would define the risky choice as a chance to try something new or a thrilling experience. For all employees to embrace risk with a common attitude, you need to learn this next truism:

> **Sixth Principle of Risk Management**
>
> Risk taking is in the eye of the beholder.

How to Create a Consensus About Risk

It took several hours for each group to finish writing their consensus-driven definition of risk. My assistant and I taped each handwritten sheet to one wall.

The next step is for everyone to walk around and study the various definitions that each group wrote down. Compare these definitions to your own group's response. You will see some terminology or concepts that are similar and terminology that is different. Next go back to your tables and write down any similarities you noted.

"I would like you all to turn your attention to the flipchart pages on the right wall of this room." (My assistant unfolded the sheets that were filled with words.) "Through our survey process we asked your employees to answer the same question that you addressed. You will notice that the range of descriptors they used for risk is similar to yours, going from pessimistic to optimistic. Remember in our survey we asked employees to think generally about their views before they responded."

The following are the most common answers to how others define risk:

- Doing something different
- Going outside of my comfort zone
- Scary
- Worth the effort
- Something that has an upside and a downside
- Putting something valuable on the line that I could lose or that could be harmed
- The unknown or X-factor
- Where I could get hurt or harmed
- A goal or destination that may not be achievable but is worth trying
- A means to an end, hopefully rewarding or beneficial
- A movement forward despite any downside
- A gamble
- Something to avoid at all costs

What You Will Discover in a Common Definition

Your primary objective is to craft a commonly accepted definition of risk that all employees will internalise and use in their daily decisions.

By going through this exercise of examining different employee's views of risk, you will discover that diversity of definitions, with opinions ranging from the optimistic to pessimistic. Some people will focus on the upside or payoff (worth the effort), and others will focus on the downside or pain (I could get hurt). Others will give you a balanced definition (something that has an upside and a downside). I am always amazed at how pessimistic some internal managers tend to be when discussing risk. Likewise I am never surprised when externally focused managers and executives see risk as something necessary, inevitable and rewarding.

When you compare all the various employees' answers, you will discover several trends in similar responses. It is important not to get hung up on the specific wording but instead to focus on the message behind the words. Your goal in Step one is to get the leadership body to arrive at a consensus on a mutually acceptable definition for both risk and risk taking. Based upon my experience, a well-conceived consensus will almost always be a balanced view.

Why Defining Risk Is Necessary in Enterprise Risk Management

Murphy's Law of Opportunity Blindness

The person who created the mess is clueless and always blames others for his or her mess.

Every organisation is striving to achieve a level of success that is uniquely and individually defined.

Because of recent changes in the world of corporate governance, boards of directors and other stakeholders of corporations are more wary of risk. Therefore, to ensure their job security, CEOs must become acutely aware of the need to develop more systemised means to measure and manage everyday business risks. Numerous experts agree that there is far less tolerance by stakeholders (especially in public organisations) for the executives who fail to prepare for a disaster of some sort. This leaves boards, shareholders and executives searching for broader and better ways to manage risk in order to achieve their goals and ensure strategy viability. Thus the entire organisation must focus on the causes of risk instead of the traditional method of treating only the symptoms or focusing on protection through insurance.

The recent economic crisis and nearly fatal events of 2008 and 2009 created a significant awareness of the need for risk management and the widespread consequences of undetected risk. Boards of directors are now focusing on risk management efforts within their organisations and are posing questions to CEOs about how their organisation identifies, assesses, monitors and manages those risks. This trend is especially evident in companies outside the financial services industries. This new focus and awareness has fostered activities such as improved governance, risk assessments, risk initiatives and enterprise risk management (ERM).

Step one of an effective risk management programme is necessary to ensure that every decision maker in your organisation is on the same page about the costs you cannot afford. As you will discover in this activity, there are many different views of what is risky. Without a common or mutually accepted view of risk, some employees will behave like they have a blank cheque when it comes to being innovative or attempting new things.

Evaluating Risk

Murphy's Law of Risk Ownership

Denial is the tool used most often to define the problem.

Now that your leadership has come to a consensus about risk, it is time to look at the risks your organisation faces and to classify these risks. Risk can be evaluated in a variety of ways, including immediacy, size, impact and scope.

Immediacy of Risk

Top risks, as identified by 168 senior finance executives in a survey conducted by CFO Research Services and Liberty Mutual Insurance Company in June 2010 and published in the July/August 2010 issue of *CFO* magazine, are as follows:

- Financial exposure (an operational risk)–51%
- Supply chain or logistics disruption (an operational risk)–37%
- Legal liability or reputational harm (a strategic risk)–35%
- Security breach (an operational risk)–23%
- Technology failure (an operational risk)–33%
- Natural and man-made disasters (an external risk)–21%
- Physical asset failure (both strategic and operational risks)–8%

A common fallacy in risk management is the belief that the more imminent risk, the more you must mitigate it, but this next truism defines reality.

Seventh Principle of Risk Management

The more time you give yourself to plan for any risk, the more options you have. The less time you provide for planning, the fewer options you have.

In ERM your risk portfolio is sorted into possible risks, probable perils, immediate threats and disastrous crises.

Right after I explained this to PJI's management team, I received the inevitable question, "How can we tell the differences?"

I replied, "It is your risk management team who assesses each risk and its consequences by conducting a risk triage with specific tools. You will learn how to use these tools before you are done with this material. What I need you to remember is the importance about time. When you provide yourself with sufficient time, you can better manage, mitigate or reduce almost any risk.

"Let's assume you face this risk. You are very concerned that a profitable line of business will be shut down because of a potential government regulation in the works. Think about ways that you could respond and protect yourself using the following time frames. Assume you have an advance notice of

- 90 days.
- nine months.
- three years."

Notice you could accomplish more in the three-year time frame than the 90-day one. This is why a systematic process for evaluating, sizing up and mitigating risk is the core of ERM and why you analyse all types of risk. How you face up to each one will vary depending on its size, impact and scope.

Size of Risk

In ERM, as your team assesses each risk using risk triage, each harmful or disastrous risk gets placed into a portfolio category. At times a risk can qualify for more than one category. Each organisation has its own definition for portfolios, but in general the sizes of risks will be sorted by the following portfolios:

- global or universal.
- specific.
- immaterial or negligible.
- emerging.

Eighth Principle of Risk Management
Formal risk management is getting in the habit of frequently and broadly asking, "What could undermine our mission and business model?"

Global or Universal Risk Portfolio

These perils are your strategic and external environment types of potholes, which makes it challenging to determine their size and impact, but you must do this because their cost can be expensive and their impact extensive.

Specific Risk Portfolio

These perils could possibly affect a specific area, such as turnover, operations, brand or intellectual capital. They are more tangible to size up and define, making your determination of the cost you cannot afford easier.

Immaterial or Negligible Risk Portfolio

These are everyday perils you face and believe will not be harmful or costly, yet it is crucial not to overlook them. Many companies make the mistake of believing that any risk in this category is unimportant and not worth effort, which is equivalent to denying the existence of Murphy's Law. Quite often a perfect storm occurs when several normally manageable risks "blowup" at the same time.

Emerging Risk Portfolio

This portfolio of risks is actually the scariest of all because they require the most attention, yet due to the numerous constraints on management's time, they rarely get managed or monitored. These risks often start out as rumours or distant rumblings, thus ignored or discredited because there seems to be no visible substance to them until it's too late.

The spring uprisings that occurred in the Middle East in 2010 and 2011 are examples of emerging risks that quickly became global ones. Later you will discover a tool that aids you in better assessing the size of a risk.

Impact of Risk

As your risk management team conducts its ongoing assessments of particular risks and determines their immediacy or size, they also attempt to define their impact. The common categories of risk impact are

- disastrous.
- disruptive.
- painful.
- negligible.

The key measure of impact is how much and how likely the risk will affect your organisation's viability. Your team must seek out answers to the question, Could this particular risk affect our

- business model?
- revenue stream?
- operational capabilities?
- reputation or brand?
- physical plant?
- financial condition or cash flow?
- intellectual capital?
- employees?
- other stakeholders?

Scope of Risk

As your risk management team attempts to get a handle on the size and impact of a particular risk, they should also analyse its scope. Scope in risk management is defined as the impact zone. This analysis is simultaneously done when assessing impact. A major risk to a key area will also most likely affect your profits, business model and one or more stakeholders. For example an earthquake similar in size to Japan's in 2011 that damages your building could also displace employees, lower earnings and distress certain physical assets.

Back to PJI

I could tell that the managers were somewhat overwhelmed by all the different ways they would have to slice and dice risk. After a long break I paused and solicited questions.

Q: Why does ERM put risks in so many different classifications?

A: You manage all risks as a combined package instead of individually. The approach you take to deal with the risk depends on its classification. A high-level danger that the whole organisation faces is managed one way, but the daily pitfalls inherent in an employee's job are managed another way.

Q: It feels like the management team will spend a majority of its time hunting for risks. Is that true?

A: If you look at risk management from the point that if it is rarely done, it may seem that the executives and others will spend an inordinate amount of time looking for dangers. The reality is that, with a systematic approach to risk, doing this becomes a normal part of everyone's job. Before e-mail became the accepted way for business communications, it was normal for the nonuser to believe he or she would spend a whole day addressing all the e-mails in his or her inbox. After we all learned how to use e-mail, it is now an ordinary responsibility of your job.

Q: Who gets to decide the classification of the risk? What happens if there is disagreement on the portfolio, size, impact or all of these?

A: It is the risk management team, sponsored and supported by the senior executives, who decide the classification of a specific risk. There will be disagreement because of the "Uncertainty Domino" I explained earlier. Some employees on this team may view a risk to be minor, but others may believe it is major. It is in the discussion about the risk's assumptions where the primary work of risk management gets accomplished.

Murphy's Law of Risk Catalyst

Denial is the greatest contributor to the existence of Murphy's Law.

How to Make an Internal Strategic Risk Assessment

When it comes to evaluating risk, leaders need to take a view that involves focusing more attention on truly understanding the risks inherent in the organisation's strategy and tactics. A risk management process must also reflect and support the organisation's culture, so the concept gets embedded and then owned by your organisation's management. If both risk assessment and risk management processes are excluded from the firm's DNA, leaders will never own or treat them as an integral part of their day-to-day management.

Risk Management Tool Three– Strategic Risk Assessment

The Institute of Internal Auditors (IIA) is a great resource for information and tools to deal with the downsides of risk. Although its primary mission is to support the internal audit community, internal auditors are valuable contributors to ERM. In large companies the internal auditor regularly examines operational areas where potholes are likely to exist.

One of the IIA's tools is the self-assessment presented in Exhibit 4-1 and designed for senior managers, executives and board members to create a global awareness regarding risk. As you go through it, see how many of these you can honestly answer "Yes" to. Each "No" answer indicates an aspect of ERM that you need to be more concerned about.

Exhibit 4-1 Strategic Risk Assessment

Is there a process within the organisation responsible for assessing and monitoring risk?

Do I have assurance that controls are operating as planned?

Is there a thorough and an appropriate reporting mechanism within the organisation that allows for adequate checks and balances for fraud prevention and risk management?

Do I have assurance that financial and other information is correctly reported?

Are risk management, control and governance processes being evaluated and reviewed for efficiency and effectiveness on an ongoing basis?

Do I have a clear understanding of enterprisewide risk and the organisation's key areas of vulnerability?

Does the organisation have an operational system for managing risk?

Is there an internal process within the organisation for adding value to and improving operations?

Are the organisation's stakeholders provided with reliable assurances that their investments are protected?

If I were not a part of management or the board, would I be comfortable with the assurances provided to me as a stakeholder?

Am I able to sleep at night without worrying about risk in the organisation?

Am I comfortable that all risks have been appropriately addressed?

Source: The Institute of Internal Auditors. Altamonte Springs, Florida. www.itaudit.org.

At the May session I asked PJI's managers and executives to complete this assessment. They discovered to their horror that the firm as a whole was not very sensitive to risk. This was not surprising because a majority of large and small organisations fail to consistently practise formal risk management.

What Strategic Risk Management Is

Now that I had their (and your) undivided attention, I presented the seven facets of a global assessment of risk. Strategic risk management is

1. a process for identifying, assessing and managing both internal and external events and risks that could impede the implementation of strategy and reaching strategic objectives.
2. a formal structure with the ultimate goal of creating and protecting value for the owners and all other stakeholders.
3. a primary component of the organisation's overall ERM structure.
4. effected by the board of directors, management and others as a component of the firm's overall ERM programme.

5. something that requires a strategic view of risk and a consideration of how external and internal scenarios will affect the ability of the organisation to achieve its objectives.
6. a continual leadership-level process that must be embedded in firm strategy by setting, executing and managing it.
7. viewed as a core competency at both management and board levels.

Three Examples of Tools to Assess Risk

Later in this session I demonstrated specific tools we could immediately apply to three specific risks that PJI currently faces.

Risk Management Tool Four–Risk Tolerance Questionnaire

This tool, shown in exhibit 4-2, is a series of layered probing questions that will aid you in determining your tolerance level or the cost you can afford. Determine, before you undertake your next urgent strategic initiative or action plan, the full consequences of the failure to achieve the desired outcome. Compare the potential losses, including the softer, hard-to-measure ones, to the alleged or expected payoffs.

Exhibit 4-2 Risk Tolerance Questionnaire

Name the goal ______________________

Why are we undertaking this goal?

What is the designed impact?

How is this goal connected to our mission?

What is the specific risk in this goal that we can afford to take?

What is the risk that we cannot afford to take?

At what point will the cost of completing this goal be considered too much to bear?

Risk Management Tool Five–Critical Risk Questionnaire

The tool can be used to identify the scope of a potential risk and consists of specific questions that will help you differently look at risk. Exhibit 4-3 shows six very important questions that need to be asked before the risk is undertaken:

Exhibit 4-3 Critical Risk Questionnaire

Specific risk or vulnerability ______________________

What is the worst that can happen?

What is the best that can happen?

What is the most likely outcome?

What are the negative effects of the likely outcome?

How can we handle the negative effects?

How will we minimise or protect ourselves against the negative effects?

Risk Management Tool Six– Critical Risk Path

This tool can be used to identify the implications of the decision to be made about an opportunity and a risk known as the critical risk path. Figure 4-2 shows the tool. Walking through this step-by-step process before the organisation takes a major risk will help you and others make smarter decisions. Please do not assume this tool is simplistic because its value lies in what comes after your initial decision.

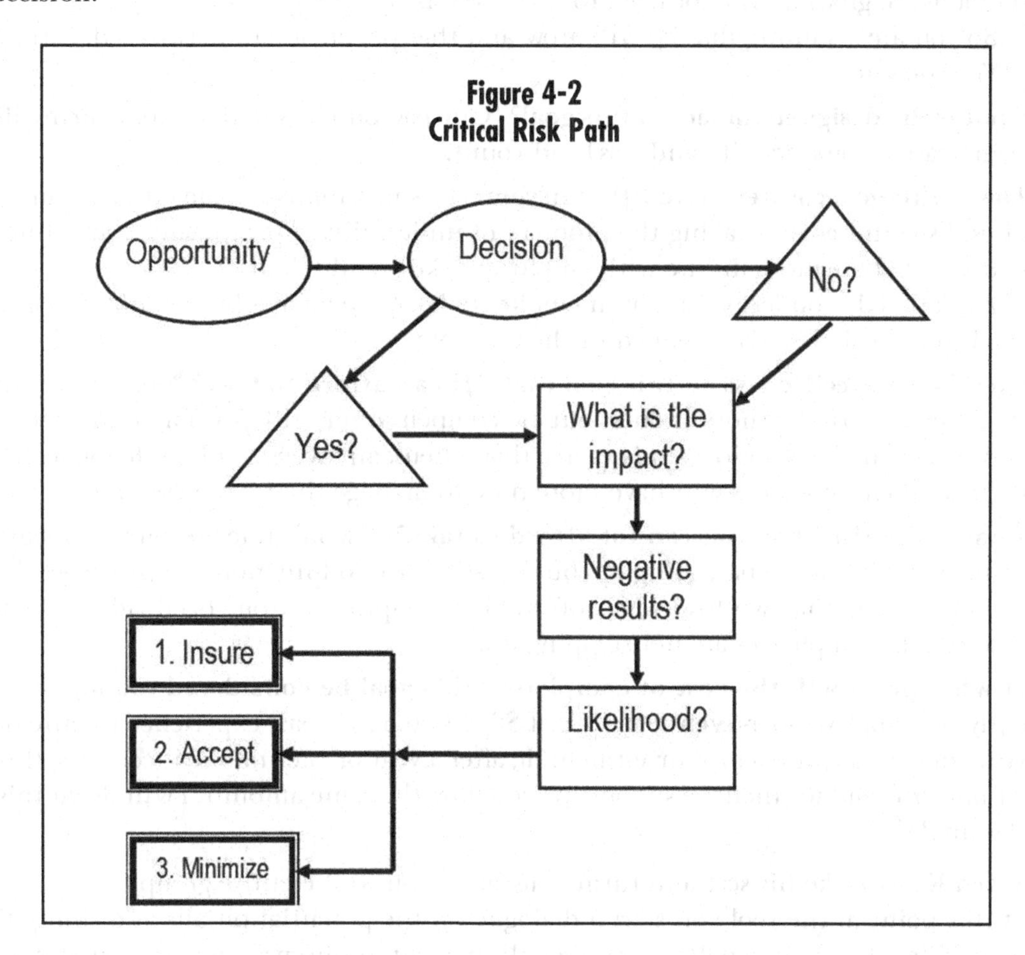

Once you have determined the likelihood, you move to the choices you have to deal with the risk. One option is to accept it (knowing the cost cannot hurt you). Another option is to minimise the risk. There are plenty of actions to take before undertaking the risk to keep its impact or cost low. A third option is to insure, but that does not mean that insurance is your only option. Sharing the risk by partnering with another firm or putting a stop-loss through a limited investment of both time and money are ways to insure the risk. Best of all your three options are not mutually exclusive. For example you could accept part of the risk, insure part of it and closely manage it, so that you minimise the potential downsides.

Three Case Studies

Case Study: The Risk in Giving Incentives to Certain Employees

Using Risk Management Tool Four to Gauge Risk Tolerance

Karl is the vice president of human resources for PJI. Weeks before we discussed a programme he was about to implement that would offer administrative employees a bonus if they met certain goals. At my suggestion Karl held off on rolling out the programme until we could test for pitfalls.

"Karl, please answer the questions in this tool."

What is your goal? "We need our administrative employees to work smarter. If they do we become more profitable, and I think we should share the saving with them. The incentive will be a carrot for them to be more productive and efficient."

Why is PJI undertaking this goal? "We want to increase the productivity of our support people, so that as we grow, we do not need to hire more people."

"So you are assuming that PJI will grow and that people are underutilised, correct?"

"Yes," he said.

What is the designed impact of this goal? "Our payroll costs will go up, which will be offset by an increase in productivity and less head-count."

How is this goal connected to PJI's mission? "PJI's mission is to convert problems into opportunities. I see this goal as taking the problem of underutilised people and converting it into work products that are more in line with employees' skills and talents."

"From this do you feel your admin employees have the talents but are not performing at a level equal to their skills?" Karl nodded in the affirmative.

What is the specific risk in this goal that PJI can afford to take? "Both Tracy (the CFO) and I believe that paying more money out in compensation will pay for itself in having a better revenue-per-employee ratio. We also agree that when employees can handle higher-level problems, the investment managers will have more time to manage their business units."

What is the risk that you cannot afford to take? "I won't tolerate our compensation, which includes the inventive pay, going up, but we still have to hire more people to get the work done. Another risk is that we lose some of our best employees from overloading them with work because other employees are not stepping up."

At what point will the cost of completing this goal be considered too much to bear? "Currently our employee-per-revenue ratio is at $600,000. From past experience we hire five employees every time we acquire a new investment. If, after a year of offering the incentives, this metric does not improve, and we increase support personal by the same amount, I will deem this programme a failure."

I asked Karl to take his seat and turned my attention to the entire group.

"At this point in the tool you start a dialogue on the potential pitfalls and things that have not been considered. In your small groups I would like you to discuss these five questions:

1. How can we deal with the productivity issue without incentives?
2. How do we strive to retain our best employees without the incentives?
3. What would employees think if we offered them an incentive programme and then, a year later, take it away?
4. How could employees obtain the incentive yet not be more productive or valuable?
5. Based on your interactions what is the likelihood that the incentives alone will induce a majority of the administrative employees to be more productive and valuable?"

The Result

After the groups reported in and presented their conclusions to Karl, he told us, "I can see I did not think this through very well. The likelihood of this getting the behaviours we desire is small. My team and will go back to the drawing board."

I thanked Karl and asked, "Aren't you glad you found out the pitfalls in your initiative before you implemented it, rather than finding them out 12 month from now?"

Karl had a relieved look on his face as he said he was glad.

Case Study: The Risk of Doing Business in a Third-World Country

Using Risk Management Tool Five to Identify the Scope of Risk

I selected an investment executive to demonstrate the power of the second tool. "Juanita, you are leading the effort to acquire a company with mineral rights in Mozambique, Africa. Would you say that this could be a major risk?"

She replied, "Yes. It is risky because we do not have experience doing business there, and I hear stories about the poverty and corruption that currently exist in that part of Africa."

"Why does PJI want to make this investment?" I inquired.

"Our opportunity is that there is a growing demand for black tourmaline in electronics. If we do not act swiftly, someone else could beat us to this company."

"The question you face therefore is, Do we go through with the purchase: yes or no?"

For everyone's benefit and to show the effectiveness of the tool, I walked Juanita through the tool step by step.

What is the risk? "We have a golden opportunity to bring a rare mineral to market just as demand for it is growing."

What is the impact of doing this? "If our geological studies are accurate,and we manage this properly, our initial $3m investment could grow to $10m within four years. However we are investing in a third-world country where the government is unstable, and there is little in the way of infrastructure. A big unknown is the potential need for a security force to protect the mine's employees and operations."

What is the worst that could happen? "We could lose all of our initial investment plus the additional money we put into the company."

What is the best that could happen? "We could generate a greater than average return of our $3m–$4m outlay within four years, plus we have an asset that we could sell."

What is the most likely outcome? *After a learning curve of six to ten months, the income stream and cash flows would become stable and then grow. Before our opportunity window closes, a company already doing business in that area might buy us out.*

What are the negative impacts of the most likely outcome? "I can think of three:

1. We would be hard-pressed to find another opportunity like this one of investing in a rare precious mineral for the booming American electronics market.
2. We would not generate our desired return on investment (ROI) of three.
3. We might be induced to sell our stake in the company at less than full value due to the political instability in that region."

How would you handle the negative impacts? "Right now I predict we could:

- position the company for sale from the start.
- get a regular appraisal of the unrecovered minerals every six months.
- lower our ROI threshold from 300% to 200%.
- strive to maximise the amount of profits and cash flows in the first two years of operation.
- induce the mine's customers to sign long-term contracts."

How would you minimise these negative impacts? "We could:

- hire an experienced geologist/mining manager to oversee the operations.
- look for a strong financially secure partner located in Africa.
- seek out the latest mining best practices and use them."

"Using this tool, Juanita, you now have the outline of a strategic action plan on ways to mitigate the risk while protecting your investment. Do you see that?"

"I do. That was not painful at all." She said this with a big smile.

Case Study: The Risk of New Technology

Using Risk Management Tool Six for Acting or not Acting

For the next example I selected Tracy, PJI's CFO. "Justin told me that you are in charge of making the 'Yes' or 'No' decision on investing in a cloud-based information system for the entire company. Have you made your decision yet?"

"No," she said.

"Let's walk through the critical path tool on the information that you have already gathered."

How would you define the opportunity? "We want to become a virtual company, so that project managers and portfolio executives can work wherever the company they manage is located. We spend nearly $1m dollars annually on airfare. Because many employees are visiting our investments, we don't need a desk for every employee. I feel we have more office space than we need. By having a company wide database that uses cloud computing, we could be more responsive and flexible by giving employees access to information wherever they are in the world."

"Tracy, assume you say 'No' to this opportunity."

What are the impacts or negative results of saying "No"? "So far I thought of three:

1. Our managers will continue to travel back and forth.
2. We will continue to rely on paper reports sent out via e-mail.
3. Our current information system is rapidly becoming obsolete, so we will still spend a large amount of money upgrading it yet not get the cost savings I want."

What is the likelihood that these negative results will take place if you say "No?" This question is very important because you now have to quantify the risk.

Tracy said, "I estimate a 50% probability that we would not acquire a cloud-based database system because not all the executives are sold on it. Plus I estimate there is a 90% probability we will have to invest nearly $500,000 to upgrade our current system."

How would you ensure that these effects will not be too costly or detrimental? "I would invest in a database that would allow us to use cloud computing later instead of now, but as rapidly as technology changes, I estimate there is a 40% probability this would be a bandage and not a solution."

How would you accept this risk? "I and others would explore other ways that allow our managers and executives to not have to travel to Phoenix."

How would you minimise this risk? "I would launch a study on alternative ways for us to end our reliance on stand-alone workstations and desktops. If we decide not to move to the cloud for our data and communications management, there must be other alternatives."

"Tracy, we now will switch gears and assume you say 'Yes' to this opportunity."

What are the impacts or negative results of saying "Yes"? "We will need to

- invest in expensive laptops for managers to use.
- beef up security.
- train everyone in the organisation on how to use the system, so we obtain a maximum benefit quickly.
- allow adequate time to integrate this new system into our operations and then change our existing processes.
- decide how best to utilise about 70,000 square feet of office space that could be freed up."

What could be the negative results of saying "Yes"?

- "If we fail to train properly to use the new system we will never obtain full value for our huge investment.
- We will face some resistance from employees who will be uncomfortable using this new system.
- If we fail to address security, relying on the cloud makes us more vulnerable than we are today.
- Of course with any undertaking like this, if we don't manage it well, it could take longer.
- If our current system 'dies' before the new one is ready, we would have a big problem."

What is the likelihood that these negative results will take place if you say "Yes"? "I like to estimate the odds:

- Not doing adequate employee training–90%
- Not overcoming employee resistance–20%
- Increasing system vulnerability–30%
- Conversion failure due to improper management–40%"

How would you ensure that these effects will not be too costly or detrimental? "Starting from the moment that the decision is made to acquire the software, we must begin training everyone on how to use it properly."

How would you accept this risk? "Recognise that there will be resistance in whatever system we switch to. Therefore we must work closely with all the managers and executives to ensure adoption through ongoing training and daily usage. In addition we must accept that by relying on the cloud, technology vulnerability increases."

How would you minimise this risk? "I think we would need to

- strengthen our security procedures.
- find ways to generate income from the extra office space, such as moving some of our smaller investment companies into that space. This will also help our cash flows.
- hire an experienced project manager to run the conversion and make sure the project gets funded and staffed and receives a top priority status."

The Result

"Tracy, what do you think of your ability to make a quick decision now?"

She said, "I can see our risks and mitigation strategies much more clearly. I am eager to spend more time on this analysis, so I can make a decision sooner." Employees who were in favour of the cloud system applauded Tracy as she sat down.

Onward

Room for Improvement

Ernst and Young conducted a survey of senior executives spanning all industries regarding their risk management efforts and the findings.

Ninety-six per cent of executives say their company's risk management processes leave room for improvement.

Only 6% of organisations planned to significantly expand risk management resources over the next 12–24 months.

Thirty-two per cent of organisations anticipate a slight increase in investing in risk management.

Source: http://www.cfo.com/article.cfm/14457815?f=search

Steps one and two of your risk management programme require leaders and key decision makers to annually sit down and examine risk. At this meeting you should dispassionately define what is considered risk taking and the costs you cannot afford. Over the life of the organisation this definition will dramatically change.

If your organisation fails to take the first two critical steps in implementing a risk management programme, you will find employees who take on more or fewer risks than they should. Employees will solely focus on either the upside or downside of a risk, depending on their frame of personal reference. Some employees will ignore or overlook activities or decisions that contain risk, but others will over dramatise the odds of failure. None of these are good outcomes because you will end up like PJI's situation: unprepared for the risks that are inherent in running an organisation.

I closed the session with the advice of another expert.

> *"The first step in the risk management process is to acknowledge the reality of risk. Denial is a common tactic that substitutes deliberate ignorance for thoughtful planning." Charles Tremper*

Your Action Plan

Step One

Complete the strategic risk assessment for your organisation. Even if you cannot answer a question, think about its implication for your company or firm. Describe, in general, what this says about those you work with and for.

Step Two

Think of an important personal or business opportunity, risk or challenge that you currently face. Use the critical risk questions on it. How did the questions help you? Is the challenge as big as you thought before going through the questions?

Step Three

Use the same important opportunity, risk or challenge as before, or select a new one. Walk your decision through the steps of should I or shouldn't I be using the critical risk path. How did the map help you? Is the challenge of saying "Yes" or "No" as frightening as you thought before using this tool?

5

WHEN Is It Appropriate to Plan for Risk?

"I wish we had taken the time to plan for the unexpected and the ridiculous." Mark R.

Just when I did not think it could get any hotter, it was. Phoenix, Arizona, would reach 45° Celsius today! I would use the heat, which Arizona natives are used to, as another lesson in enterprise risk management (ERM).

Plan for Risk before It Happens

Standing in front of PJ Investment's (PJI's) management team, I asked them, "How do you plan for this intense heat?" I received many puzzled looks, which was my intent.

"Let me restate this question. Imagine that a cousin of yours, Vanessa, who lives in Reykjavik, Iceland, announces she is moving to Phoenix and wants you to advise her on how she should adapt to the summer weather, something Vanessa has never experienced. Think about this question as I relate a story about a client's pitfall."

Mark's Failure to Anticipate Risk

Mark and Mary had a passion for helping others. Early in their marriage, even though they were living pay packet to pay packet, they committed to one day starting a foundation to help children afflicted with Apert syndrome.

Mark's younger sister was born with this rare disease. Catherine, or Cat, as her family called her, was never treated for it because her parents could not afford the expensive test and surgeries. At that time there was no funding or other form of support for young victims of this random disease. Cat's life, as Mark saw it, was one misery after the other. Due to her abnormally shaped head and fused fingers that resembled fins, Cat was frequently made fun of and spent most of her life indoors as a way to shield her from the embarrassment and unwanted attention.

When Mark and Mary made this pact to fund early medical intervention for infants born with Apert's syndrome, they had no clue where the money would come from, but that did not deter them. Over their first 30 years of marriage, they saved what they could (approximately $750,000), which got the M&M Foundation started. Then three unrelated events took place that Mary considered a blessing and Mark called good timing. They could now afford to fund their dream.

First, Mary won the state lottery in which she collected $5m after taxes. Next, Mark patented one of his many ideas and sold it for $1m. The most surprising gift was from Mark's aunt, Minnie. Upon Minnie's death her family discovered she was a saver and died with over $2.3m in her savings account. She willed this money to the M&M Foundation because she also had witnessed the sad impact the syndrome had on Cat's life.

On his fiftieth birthday Mark retired and devoted his full-time attention to running the foundation, which had accumulated $10.2m in cash resources. Mark, who is more of a dreamer and visionary than a planner, spent most of his time managing the investments and meeting with Apert syndrome research organisations. He also brainstormed with doctors and hospitals to determine the best ways to fulfil the numerous requests he received to pay for early detection and surgery. These came from anguished parents, similar to his Mom and Dad, who could not afford these costly procedures.

Once he took the CEO role full time, Mark was frequently reminded by Mary to write out a management plan to ensure that the foundation was properly managed and would continue to exist beyond their lifetime. Each time Mark promised her that he would, but he didn't. Because he hated sitting behind the desk and writing out his thoughts, Mark procrastinated on this obligation.

In its fourth full year of operations, the M&M Foundation was hit by two unexpected lawsuits. One was from a family whose son died from complications of the surgery to correct his cervical spinal fusion. Their punitive damages claim for $10m was directed at the hospital, the surgeon and the foundation that funded the surgery. Seven months later an ambitious solicitor convinced a potentially unethical research organisation to sue the M&M Foundation for $5m. The reasoning, as stated in the lawsuit, was that "Mark's decision to not fund their research was a capricious and badly researched decision."

These lawsuits put Mark into a state of panic. He had never considered that the people and organisations he dealt with wouldn't always take the high road.

For the next year Mark and Mary spent considerable time and personal and foundation money to defend their dream from the two lawsuits that their solicitors described as "frivolous yet winnable."

Mark's Pitfall

Mark assumed that the compassionate purpose of this foundation, its reputation and deep pockets could never be a magnet for people who want something for nothing. He was unprepared to deal with time-consuming and wasteful events, such as defending his foundation from these lawsuits.

Mark was correctly spending his time setting the vision for his foundation, but he also needed to spend time envisioning the best way to protect his organisation's future. Both are vital leadership responsibilities that are done simultaneously.

Back to PJI

"Let's return to my question. Walk through your thought process, on paper, of how you would prepare cousin Vanessa for a typical Phoenix summer. Remember she spent her life in Reykjavik, where the winters get down to –15° Celsius, and the summer temperatures rarely rise above 20° Celsius."

I broke them into small groups and provided each with a flipchart, requesting they list a step-by-step process to help Vanessa prepare for a Phoenix summer. When they were finished we reviewed each team's process and then condensed those into a comprehensive process. The major steps were

- establish a new mind-set.
- change her wardrobe.
- relocate in fall or winter.
- live in a house or an apartment with a good air-conditioning system.
- drive a car with a working air conditioner and park it out of the sun.
- adjust her diet, and tell her to drink a lot of water.

- adjust her daily schedule (eg, do not go outside between 10.00 am and 5.00 pm).
- never put herself in a situation where she is outside for long periods of time.
- monitor her health (heat stroke usually is detected after it's too late).
- make the transition one step at a time (it will take several summers to fully acclimate herself).

After we reviewed the steps I pointed out, "Please notice that in your plans for Vanessa's care and ability to deal with the extreme change in climates, she would need to prepare herself before she encounters the intensity of a Phoenix summer."

In ERM you must examine risk where it starts. If you consistently do this, you quickly will have the capability to prevent, avoid or minimise costly perils. Then as you drive down the road, any inevitable potholes you encounter will be less detrimental to your journey because, like Vanessa, you will face them with a sense of confidence and preparedness.

> **Murphy's Law of Risk Timing**
>
> Disaster seems to occur on Friday afternoons, weekends, holidays, vacations and when you are away from your desk.

Risk management is not a programme, but it is an attitude and awareness. It is not enough to have a risk management structure in place, you must practise risk management. According to conventional wisdom the pessimist sees the worst, the optimist sees the best but the realist sees the best of both, which is the attitude you want to instil in your own risk management programme. If employees believe the sky is falling, they will pick apart every action and decision while looking for the pothole. If employees think nothing can go wrong, they will miss or ignore the potholes. Your goal is to propagate the attitude that we will take risks and be on the lookout for the potholes along the way because they exist. The confidence to act with realism is built by seeking out the true sources of risk.

ERM Step Two– Seek Out the Global Sources of Risk

ERM is a broad set of processes that apply across the entire organisation. It enables the achievement of the entity's objectives in four realms:

1. Strategic objectives
2. Operational objectives
3. Reporting objectives
4. Compliance objectives

The first two objectives are covered in this chapter, and the latter two will be covered in later chapters.

ERM is the best practice for overall risk management in highly successful organisations and is quickly becoming the standard as an integrated approach to managing a broad spectrum of risks called a risk portfolio. It is a strategy for overcoming the preferred and dangerous "silo" approach to risk management in which different groups or teams within the company focus on different sorts of risks, with little or no interaction between them: "siloed" risk management.

Risk portfolio is a view of risk in an aggregate manner. In ERM, risk is viewed from an organisation-wide perspective, known as a holistic, an integrated or an aggregate approach. Risk is addressed in a portfolio manner to create a consistency of approach and communications. In most companies informal risk mitigation is more likely to be performed on an ad hoc basis and done separately, described as a "silo" approach. This is where managers are responsible for managing only the specific risks of their individual functions. For example, the purchasing department is responsible for managing the commodity price risk, and the treasury department takes ownership of foreign exchange and interest rate risk. This approach lends itself to certain risks going unnoticed because no single employee is uniquely accountable.

If an organisation adopts the integrated approach to risk management, it must evaluate the entire portfolio of risks that it faces globally and locally.

ERM offers you a holistic methodology for identifying, assessing, quantifying and addressing strategic, operational, market, financial and human risks in order to optimise your organisation's risk-reward profile.

Organisational value in ERM refers to the ongoing worth of your organisation. In a public company this is measured by its market capitalisation. In a privately held company it can be measured by tangible net worth. A non-profit making company's value could represent the nonprofit's fiscal health or viability. In formal risk management you are attempting to protect this predefined value from being harmed or diminished by unwarranted risks.

Strategic Objectives and ERM

Just as a river has a source, all your highest-level risks have one too: the way you define your organisation in your mission or purpose and business model. A company's business model is made up of two components:

1. The organisational structure and processes
2. The impact from opportunities faced and decisions made

If your organisation is unable to perform or execute its strategy, you risk execution failure. To prevent this you need to focus on the results generated from the structure of your marketplace and business model. Three specific global risks reside within the theory of your business model:

1. Strategic risk
2. Operational risk
3. Innovation risk (this topic was covered in chapter 3, "WHY Is Risk Management Important to Us?")

Strategic objectives are 10,000-metre goals aligned with your organisation's mission. Any internal and external events and scenarios that can inhibit your organisation's ability to achieve its intended objectives are named as strategic risks. Strategic risk management is a critical part of the organisation's overall ERM process. Strategic risk starts the moment you create a business model from a mission.

Today's leader needs this high-level view of his or her road to success because it is easy and dangerous to lose sight of the big picture. As you fly over to see things like detours, avalanches and washed-out roads, you are looking far ahead, so that your journey is safe and prosperous. Traditionally, senior leaders do some of this work as they conduct strategic planning that generates a budget.

Relationship of Strategic Planning and Risk Management

Strategic planning is managing change and overcoming risks and must become a process in which global risk can be identified and dealt with. The standard flow of strategic planning is shown in Figure 5-1:

Figure 5-1
Strategic Planning Flowchart

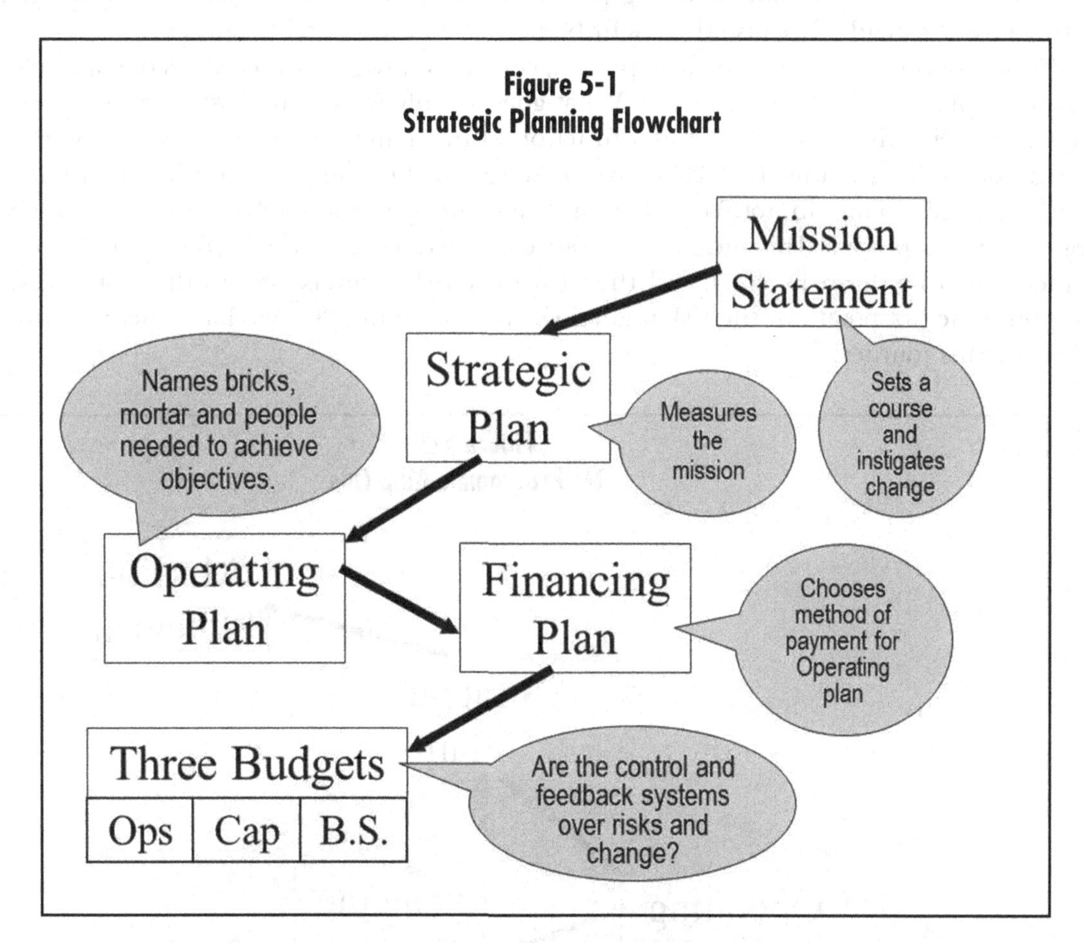

Strategic planning starts with your mission statement because it sets your organisation on a course and instigates change from today's status quo to where you want to be in the future.

A basic outcome when you engage in strategic forecasting is your actual strategic plan: the measurement of your mission. In this document you identify specific metrics and methods of measuring whether you are accomplishing your mission over the next 18–24 months. Specific global risks can be measured, so you can monitor them.

Information from the strategic forecasting flows into the second product—your operating plan—that identifies the bricks, mortar and people you need to achieve each specific objective in your strategic plan. The annual operating plan defines where you are heading and what you will commit to accomplishing in the next 12 months.

Out of your operating plan comes the third product: your financing plan. In this document you highlight the methods of payment for the bricks, mortar and people required to fulfil your operating plan. These are the questions that get answered in the financing plan:

- How much of the money will come from internal sources and profits?
- Will some of the funds come from outside investors?
- Will additional funding be required from our banks or other lenders?

Finally, after the financing plan, you produce three more products detailing your fiscal plans: the operating budget, capital budget and balance sheet budget. These three documents become your control and feedback systems over the risks and changes you instigated with your mission and strategy.

This holistic view of your planning process serves to remind you that you really need to plan your journey carefully because there will be potholes on the road to success.

Because of the necessary holistic approach, your ERM programme consists of your operating plan, financing plan and the three budgets. What goes terribly wrong in most organisations is that your leaders perceive risk management as a function of insurance. From this flawed view the job of risk mitigation is delegated to the CFO or risk manager, if the company even has a formal position for a risk manager; many do not. Yet, CFOs and risk managers are rarely included in the leader's strategic planning process. This means that your executives embark on a global plan, ignoring risks or underestimating the risks' costs, and then turn the risk analysis over to the employees, ultimately dropping the hot potato in the risk manager's lap and asking, "Do we have adequate insurance coverage for this journey?"

Figure 5-2
ERM Programme Map One

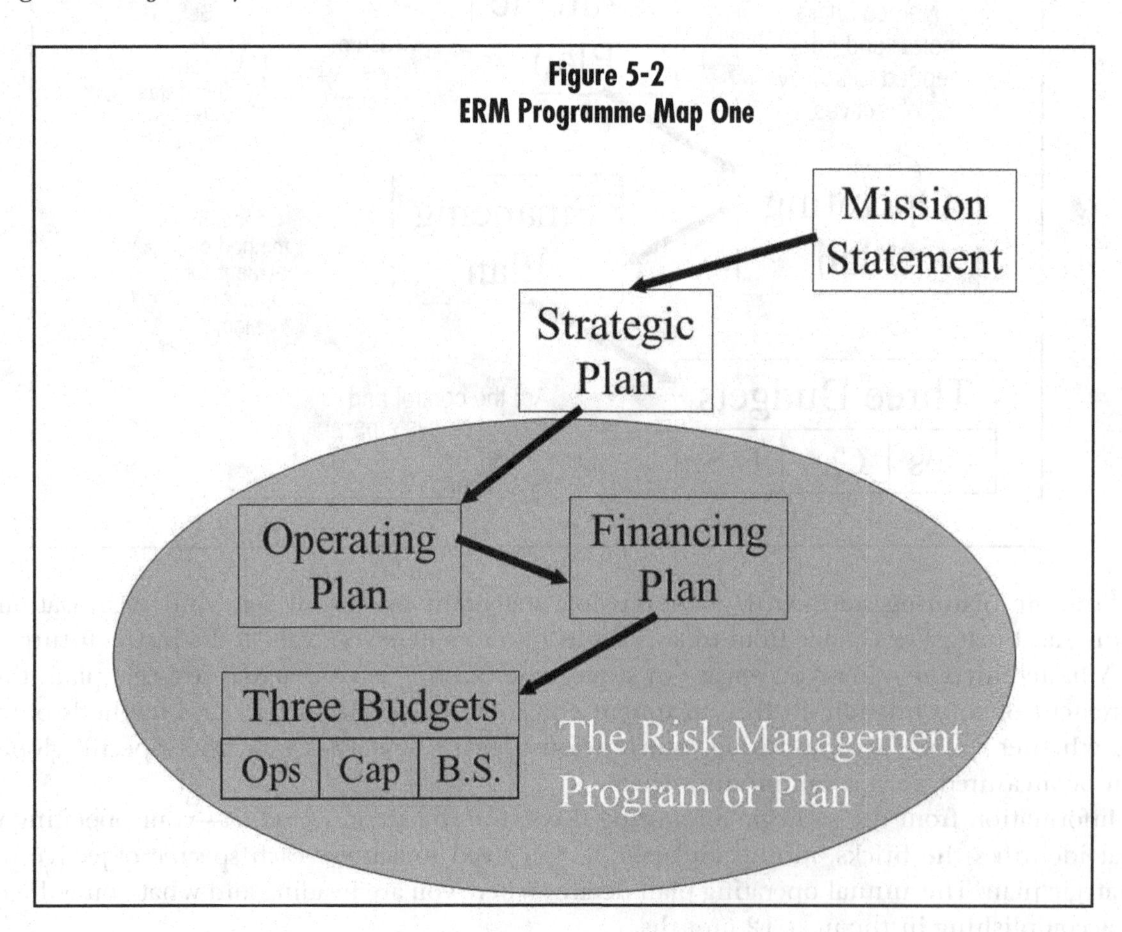

As you can see from Figure 5-2, making this fatal blunder will not really protect the firm from potholes. Your ERM programme needs to be a key agenda item at all strategic thinking sessions when the leaders are devising their plans for next year. This is when they must define risk, as we did in Step one.

Assessing Your Strategic Risk

Strategic risk is defined as the inability to prepare your organisation for competitive pressures and customer satisfaction. Three threats may compromise your strategy:

1. Integrity risks, including ethical lapses, that harm your reputation and brand
2. Reputation risks that harm your reputation and brand
3. Intellectual capital risks that harm collective wisdom and trade secrets.

The executive team should focus on the identification and management of strategic risks, which are those risks that are most consequential to your organisation's ability to carry out its strategy, achieve its business objectives and protect or build value. The 10,000-metre level focus of strategic risk management is not intended to identify every risk that you face but only to identify those that are most significant and can harm your organisation's ability to achieve its core business strategy. A focus on strategic risk reinforces the direct relationship and critical linkage that connects your strategy to the execution and then to your risk management structure, as shown in Figure 5-3:

Figure 5-3
The Cause and Effect Chain

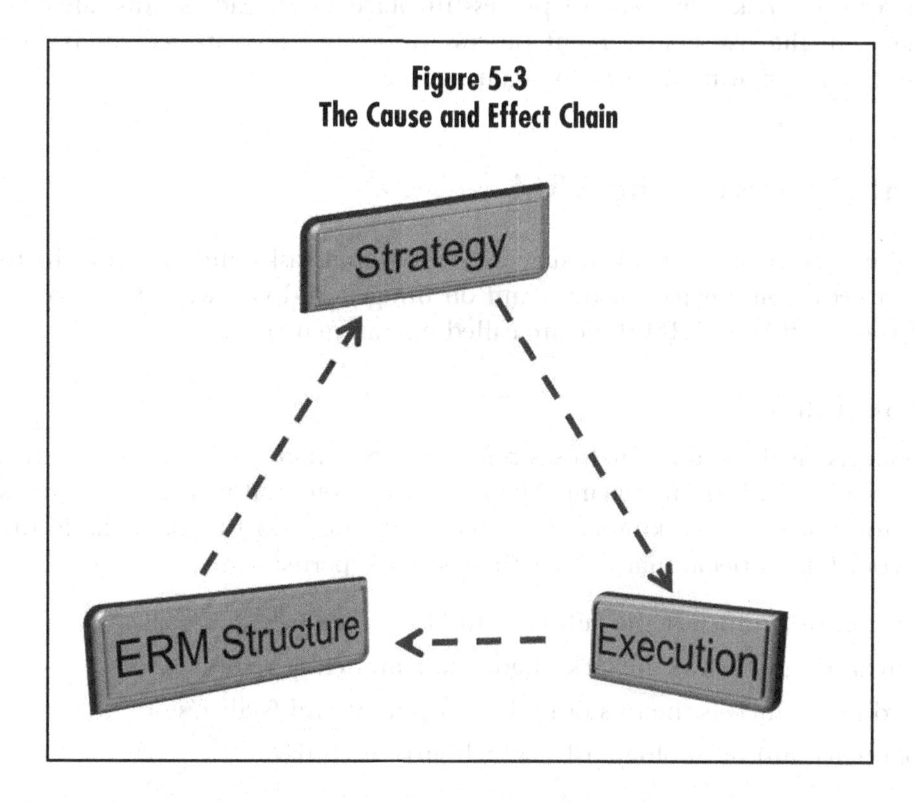

The entry point of a strategic risk assessment is designed to identify your organisation's strategic risks and action plans that will address those risks. The strategic risk assessment tool is described later in this chapter. Your strategic risk assessment is a systematic and continual process for assessing significant risks that an organisation faces and will provide valuable insight to both your executives and board. A key responsibility for a board of directors is to deeply understand the organisation's strategies and associated risks and to verify that the management team practises proper risk management.

These steps you go through define a basic high-level critical process that allows for tailoring and customising the plan's execution to reflect the maturity and capabilities of your organisation. The steps also show that your strategic risk assessment is an ongoing process, not just a singular event. It is a process designed to reflect the dynamic and ongoing nature of risk and to become a circular process that should be ongoing while continually improving as learning takes place.

> The National Association of Corporate Directors published the article *Key Agreed Principles to Strengthen Corporate Governance for US Publicly Traded Companies* in September 2011, which states the following:
>
> "For most companies, the priority focus of board attention and time will be understanding and providing guidance on strategy and associated risks . . . and monitoring senior management's performance in both carrying out the strategy and managing risk."
>
> *Source:* www.nacdonline.org/Resources/Article.cfm?ItemNumber=2686.

Increased expectations from shareholders, regulators, rating agencies, employees and the general public directed at both directors and executives demand that they understand and manage risks and have a formal risk management process in place. Your leaders must also ensure that there is transparency in the risk management process. Strategic risk management is focused on the most consequential and significant risks to organisational value.

Operational Objectives and ERM

As your firm travels on its road to success, operational tasks and activities in the form of action items must get accomplished on time and on budget, and you want to know about the potholes that will prevent this. In ERM these are called operational risks.

Operational Risk

Operational risk is defined as the losses resulting from inadequate internal control, poor processes, deficient people and broken systems. Managing this potential meltdown requires examining your business from the inner working's perspective. Sadly most existing financial feedback is inadequate to gauge your firm's operational risk for these specific perils:

- Execution risk, which is the failure to fulfil your strategy and goals
- Financial risk, which is the lack of adequate monetary resources
- Hazard risk, which is the loss of tools, equipment and facilities
- E-commerce and technology risks, which grow each day

The value of managing operational risk is only now gaining recognition. All firms incur operational risk simply when choosing their marketplace and customer base. Business complexity and revenue volatility increase operational risk and so do technology, regulations, your consumer and the global economy. Because they all affect risk, these must be factored into the assessment of your operational risks.

Operational risk management is managing the potential hazards resulting from

- inadequate or failed processes or systems,
- human factors and
- external events

and it requires clearly defined authority and accountability for each sort of identified risk.

Mitigating Operational Risk

Managing operational risk requires a systematic framework that assesses all the non-financial variables that could contribute to your risk portfolio. Timely, accurate and unbiased information is the underlying support system for these next solutions.

The starting point to managing operational risk is to make sure you are collecting the right data. This requires a complete and balanced view of your key business metrics and must include a mix of leading and lagging indicators. Your operational feedback data must be able to describe how all key operations are conducted. By tracking operational indicators and metrics, you will identify opportunities and threats before they affect the company's finances.

Your risk management programme requires a reporting mechanism for it to work as designed. Here are four solutions that will lower your operational risk while increasing transparency and decreasing rash or unwarranted risk taking:

1. To minimise any inability to execute, such as insufficient internal capability to deliver as promised, your executives must develop acute foresight and conduct regular in-depth self-assessments on the ability to bring their plans to fruition.
2. To overcome any information deficiencies, your organisation must combine operational and financial data in order to gain a complete and timely picture of operational risk. This means your managers must decrease their reliance on historical financial data. You need to assemble a list of possible and predictive metrics for your business and then test them to ensure that they correlate the activity to a particular financial impact.
3. To overcome the danger of not succeeding, your leaders and employees must grow in their ability to both spot and manage risks and convert them into opportunities. By understanding and then assessing your risk profile via regular updates, your tough resource allocation decisions benefit everyone, including your shareholders, customers and suppliers.
4. To ensure your success is multidimensional, the leaders must routinely access many non-financial factors, such as the quality of corporate governance, employee morale, customer satisfaction, implementation and execution of goals, and applications and deployment of new technology. In ERM a firm cannot afford a singular approach to measuring its operational risk; therefore, you must update your existing accounting system and reporting technology. As you implement ERM you employ numerous tools that enable you to easily measure your operational risk, such as the balanced scorecard, activity-based costing or driver-based forecasting.

No one likes to be in a vehicle in which the person at the wheel drives with his or her eyes closed. Yet most companies rely on accounting and budgeting processes and historical reporting techniques created in the 1930s. The ultimate payoff of relying on multiple and varied operational metrics to predict risks is the strengthening of your overall budgeting process.

When to Apply Risk Management

> **Murphy's Law of Foolproof Risks**
>
> The failure of only one system will never happen. Instead you will experience the failure of numerous systems that were failure proof.

Once you have established a risk management programme, you will notice numerous everyday activities where you can apply the principles and tools. This next section will define several areas where you can begin to impact and reduce the risk of doing business by applying ERM:

- When setting goals
- When implementing strategic initiatives
- When making everyday business decisions
- When identifying opportunities
- When tackling threats to your business
- When conducting scenario planning
- When practising governance

Daily, Monthly and Annual Goals

Operational objectives are the goals and targets established in the conduct of normal business operations. Executives set goals for themselves and their employees as indicators of achievement. These targets or milestones could be related to sales, production, customers or members, or expenses. An organisation fails whenever these goals go unmet; therefore, a huge risk exists if there is no way to determine if operationally oriented goals are not being met. If the goals are unrealistic, and employees waste time working on them, failure is also inevitable.

Managing operational risk is then simply managing the goals and objectives to ensure they are supported, realistic and achievable and then consistently making sure they get accomplished. In every organisation execution of goals related to the operation of the business is priority number one.

New Initiatives

Risk management becomes a way of operating so any time your organisation decides to take on a new project, a major activity or an initiative, the group of people who are making the decision automatically will do a risk analysis. By maintaining an awareness and a global mandate, potholes and perils will need to be addressed. The advantage of ERM is that this becomes a standard way of thinking, and over time people will soon forget they are doing a risk assessment. Analysing how Murphy's Law can affect your future becomes part of your daily work routine.

Everyday Business Decisions

Similar to how risk assessment enters into your big long-term decisions, the act of sizing up potential perils in your everyday business decisions also becomes a standard protocol. It can be difficult for those who have never been through a risk management process to understand that in every key business decision, there could be a potential pitfall.

In ERM, because you have embedded in your organisation's cultural awareness that risk could be costly and must be addressed up front, people will adopt the habit of reflecting on the potential downside of their decisions. ERM does not prevent decisions nor slow them down. It does help decisions to be comprehensive, and it makes employees, especially key decision makers, aware that their decisions have repercussions beyond the present moment.

Opportunities and Threats

Practising ERM, as it is designed, means your firm is alert to opportunities. Each day your employees miss out on lucrative opportunities. Do you recall a time when you saw an opportunity, missed it and later found out that someone else grabbed it? Frustrating, isn't it? This regularly occurs because of a natural tendency known as confirmation bias. We tend to notice data that confirms our existing belief system and ignore or discredit information that challenges that bias.

Being able to capitalise on the opportunities in your strengths, limitations, opportunities and threats (SLOT) analysis starts with paying attention to subtle clues, such as contradictions, incongruities or anomalies, which are all information that does not agree with conventional wisdom or what everybody else believes to be true.

Every day your employees encounter opportunities, but because they are not paying attention, they go to waste. Recall that in risk management, awareness is a fundamental way to uncover risk.

An article written by Donald Sull, professor of strategic and international management at the London Business School, in the autumn 2011 issue of *strategy+business* magazine names ten opportunities that organisations frequently miss:

1. A product should exist but does not.
2. The customer experience is time-consuming or annoying.
3. The product, service or resource is underpriced.
4. An innovative idea has not gained traction.
5. A product or service should be everywhere but is not.
6. Your customers have adapted a product or service in ways you did not plan for.
7. Customers (members) should not want a product or service, but they do.
8. Customers (members) are excited about a product or service you do not offer.
9. A product or service is in demand elsewhere but not locally.
10. A product or service, on paper, should not make money but does.

Awareness of information that goes against conventional wisdom is a critical clue that your organisational assumptions need updating. Any situation in which conventional thinking differs from reality is a huge indicator of risk. Leaders who consistently notice and explore anomalies usually are able to capture emerging opportunities before everyone else. Similarly they have less risk exposure.

In Chapter 6, "WHERE Do Our Efforts Need to Be?", you will be introduced to the SLOT analysis in which two components are your opportunities and threats. In ERM, each time that you go through a SLOT analysis, you are conducting an aspect of risk management by being aware of major threats to your business.

For leaders who are optimistic, the opportunities outcome of the SLOT analysis is where they put their attention. If your organisation has a viable business model, there will always be opportunities to sell more products, provide more services or lower your expenses. In the thoughtful process that goes into a SLOT analysis, as you identify each opportunity and decide when to pursue it, it is natural to do a risk assessment to determine what could undermine the opportunity or prevent you from capitalising on it.

Risk Assessing When Scenario Planning

Running through risk scenarios is one sure-fire method to help you understand risk and its likelihood at the 10,000-metre level. This helps you establish a clear high-to-low internal metric that represents the acceptable and unacceptable costs for the organisation. The more your leadership team runs through scenarios, the better it will understand the causes and forces of risk. Great information will be found in these scenario discussions. Of course leaders need to include not only financial implications of risks (earnings and cash flow) but also operational implications, such as brand, reputation, employment, and oversight of regulators and government agencies.

Scenario planning traditionally has been used by organisations in their budgeting, forecasting and financial planning processes. Today, however, scenario planning is being widely used by both large and small organisations that operate in uncertain or volatile markets.

Two driving forces behind the increased popularity and use of scenario planning are the

1. rapid and global impact of totally unpredictable events, such as September 11, the Japanese earthquake and resultant nuclear plant meltdown, and the global credit crisis.
2. accelerating pace at which new trends have an impact.

This scenario planning is focused on finding reasonable and viable answers for three critical questions:

1. What could happen (define the event)?
2. How would the event affect us beyond our strategies, plans and budgets?
3. How should we respond to the event?

Scenario planning is often used as an evaluation tool for an overall risk management process and can aid in the areas of risk appetite determination; capital planning; and credit quality, cash flow forecasting, hedging strategies and insurance coverage selection.

Finance professionals are vital to a scenario planning programme because they help managers better understand the current and future threats and opportunities and convert them into the potential financial impact. Your CFO's team (or accounting firm) can effectively support a scenario planning effort with these vital tasks:

- Analysing the financial implications of alternative strategies under different future scenarios
- Testing the sensitivity of key assumptions, financial measures and variables under different scenarios
- Developing alternative financial plans and forecasts using different selected scenarios
- Defining key performance indicators (KPIs) and leading indicators to track potential triggers
- Defining, measuring and monitoring key risk indicators (KRIs) to serve as early warning signals
- Monitoring and reporting on internal performance and external indicators likely to impact the current strategy.

As your organisation struggles to deal with an increasingly uncertain world, you can use scenario planning to help you understand your risks and then layout your choices for each one.

We recommend a simple step-by-step process for conducting a scenario analysis on a selected issue that concerns you. Each step describes the outcomes and tasks. Steps two and three can be simultaneously accomplished. The most important step is the first one because everything you do after this one is based upon consensus on the basic principles or assumptions.

Step One: Define Your Objective and Scope. Write out the issues, decisions and key variables to be evaluated. Set the scope of the study and the time horizon to be considered. Obtain consensus on the approach, select the team members and seek senior management's commitment if they will not be intimately involved. Finally select the tools you will use to test the scenarios.

You can address four broad types of scenarios in your scenario planning exercise:

- Social conditions
- Economic conditions
- Political conditions
- Technological conditions and changes

After you have agreed on the issue(s) to be studied and defined the scope and time horizon, these key information bits should be documented, confirmed and communicated to everyone involved in the scenario planning process.

Before conducting a scenario planning exercise, be clear about the issue that you want to address, and define the appropriate scope and time horizon for the scenarios you will construct. Be sure to answer these four questions that will help you determine if scenario planning makes sense and assist you in defining both the scope and objectives:

1. What decisions are we trying to make?
2. Is there a high degree of uncertainty about the future?
3. Is there is high uncertainty?
4. What is the time horizon for making decisions and executing them?

Step Two: Define Your Key Drivers. Identify the key external drivers that are likely to influence the scenarios. Define the major internal variables that need to be addressed. Establish critical relationships between the drivers, looking for relationships of cause and effect.

Scenario planning is a projection of things that will shape your organisation's future and a tangible way of understanding the driving forces or causal factors that affect your desired future, such as

- changing demographics.
- war, conflict or hostilities.
- weather conditions.
- political pendulum swings.
- globalisation.
- technology changes.
- environmental sustainability efforts.

Step Three: Collect and Analyse Data. Collect both quantitative and qualitative data, as well as expert opinions. Assess the predictability and impact of the selected key drivers. Define the appropriate measures to keep track of your key drivers.

Step Four: Develop Scenarios. Construct different scenarios and develop a narrative description for each one. Test these scenarios using the data you collected. Update each scenario as necessary, and set the criteria for evaluating both the strategies and tactics. You will likely need to use a technology tool that allows you to easily and quickly conduct sensitivity analysis.

Step Five: Apply Scenarios. Test the sensitivity of the strategies and tactics under each scenario. Formulate contingency plans, and establish risk mitigation strategies. Communicate these plans and strategies to all stakeholders.

The scenario plan you produced from these activities allows your organisation to make fast, confident decisions by providing a sound basis for evaluating the impact of changing conditions.

Step Six: Maintain and Update. Integrate the KPIs and KRIs into your regular management reports. Refresh the data, and update scenarios as needed over the selected time horizon. Repeat as needed.

Tool for Measuring Risk

It was time for the managers to learn another risk management tool.

Risk Management Tool Seven–Risk and Opportunity Measurement and Management Strategy Grid

A risk measurement and strategy grid is a common matrix that is often used to assist decision makers in fostering smarter decisions. It also applies to effective risk management.

This tool comes in three parts. The first, represented by Figure 5-4, is to help you determine the significance or impact of a particular risk. Each risk you analyse is defined by its probability or likelihood of occurring and its impact on your business or future. If a particular risk is both impactful and highly probable, it will be a high risk. If the risk is impactful but has a low probability of occurring, that it is a medium risk, as is a risk in which the likelihood is high, but its impact is low. Finally a low risk has a low probability and impact. Even small risks need to be analysed because they could grow, worsen or be underestimated.

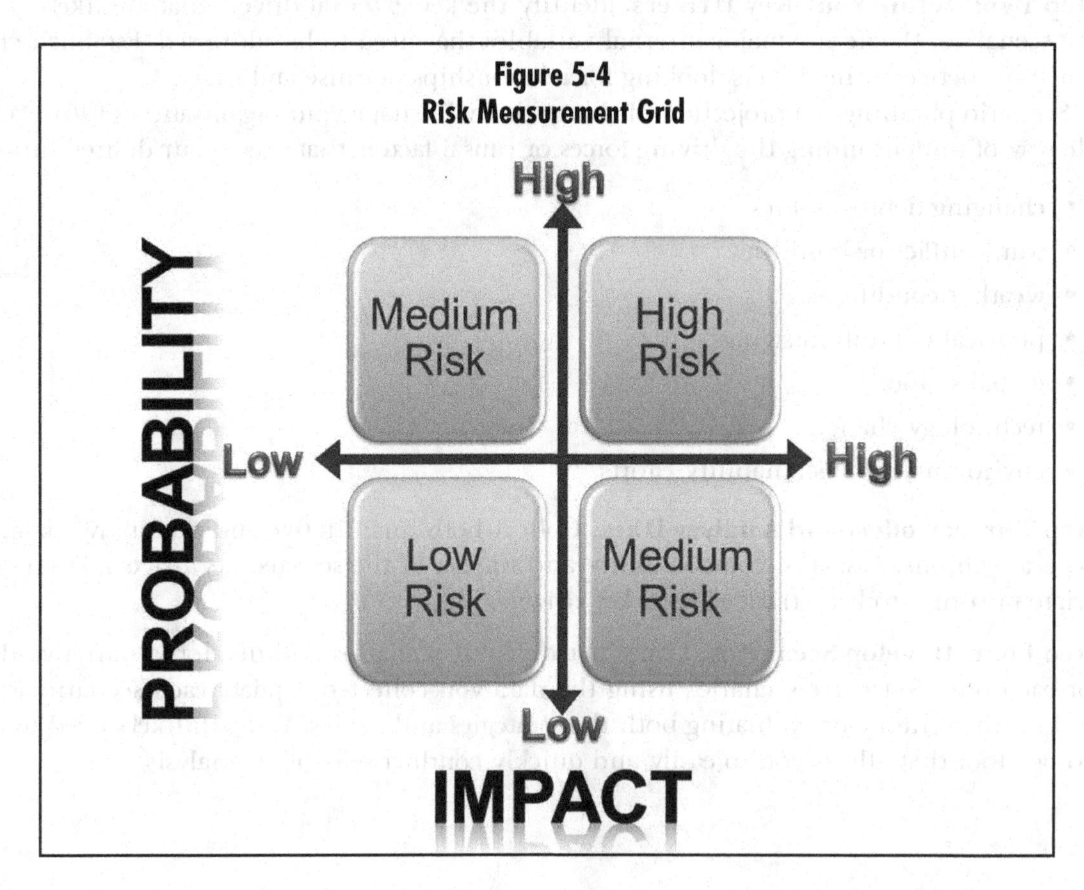

Part One–How to Use the Risk and Opportunity Measurement Grid

Step One: Identify the risk and/or opportunity. At times, they can be one and the same.

Example: Your organisation is seeking to obtain a long-term contract with a government agency for your products. You are one of two suppliers that submitted sealed bids. However, your competition is more experienced in this arena. The future of your company depends on winning this business. If you do not get the order, you will need to lay off employees and significantly cut spending.

Step Two: Estimate the upside for an opportunity or the downside for a risk.

Example: If you win this contract, it could mean about $50 million in new business.

Example: If you do not get awarded this contract, you will have to cut the operating budget by 20%.

Step Three(A): Determine the likelihood of the upside as a probability.

Your marketing director estimates that you have a 65% chance of being awarded the entire contract. However, the agency has the right to split the overall contract between your firm and the competition. The marketing director has no idea how much business you could get if the split happens.

Step Three(B): Determine the likelihood of the downside as a probability.

If you do not get any part of the order, there is a 90% chance you will need to cut spending immediately.

Step Four: Determine where the upside and downside risks will have their biggest impacts to your organisation. If there is more than one, you can apply this step to each area. The impact could be to something tangible such as sales (turnover), profits or cash. And it could impact things such as your brand, reputation, or viability.

Example: If you are awarded the full order, it will significantly improve the viability of your organisation. If you do not get any part of the order your cash balances will take a big hit.

Step Five: Use the grid to determine the size of your opportunity.

Example: Regarding winning the business, you think the probability is high (left side) and the impact will be high as well. Your opportunity falls into the "high risk" category, as shown in the upper right-hand quadrant.

Step Six: Use the grid to determine the size of your risk.

Example: Of course, if you do not win the business, you will be in dire straits. That can be slightly tempered in that you might be awarded part of it. Based upon thoughtful analysis, you think the probability of running out of cash is low and the impact on your business, should it happen, is high. Therefore, this risk falls into the "medium risk" category, as shown in the lower right-hand quadrant.

Step Seven: Next you turn to the second grid for your approach to managing the risk.

Part Two–How to Use the Risk and Opportunity Management Grid

The second part of this tool, in Figure 5-5, assigns each quadrant a number, which indicates a management strategy to use. This tool focuses mostly on the negative impact of both opportunities and risk. Remember, even upsides and windfalls have a cost attached to them that you may not be able to afford.

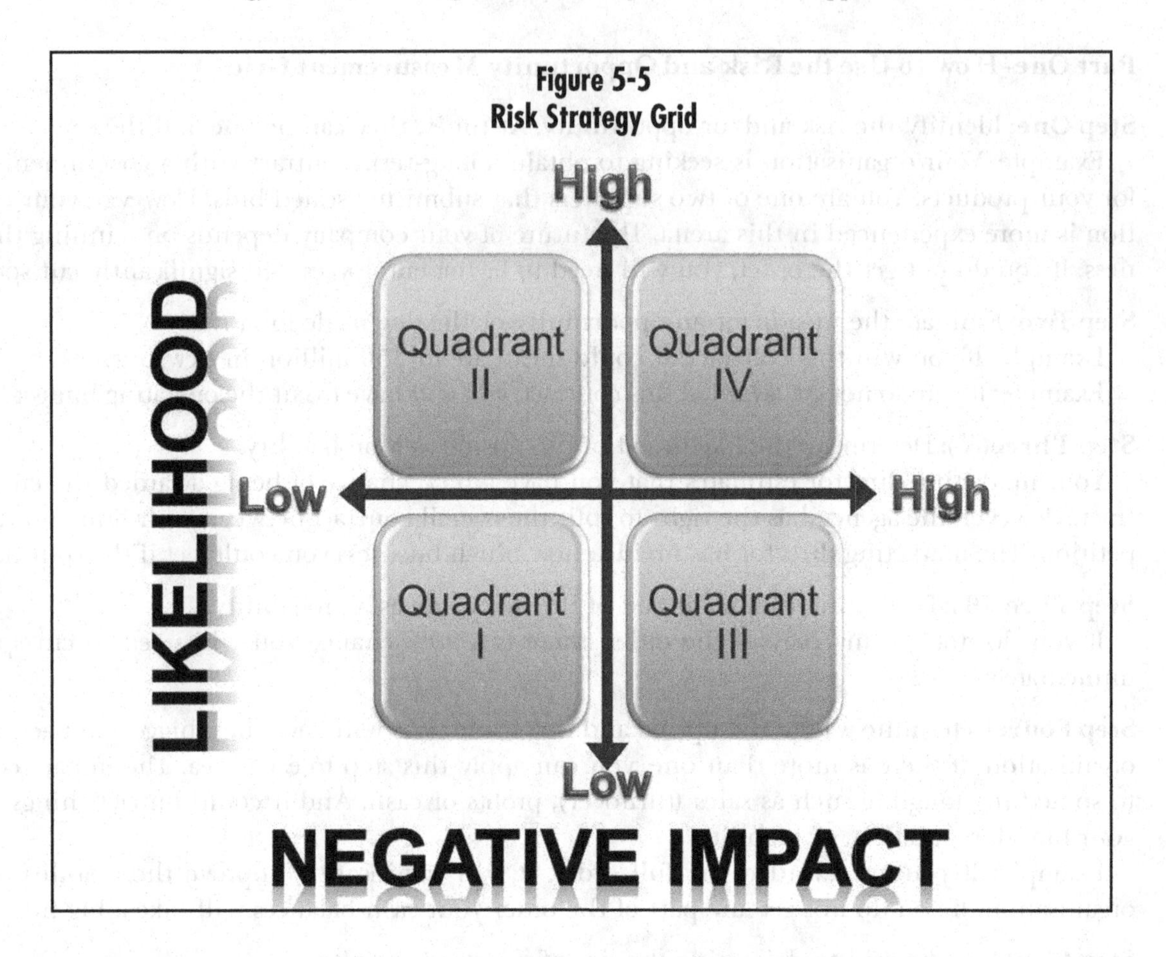

Step Eight: As before, go through the same thoughtful process for the opportunity. Focus on the potential negative impact of it.

Example: If you are awarded the entire contract, you will have to ramp up production quickly. Since there has been a hiring freeze for some time, getting your production facility up to speed will requiring hiring expensive temporaries, buying large quantities of materials and depleting your cash balances (and tapping lines of credit) until you get paid by the agency.

Step Nine: As before, go through the same thoughtful process for the risk.

Example: You are feeling some pessimism that you will get the full order and assume that your firm will be awarded about 20% or $10 million in new orders. This will mean no further layoffs but you will need to carefully watch cash balances and expenses carefully for the next year.

Step Ten (A): Use the risk management grid tool to determine how you will manage the risk inherent in this opportunity

Example: Since you believe you have a 65% chance of being awarded the entire order you think that the likelihood of the drain on your cash will be high. You also think that the negative impact on your liquidity will be high as well. This means this opportunity falls in Quadrant IV (upper right hand quarter).

Step Eleven (A): Next, you turn to the Risk and Opportunity Management Strategies Matrix, in Table 5-1 to determine how to best manage the "cost" of your opportunity.

Table 5-1 Risk and Opportunity Management Strategies Matrix

Quadrant	Risk Level	Meaning	Management Strategy
I	Low	This is a small pothole.	**Acceptance:** Accept this as a normal operating reality.
II	Medium	This is a large pothole that could hurt you.	**Awareness and Monitoring:** Stay aware of this, conduct regular monitoring, and consider reassessing in the near future.
III	Medium	This is a large pothole that could hurt you.	**Awareness, Monitoring and Planning:** Increase awareness of this, conduct ongoing monitoring and develop a contingency plan.
IV	High	This is a major pothole that could seriously undermine your success.	**Managing, Insuring and Exiting:** Appoint a manager to manage it, "insure" it by partnering, sharing or purchasing insurance coverage, and develop an exit plan.

Example: The downside of your opportunity falls in Quadrant IV. Therefore your strategy for managing it becomes "Managing, Insuring and Exiting." This means you appoint a responsible senior executive as the point person of this risk, you consider ways to insure yourself as well as develop an exit plan should Mr. Murphy make his appearance in the form of an employee strike, fire in your production facility, the inability to obtain a much needed raw material, etc.

Step Ten (B): Next you turn to the risk of getting only part of the order. After careful study, you think that the likelihood of the strain on your working capital will be high and the negative impact will be low. (Your organisation has been on an austerity budget for 16 months, so what is another 12?). Therefore the risk falls into Quadrant II.

Step Eleven (B): Using the Risk and Opportunity Management Strategies Matrix again you determine the best management tool for the "cost" of your opportunity is "Awareness and Monitoring."

Step Twelve: This last step is to move ahead with your plans. Should any conditions change significantly up or down, go through these steps again.

Example: The downside of your opportunity falls in Quadrant IV. Therefore your strategy for managing it becomes "Managing, Insuring and Exiting." This means you appoint a responsible senior executive as the point person of this risk, you consider ways to insure yourself as well as develop an exit plan should Mr. Murphy make his appearance in the form of an employee strike, fire in your production facility, the inability to obtain a much needed raw material, etc.

Part Three–How to Use the Matrix Values and Impact Zones Tables

Some organisation's leaders want a more statistical method for measuring their risk before deciding what to do. That is where the rest of this tool comes into play.

The third aspect of this tool, Tables 5-2, 5-3, and 5-4 are used to assign numerical rankings and management responsibility to particular risks and opportunities.

Step One: Define the risk or opportunity in as much detail as possible.

Step Two: Use the Risk and Opportunity Measurement Grid (Figure 5-4) to decide the level. First select the probability as either high or low. Be clear about how you define each of these terms. Then do the same for the impact or significance, as either high or low. Be clear about how you define those because you want to use consistent definitions as you examine a portfolio of similar risks.

Step Three: Use the Matrix Values from the Criteria Ranking Table (5-2) to assign your risk or peril a relational number from 1 to 9 with nine being the highest.

If you believe your risk is a level 10, then it needs to be treated as a crisis, eg, the explosion at the Japanese nuclear power station.

Table 5-2 Criteria Ranking Table

Area of Significance	Probability	Priorities	Ranking
Global or strategic or cultural (10,000 metres)	High	High	9
Global or strategic or cultural (10,000 metres)	Medium	High	8
Operational or capability or marketing (10,000 metres)	High	High	7
Global or strategic or cultural (10,000 metres)	Low	Medium	6
Operational or capability or marketing (10,000 metres)	Medium	Medium	5
Administrative or activity (100 metres)	High	Medium	4
Operational or capability or marketing (10,000 metres)	Low	Low	3
Administrative or activity (100 metres)	Medium	Low	2
Administrative or activity (100 metres)	Low	Low	1

The second table (5-3) is the Alternative Matrix Criteria Ranking Table. They both show the same numerical rankings. The first is more linear than the second. Use the one that is easier to explain to people.

Table 5-3 Alternative Matrix Criteria Ranking Table

Probability is...	Numerical Ranking		
High	6	8	9
Medium	3	5	7
Low	1	2	4
Significance	Low	Medium	High

Step Four: Define where the greatest impact of the risk or opportunity will be. You have three choices: 1) the Global or Strategic or Cultural (10,000 meter) level; 2) the Operational or Capability or Marketing (3,000 meter) level, and 3) the Activity or Administrative (100 meter) level.

Examples: A natural disaster will be detrimental to all three levels so it has global impact. A limited general strike could be detrimental to making or delivering your products so it is classified as having an operational or capability impact. A fatal car accident involving a key non-executive employee will likely have the lowest level impact, so you classify it as activity or administrative.

Step Five: Use the Risk or Opportunity Management Responsibilities Matrix (5-4) to define who would be responsible and accountable for both monitoring and managing the specific risk.

Table 5-4 Risk or Opportunity Management Responsibilities Matrix

Matrix Value	Area of Impact			Opportunity or Risk Managed by	
	Global	Operational	Activity	Primarily	Secondarily
7–9	✓			Senior executive	Manager or Director
4–6	✓			Manager or Director	Informed employee
1–3	✓			Informed employee	Informed employee
7–9		✓		Manager or Director	Informed employee
4–6		✓		Manager or Director	Senior executive
1–3		✓		Informed employee	Informed employee
7–9			✓	Manager or Director	Informed employee
4–6			✓	Informed employee	Informed employee
1–3			✓	Informed employee	Informed employee

Step Six: To communicate what your analysis looks like and support why you chose a specific way to handle it, use the next two views of this comprehensive tool, shown in Tables 5-5 and 5-6.

For an effective risk management programme it is wise to appoint a primary manager over the risk that is supported by a second employee. Here is what your final product or report will look like.

Table 5-5 Tool Report Part 1

Risk Examples	Probability	Significance	Matrix Value
1) Earthquake or other natural disaster	Low	High	7
2) Unauthorised entry into company database	Medium	High	8
3) Unexpected loss of CEO	Low	Medium	4
4) Vehicle accident	Medium	Low	2
5) Employee strike	Medium	Medium	5

Table 5-6 Tool Report Part 2

Risk Examples	Matrix Value	Managed by	Supported by
1) Earthquake or other natural disaster	7	Senior executive	Manager/Director
2) Unauthorised entry into company database	8	Senior executive	Manager/Director
3) Unexpected loss of CEO	4	Manager/Director	Informed employee
4) Vehicle accident	2	Informed employee	Informed employee
5) Employee strike	5	Manager/Director	Informed employee

This comprehensive tool provides several solutions. It is a tool that a key employee, supervisor and director can easily use and teach to others. It also quickly points out the optimal strategy to manage the opportunity or risk and then shows the most viable employee to take on that responsibility.

Regular use of this tool leads to quicker decision making once specific risks and opportunities are identified.

Case Study: The Opportunity to Invest

For our first case I selected Grace, the treasurer of PJI. Grace said, "I am concerned about temporarily placing $750,000 of our money in a fund that has a wildly fluctuating rate of return."

I walked her through the tool. "Grace what is your average rate of return on the excess cash you invest?"

"On an annual basis we earn about 2.9%. This fund could provide a return of 7.9%, or we could earn nothing. That is how volatile this fund is."

"And how much is that in terms of dollars?"

"Roughly $9,000 for the 90 days our money will be in the fund."

"Grace, what is the likelihood that you would not gain that differential?"

"Based upon my research, the probability I would say is medium to low."

"Before I ask about the impact, what could happen if you only earned 2.9% or less?"

"I might lose respect for my financial acumen."

"Is this overall impact to you and the company high or low?"

"The dollars we do not earn would not be large, and when compared to our total earnings from our investments, I would describe this as low."

"Therefore, Grace, what quadrant does your risk fall into?"

"This would make it a low risk."

Case Study: The Risk of Losing Qualified Talent

For our second case I asked Mario to describe his concern.

"We own a clothing company that makes an extremely popular high-end hunting jacket. My concern is that sewing is a dying art in the United States, so we will have a hard time finding trained workers with the skills to make a high-quality product. Many of our skilled sewers are retiring in the next 18 months."

"Mario, what is the probability or likelihood that you will be unable to find qualified employees?"

"In the short run the probability is high, in my opinion."

"What and where is the impact?"

"Our jackets command a premium price due to their quality. If we are unable to find trained sewers, it could hurt both our profits and brand. Its impact is almost immeasurable because without quality products, we would no longer have the edge over the competition."

"Therefore, Mario, based on this tool would you say that your risk is a high one?"

"Yes, I agree with you."

Case Study: Avoiding Termination Blowback

The third case was offered by Letitia, an investment manager.

"I have a performance issue with the VP of operations of my technology company. She is a 65-year-old woman who clearly does not have the talent or interest to run a fully automated production plant. My concern is if we demote her, she would claim age discrimination."

"Letitia, what is the likelihood that this employee would do this?"

"Very high."

"And what is the likelihood that the Department of Labor would penalise your company if it believes her story that your decision was based on her age and sex, rather than her competency?"

"I would say that the probability is low because we have documented this issue well."

"Assuming that the agency did rule in her favour, what is the impact on the company you manage?"

"I would say that the financial impact on us would be negligible."

"Letitia, based on what you told us what is the size of your risk?"

"It would be a moderately low risk. I now understand how this tool works."

Lessons from the Case Studies

I asked each manager to summarise for the rest of us how this tool could assist him or her in determining the approximate size of his or her risk.

Grace: "This great tool would help me isolate specific concerns regarding where I place our excess cash. I can use it before I make an investment and later to analyse if I should switch."

Mario: "I can see that I need to address this now instead of later. This tool helps me to focus specifically by looking at it as two dimensions. This shows me that my risk is a major one, and I must make it a priority."

Letitia: "I have been stressed about this coming termination but don't need to be. Due to this analysis I do not need to be afraid of facing this issue, which I have been dreading."

Onward

I explained today how risk starts with your business model, which is a primary source of strategic risk. Risk management is especially important in business turnaround situations and during turbulent and unstable times. ERM suggests that you use the team approach in assessing strategic and operational risk because proactive cross-functional risk management allows an organisation to deal with potential land mines with optimism.

I ended the day with another quote about risk taking.

"Progress always involves risk; you can't steal second base and keep your foot on first." Frederick Wilcox

Action Plan

Step One

Does your organisation do the form of strategic planning as shown in the Strategic Planning Flowchart? If it does, how well does it prepare the organisation to deal with risks and opportunities?

Step Two

Think about where you and/or your organisation conduct scenario planning. Does the process generate a list of reasonable alternatives? Does the process consider the cost and size and impact of each option? What aspect of this scenario planning process needs improving?

Step Three

Think of an important opportunity, risk or challenge that you face currently—personal or business. (You can use one you used before.) List the significant impacts, good or bad, it could have on you or your company. Think about the probability of these impacts. Use the Risk Measurement Grid to determine which quadrant the risk falls into.

Step Four

Continuing with the opportunity, risk or challenge in the previous step, focus only on a bad outcome or negative impact. Again think about the likelihood of this occurring or coming to fruition. Using the Risk Strategy Grid, what are your "best" options for dealing with the unpleasantness of your risk or opportunity?

6

WHERE Do Our Efforts Need to Be?

"The person who invented that device lost more brains before breakfast than you and I will ever have." Harry A.

Rain in the desert is rare, so when the clouds show up bringing rain, people who live in the desert are happy. In most places where I travel, rain is not so desirable; however, there is a cost to this rain, and I arrived in Phoenix, Arizona, to witness the wonders of an intense desert rain storm.

Sources of Jeopardy

Crack! The slate grey sky flashed a brilliant white warning of a powerful storm that could bring rain. I could feel electricity in the air as I entered the conference centre. I decided to use the storm as an introduction to today's session with PJ Investment's (PJI's) managers. When everyone settled in I greeted them. Then we heard a loud *BOOM* that seemed to shake the building and got everyone's attention.

"Please imagine that you are standing out in the middle of an open field when this lightning storm arrives. What would you do? How would you react?"

They shouted out responses of

- run for cover!
- get as low to the ground as possible!
- get the heck out of there!

"What if you could not leave the area? What would you do if there is no shelter for miles? In other words how would you protect yourself?"

Jacob responded, "If I found myself in a situation like that, I would pray that the lightning would miss me." His peers laughed.

"Thanks, Jacob. Companies that choose not to practise risk management are like Jacob, hoping and praying silently that nothing bad happens each time a lightning storm arrives. They do what Jacob's prayers are meant to do: cover your assets (CYA)." With the added laughter Jacob turned red.

"Peril or risk in business can at times be like the lightning storm taking place today, but the deadliness and power of the storm is not just dangerous for the individual. The jeopardy can be felt at multiple levels."

Level 1–The Individual

Even if you are not anywhere near where the lightning hits, you still feel static electricity and energy. In risk management we protect ourselves against deadly or costly risk at the employee level because employees often see the indications of a storm first.

Level 2–The Team

Imagine that you are driving when the lightning storm hits. Your vehicle and its passengers could be in jeopardy from the lightning, as well as the storm's strong wind, intense rain and decreased visibility. In risk management, risk is examined and managed at the team level because any costly risk could undermine important processes like selling, production or communication.

Level 3–The Entity

If a storm in the desert dropped 7.5 centimetres of rain, it would flood streets, back up sewer lines and create havoc that could affect any company or family in the immediate area. In risk management we seek out and manage costly risk that could cause harm to the company and those who rely on it, such as customers and suppliers.

Level 4–The Environment

Today's storm has the potential to knock out power to parts of the city, which will create problems for people and companies beyond the immediate impact zone. That is why enterprise risk management (ERM) requires constant vigilance against risk at what I refer to as the 10,000-metre level.

Today we will learn how to use the strategic planning tool called the strengths, limitations, opportunities and threats (SLOT) analysis to discern potential risk at all four levels. The SLOT analysis is something many of you are familiar with. Before we get to this tool, here is a story about someone who knew where to look for problems.

Harry

Harry is a practical man. Even though he retired after selling his trucking business, he wanted to stay active. He was hired to be the janitor of the office where I worked. As I got to know him, I could tell that Harry cared a lot, even though at this stage of life he could easily "phone it in." At the time I surmised (proven years later to be true) that Harry displayed the attitude of someone who had an emotional investment in his job.

Harry unintentionally took me under his wing and provided me with many insights about where to look for potential problems and risks. The first time I witnessed this was with a small construction project going on just outside our office building. The contractor's employees were installing a drainage line to move water, now collecting at a low point, to the newly installed drain approximately 68 metres away. Even though this project was none of his business, Harry would walk past the area on a daily basis and watch the contractor's employees as they dug the 45-centimetre deep ditch and installed the drainpipe.

One day when the installation was near completion, Harry invited me to walk with him. We headed over to the ditch, and he pointed to the middle section and asked, "Does that pipe look straight to you?"

I stared at it for a while and said, "No, it seems to be tilted." He handed me a level and asked me to place it on the pipe to see which way it was tilted. The entire drainpipe was tilted towards the low spot and away from the drain.

Harry asked, "What will happen the first time it rains and that low spot fills with water?"

I thought about it and replied, "The water won't move to the drain because the entire pipe is tilting the wrong way."

"That's what I thought," Harry said. He added, "I saw this goof-up and hoped that the contractor's employees would notice their mistake. They haven't, and tomorrow they will fill in and pave over the trench. I just wanted another person's opinion before I pointed this out to Ken, the warehouse manager."

Later, when I asked Harry about his conversation with Ken, he said, "After I demonstrated the mistake with my level, he contacted the contractor. Within an hour the contractor's employees were reinstalling the pipe correctly."

Several weeks later in a staff meeting, the production manager, Pete, was complaining about the high cost of repairs to our fleet of service trucks. He asked me to do some investigation on the reasons repair costs were high. At lunch the next day I chatted with Harry about my assignment. He suggested that I pull all the repair bills for the last couple years and look for any work done on the vehicles' clutches. I did this and discovered that most of the repair costs over the last 18 months had been to fix the clutch and gearbox in over 75% of the vehicles, many of which were relatively new.

Before I took my findings back to Pete, I asked Harry why he had suggested this to me. Harry said, "Each morning I clean the lot where the trucks are parked at night. I always detect the smell of a burnt clutch. It's a smell you will never forget." Harry showed me the indications that proved many of the employees assigned to a service vehicle were incorrectly shifting and using compression to slow their vehicle instead of the brake system.

He suggested that when I present my cost analysis to Pete, I also report his suspicions regarding how vehicles were incorrectly driven. Harry instructed me to report this as if they were my conclusions and leave his name out of the conversation. I didn't see any harm in his suggestion, so I did as instructed. Within a few days all our drivers were required to take several classes on proper driving techniques, and from that day on Pete would randomly ride with an employee to see that the lessons were taken seriously. The clutch problem quickly disappeared, and our vehicle repair costs dropped dramatically.

It was right after this incident that, for the first time of many, Harry told me, "When employees don't give a s---- about their work or tools, all kinds of problems crop up. The careless employee causes headaches for the next person because they have to clean up the mess left behind by the first employee's neglect or inattention." He added, "When I was the boss of my trucking company I used to regularly remind my employees who drove our trucks or operated our equipment, 'I expect you to put your brains into your work. Think about what you are doing and why you are doing it. The person who invented that device lost more brains before breakfast than you and I will ever have. Use your tool the way that it was designed to be used.'"

Holistic Approach

Supervisors and managers frequently neglect that their employees' risky behaviours that could lead to losses or waste. That is a risk no organisation can afford today and the reason why simply giving risk management tools to employees will not reduce risk. Your employees must be trained in how to properly use them, so that risk is detected before its cost gets too steep.

A requirement of ERM is that it become a standard way of operating and managing throughout your organisation. It is a holistic view of risks, and you need information about where it exists from all parts of your organisation: bottom to top and across all levels. The best way to make sure this widespread adoption takes place is to study your culture because it provides clues. This is your third step when implementing ERM.

Murphy's Law of Risk and Brains

People are smart, except when they fail to use their brains.

ERM Step Three–Analyse the Ability of Your Organisation to Handle Risk

Every employee, or at least 80% of them, must adopt and use risk management for you to obtain the full benefits. You may not be able to ask each employee if he or she will do risk planning because your population may be too large,or you will not receive honest answers. By managing your culture mosaic, studying people's behaviours and being very vocal about risk management, you will know if and when ERM is part of your culture story.

> "Companies like J.P. Morgan and Goldman Sachs didn't fall down the same rabbit hole as other investment banks, because they had a culture of intelligent risk-taking, where employees were accountable for sounding a warning if something didn't seem right. Risk management has to be in the fabric of the company." William Bolan junior, president and CEO of Integrated Governance Solutions
>
> *Source:* http://www.cfo.com/article.cfm/14457815/c_2984294/?f=archives

Risk Management Tool Eight– Culture Assessment

I introduced the managers to another tool that consists of a self-rating. It serves as an entry point for the third step of a risk management programme.

Part One: Read the following statement. Then check off any of the required attitudes that your fellow leaders currently have. Base your answer on what you experience, not what you feel.

We must believe in ourselves to take successful risks!

This requires us to have the

- ☐ courage to believe in abilities and talents.
- ☐ belief that we can take risk.
- ☐ belief that we should take risks.
- ☐ belief that we can be better than we are now.
- ☐ belief that our clients are the most important.
- ☐ belief that employees are as valuable as clients.
- ☐ belief that employees can think for themselves and be trusted.
- ☐ belief that by collaboratively working together we can grow our profits.

Part Two: Answer this question using Table 6-1 and this scale: 4 means you strongly believe the statement, 3 means you mostly believe it, 2 means it may or may not be true and 1 means you do not believe the statement.

What is your level of belief that this organisation can practise proactive risk management?

Table 6-1

I believe we											
can follow an ERM plan.				will eventually embrace ERM.				are doomed to fail at ERM.			
4	3	2	1	4	3	2	1	4	3	2	1

This assessment gave me data for the amount of cultural support, scepticism or resistance that existed in PJI's culture.

Embedded in the Cultural Fabric

People who have consistently implemented ERM say that formal risk management will fail when it does not mesh with a company's culture. When leaders attempt to impose a risk management structure in an organisation that is not ready for it, the programme will not be utilised. Similar to quality, ERM is built in, not added on.

Creating risk awareness and facing it head on must become part of the consciousness of your organisation and get integrated into its DNA. True success in an effective risk management programme comes from an organic process. In other words it cannot be another management programme or "flavour of the month" leadership idea. It must be described and accepted as the way things work here.

What Is Culture?

I asked the managers of PJI to complete this sentence:

To me workplace culture is...

Several employees read aloud what they wrote, and as I suspected they had a general sense of what it means. Then we looked at the true definition.

Workplace culture is the mood, attitude and atmosphere of an organisation. It is the story of who we are as enacted by each employee. A shorthand way of describing culture is how things are done around here.

Your own definition of culture will be similar to mine because culture is instinctual in us. Any time two or three people join to work together on something, they create a culture. It is something we humans naturally do. What you may not know about culture, even though you have a good intuitive sense of it, is that culture is made up of ten unique parts that give it an intangible yet measureable quality made up of these interrelated elements. These ten pieces fit together like a mosaic, and each one both touches and affects the others. They all must be in place for the mosaic to exist, and they must create a cohesive picture or story for an organisation to be considered functional and healthy. No two mosaics are alike. They all differ. In a large decentralised organisation like PJI, different culture stories will be told by employees in different business units.

Exhibit 6-1 is a representation of how the mosaic pieces meld together. The centrepiece of all culture mosaics is the leader's attitudes, behaviours and beliefs. This leader can be one person, a team or a family.

Exhibit 6-1 Culture Mosaic

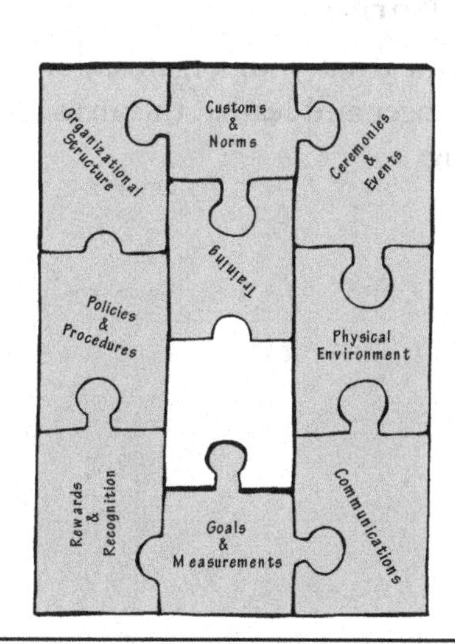

The components that make up your cultural mosaic are:

- ceremonies and events.
- communications.
- customs and norms.
- goals and measurement process.
- leaders' attitudes, behaviours and beliefs.
- organisational structure.
- physical environment.
- rewards and recognition.
- rules and policies.
- training.

How a Culture Story Is Developed

When individuals decide to form an organisation or start a business, they gather other people around them who have a similar mindset. You have heard employees describe their employer as a family. This describes a firm that consists of like-minded people sharing the same values and visions. All business starts out this way, even Walmart, IBM and Ford Motor Company.

Then as the organisation grows and matures, the leader, realising the need for additional help, installs channels of communication. The firm grows into different physical locations, each with its own environment. The leader has to set rules and policies to shape other people's behaviours. The organisation sets goals and tools to measure those goals. Because of the desire to reward people for their efforts and perhaps share the profits, awards and recognition programmes get established. The leader creates an organisational structure hierarchy because people have to fill specific slots, wear fewer hats or take on certain roles. Of course to promote fun, the leaders sponsor a Christmas party, summer picnics or monthly potluck birthday celebrations. Sometimes on their own or with guidance, employees start forming customs and norms, like the end of the month beer bash and casual Fridays. Notice the core of the culture is still the leader's attitudes, behaviours and beliefs. This centrepiece drives the entire culture from the beginning. In other words a firm's emotional attitude, its DNA, resembles the emotional attitude of its founder, but that will change.

As the company grows older, and the leader decides to hire professional managers because current leaders cannot do everything themselves or perhaps have become less able, new leaders come in and start putting their imprint on the culture with new attitudes, behaviours and beliefs. Even if this occurs it takes years for the attitudes, behaviours and beliefs of the original founder to be fully removed.

For example, even though Bill Gates has not been Microsoft's CEO for quite a while, a lot of Bill Gates is still in the DNA or culture story of Microsoft. The same holds true for Sam Walton's impact on Walmart's DNA. In the UK, Sainsbury's Supermarkets Ltd. is well over 100 years old and members of the founding Sainsbury family still own 15% of the company. The DNA or corporate culture of Sainsbury's to this day contains the imprint of its original founders.

Louis stopped me and said, "Well this is great, Ron, but I am in not charge of this place. I am only a small cog in the wheel, so what can I do about our culture?"

"I am glad you asked that question because that is where we are going next."

Visible Clues about Risk in Your Cultural Norms

Many visible outcomes in your culture will tell you what your organisation is like and what the culture says about its ability to handle risk. As manager and leader, the areas you need to keep your eye on and carefully examine include the following:

- Morale
- Employees' attitudes
- Level of cooperation
- Level of loyalty
- Level of integrity
- Level of fun
- Level of trust

- Level of openness and honesty
- Sense of urgency
- Internal reputation
- Commitment to ethics
- Turnover rates

I walked over to where Louis was sitting and asked, "Why would knowing how this company's culture is built help you in analysing PJI's ability to handle business risks?"

Louis didn't have an immediate answer, so I asked his peers to come to his rescue.

His fellow managers provided these answers:

- I would know if I should be concerned about something specific.
- I could determine who most likely would follow through and who wouldn't.
- I could change our reward system to reward more risk taking.
- We could evaluate the risky goals and get better feedback to determine if we're on track or off track.
- I believe that if employees are behind us, then we will more likely be successful, but if employees are against us, then our risk becomes greater.

That leads us to more truisms of risk taking:

Ninth and Tenth Principles of Risk Management

Assessing and monitoring your culture will give you information about where you are vulnerable.

Assessing and monitoring your culture will give you information on how your organisation values risk taking.

Culture Must Never Be Downplayed

Culture is important because your culture brings forth success and failure with equal efficiency. In essence your culture can support your efforts to survive risk or make you succumb to its perils. Knowing about your firm's culture story is important because the culture needs to expose risks rather than hide them. Think what could happen if your employees were not honest about the pitfalls they fell into and about what might cause that risk-laden behaviour.

I worked for several organisations where the norm was to hide risk because the leaders always shot the messenger. Rather than hear bad news, the leaders wanted people to dwell on the good news. In addition they never wanted anyone to question or critique the strategies they conceived. So the prevailing culture became one in which employees would do anything to save their jobs, which included sweeping unnecessary risks and problems under the rug. The firms were always in hot water, yet the managers were clueless about why Murphy's Law kept haunting them.

Risk management must be built into your organisation's consciousness and become part of its DNA or culture. The programme's efforts and intent must have support and sponsorship by your executives and become an organic process. You do this by building both formality and informality into the programme.

Determining Your Culture's View of Risk Taking

To ensure that your culture supports your risk management efforts, you must have one that balances risk taking with risk exposure. Without this balance it is easy for your employees to flock to one side or the other of the scale, which is another truism.

> **Eleventh Principle of Risk Management**
>
> If employees take too many risks, the inherent dangers exponentially grow. If employees take too few risks, the inflow of opportunities exponentially declines.

Figure 6-1
Balanced Risk Taking

As you can see in Figure 6-1, someone is attempting to find balance between risk and innovation on one side and control and security on the other side. Every organisation struggles with finding the right balancing point. Proper management of risk, such as by using ERM, greatly aids you in discovering the healthy balance for your organisation with a lot less painful trial and error.

You cannot be everything to everyone, so being in balance is important so that you will know what to do when confusion sets in. You can focus on what you do best by asking yourself these questions:

- What is most important right now?
- What have we done best in the past that worked?
- What are we trying to become best at in the future?

The answers you generate will help you remember your number one priority.

I posed a question to PJI's management group, "Based on what you have learned about risk management, what would an environment that balances risk taking and controlling unnecessary risks look like? I would expect to see..."

They provided the following responses:

- Managers leading by example
- Practical tools for employees to use
- A team approach to risk management
- A culture of honest reporting
- A culture where we do not shoot the messenger
- A balanced approach to risk taking
- A widespread concern that every risk has a cost
- Awareness about what a risk is and what it could look like
- Sensitivity to risk
- Accountability
- A culture where employees are encouraged to raise their concerns and issues
- A culture of sharing information
- Leaders who are more concerned about the company's success than their own success

The culture that balances risk taking and exposure has all these traits and more. Now that you know what to look for you can determine if this healthy attitude exists. If you do not see these important behaviours, you must seek out why they are missing. Does your organisation currently have these traits? We will now find out.

Risk Management Tool Nine– Assessment of a Balanced Culture

I pointed out this tool (Table 6-2) in the workbook and asked them to fill it in to determine which aspects of their culture needed fixing.

Table 6-2 Assessment of a Balanced Culture

Instructions: For each trait below check off whether it exists.			
Culture Trait	**Does Exist**	**Does Not Exist**	**Do Not Know**
Accountability to standard and policies and goals			
Encouragement to raise concerns and issues			
Encouragement to take rational risks			
Encouragement to think before acting			
Honesty and openness			
Leaders setting the example			
Penalties for disregarding the rules			
Review of end results against the actions taken			
Rewards for innovation			
Sensitivity to the cost of risks			
Sensitivity to risk			
Sharing of information			
Team-based problem solving			

Once their answers were compiled I informed them of two critical findings.

"First, a majority of you said encouragement to think before acting does not exist. This explains why in the recent past you had employees who took on too much risk or disregarded it. Second, over 30% of you felt that sensitivity to risk and sensitivity to the cost of risks does not exist in this culture. This is why only 19% of your employees believed that PJI could handle unexpected surprises."

I could see the glow of enlightenment shine in the eyes of many of them.

"By this time in the process of establishing a risk management programme and seeing it through the eyes of the ones who set the tone for employees' actions, you will experience many AHA moments. One is discovering how the management team's behaviours and decisions impact the ways employees react to risks and to the standards you want them to follow. Your eyes will also be open to what aspects of your culture cause everyone to resist new ideas like ERM."

Barriers to ERM Implementation

Murphy's Law of Risk Behavioural Science

Just when you figure out how people behave, they do not behave like you expect.

Just because it is a wise and profitable idea to practise formal risk management, it will not easily embed itself into your culture. There will be many barriers rooted in your culture story that you must overcome.

Obstacle One: Perceived Cost in Dollars and Time

The recent study *Report on the Current State of Enterprise Risk Oversight* conducted by North Carolina State University's ERM Initiative faculty and supported by a research grant from the AICPA Business, Industry and Government Group shows that it will be a while before ERM is embraced and supported even in large, resource-rich organisations. The survey's responses came from CFOs who often describe themselves as risk averse and profit oriented. The study received answers from 701 individuals representing organisations in a wide variety of industries and sizes. When asked for the reasons why ERM had not yet been implemented in their companies, they responded as follows:

- Competing priorities (61%)
- Insufficient resources (60%)
- Lack of perceived value (48%)
- Lack of board or senior executive risk management leadership (38%)
- Perception of risk management as bureaucracy (37%)
- Leader or regulatory barriers (5%)

Justifying the investment in risk management is their main challenge because respondents most often cited the inability to determine their return on investment on risk management spending as an obstacle to making risk management a priority.

Obstacle Two: Denial That ERM Is Necessary

A recent Arthur Young survey concluded that there is "an urgent need to evaluate existing risk management processes in light of perceived increases in the volume and complexity of risks and operational surprises being experienced by management" (http://www.journalofaccountancy.com/Issues/2009/Sep/20091792.htm). The organisations described themselves as having a high aversion to risk. Despite this awareness organisations are still hesitant to face up to risk and incorporate the appropriate infrastructure and processes required by ERM.

Obstacle Three: Leaders' Resistance

Employees will embrace ERM when they see visible proof that their leaders also embrace it. Recall that the culture story always starts with the leader's attitudes, behaviours and beliefs. Therefore instilling an attitude that risk has a cost that must be determined before we risk starts once your senior leaders and managers also believe it.

Obstacle Four: Employee Attitudes

You will encounter four distinct attitudes or mindsets as you go through the process of properly integrating risk management in your culture:

1. Risk taker
2. Risk averse
3. Custodian or guardian
4. Indifferent

The Mindset of the Risk Taker

Call it a genetic compulsion, defensive reaction or simple optimism, but the reality is most visionaries, business owners, entrepreneurs and sales executives refuse to contemplate the possibility of failure. It is as if the word does not exist in their vocabulary, but failure is an option. The downside of this never say die attitude is that it can be ruinous, wasteful and costly; hurt people; and spoil opportunities for future success.

Most people who refuse to concede defeat see themselves as the type of person who puts his or her head down and charges full steam ahead; however, you can badly injure yourself with that mindset. This person does not avoid risk but ignores it at every opportunity.

This person tends to be emotional, confident and impulsive, so he or she fails to recognise that failure is an option, which is why risk can be mismanaged or unacknowledged.

In facing up to the possibility of failure when taking a risk, there is a very delicate line to walk. It is better to assume that failure can occur than to resign yourself to it. It is okay to acknowledge your fear, but don't let yourself be overcome by it. Walking that line requires courage.

The Mindset of the Risk-Averse Person

Just as there are some people who tend to take risks, there will be a group of employees in your organisation who tend to be risk averse. They say, "I don't like to take risks." Those who are risk averse may feel they should take more risk because they see risk taking can lead to great rewards. Just look at the honours bestowed on Olympic athletes and poker players as examples. However, when reality sets in, this person realises that he or she could actually lose money, and generally people hate to lose money. More specifically people hate to look stupid or incompetent. That is what the risk-averse person is really afraid of when it comes to facing risk. If this person didn't plan on losing money and does, the feeling of incompetence is overwhelming, and this person refuses to let go of embarrassment because he or she is rational, anxious and reflective.

The Mindset of the Custodian or Guardian

Employees in finance, accounting and other technical professions own the mentality, "I am the guardian of the assets, processes or results," and this attitude leads them to look at risk differently. Risk is inherent in nearly everything that a business does, including expansion, merger, investment or contraction. This means that no matter how much the technical expert researches a decision, he or she must face the fact that there will always be uncertainty in any strategy and decision. This ambiguity of the outcome is hard for the guardian to accept because this person generally is rational, confident (in his or her knowledge) and reflective.

The custodian wants to make sure he or she doesn't do anything stupid, and that is very different from taking a risk. The technical professional's job is to put forth the best alternative, suggest the pros and cons, identify the opportunities sought, and then show what the future could look like in all scenarios. While doing this evaluation of a risky situation, the guardian must keep an eye on potential gains or upsides, as well as the potential losses or costs.

The Mindset of the Indifferent Employee

This employee claims not to care about taking risk yet in actuality does but feigns detachment because he or she is afraid to take a risk, has no experience in taking a risk or has been overmanaged. The two reasons why taking a risk is difficult for this person are because his or her definition of a risky event is inconsistent, and this person wants someone else to be responsible for what he or she does or says.

Although the conditions significantly vary, the indifferent person can be seen as emotional, anxious and impulsive.

Ways to Integrate ERM into Your Culture

Assume you have to relocate your entire company to a new building across town. You would need to compare what you have now to what you will have soon, in terms of space and constraints. Then you would go through everything you have in your existing space as you conduct the relocation. Finally you would make a set of new decisions regarding ways to ensure the move is a success.

As you start implementing ERM, just as in relocating, you define what you currently have or do. You then compare this to what you will soon have or want to have. Finally you examine every major process and culture element as you "move" into your new space: a culture committed to ERM.

The processes, systems and tools that enable your employees to detect, measure, monitor and finally mitigate risk must be integrated into the work of every employee. This is not easy, yet doing it is crucial to reaping the benefits of ERM.

Bring Your People Resources Together

A major benefit of ERM is that it brings people together, not for endless meetings but in a framework for assessing, sizing up and reducing risk. Because ERM is holistic, it requires many sets of eyes and ears to detect potential risk. ERM's global approach requires numerous brains to conduct scenario planning and what-if analysis. Finally collectively examining your organisation from top to bottom requires many talents to come forth to assist in creating a complete realistic picture of where you are and where you are headed.

Ensure Employee Acceptance through Training

As you integrate risk management into your culture and existing systems, every employee must be involved, and this is accomplished through ongoing and mandatory training. If only a few people know about the inner workings of a risk management programme, guess what? Only a few people will practise risk management. Because you want every employee to embrace it, in step three you begin to train all employees, starting with executives and senior leaders.

Build Enthusiasm

Enthusiasm to practising risk management does not arrive until it is embraced, and embracing comes when everyone understands that it is part of their job duties. To instil ownership of the practice of risk management, you must sell it to employees in a way that they will see they are better off with it than without it.

When integrating risk management, you must do many things to ensure that employees and others buy into the understanding that this is the way your organisation will operate. As mentioned before, employees take their behaviour cues from the people they work for. To ensure everyone sees risk management as a priority and normal way of operating, your executives must buy into it from the outset.

Here is how to get executives' attention about the importance of risk management.

Make it a Bottom-Line Issue

I still had to get Paul and Justin to provide proof to their employees that they embraced and would support this programme. My opportunity was now. The best way to get someone's attention is to speak about his or her greatest fear or concern. An executive like Justin who was concerned about integrity would pay heed to advice on how to preserve it. A mover and shaker like Paul always worries about profitability. I spoke to the group about this.

"One way to get risk management on the agenda of a group of executives is to make it about their bottom line. Unmanaged risk undermines your organisation's ability to generate a profit and also affects your ability to have a sustainable business model.

"Understanding that there is a fundamental relationship between risk and reward may help some executives realise the strategic benefits of strengthening their risk oversight because when risk is managed thoughtfully, your firm is more likely to achieve its strategic goals. Paul, as a person who sets the vision of what this company can accomplish, what is the cost to PJI of not reaching your ultimate goals?"

This caught him by surprise, but he recovered quickly.

Paul answered, "If the people in this room are unable to carry out our primary strategy of finding undervalued businesses and making them more valuable, then we might as well close the doors."

"Does that statement apply to you Paul?" I asked.

"Yes it does. I feel that the cost is immeasurable, and I would take it as the ultimate failure."

It was Justin's turn on the hot seat. "Lapses in business ethics can lead to higher costs, damaged relationships with important stakeholders and lost opportunities that can significantly harm financial performance. Justin, is that a cost you are willing to pay as an owner?"

Justin seemed to be ready for this question and replied, "No amount of money could induce me to do anything unethical. To me this is the biggest asset we put on the line every time we make an investment in or buy a company. I am not willing to sacrifice our reputation for anything."

I said, "It is good to hear you profess that because many business people fail to see the direct connection between ethical conduct and profits. Business misconduct can lead to incurring legal fees, monetary fines, sanctions and reputation recovery. Given a choice of those they partner with, stakeholders are more likely to prefer a relationship with an organisation that has a reputation for integrity."

Here is a representation of that symbiotic relationship, as shown in Figure 6-2:

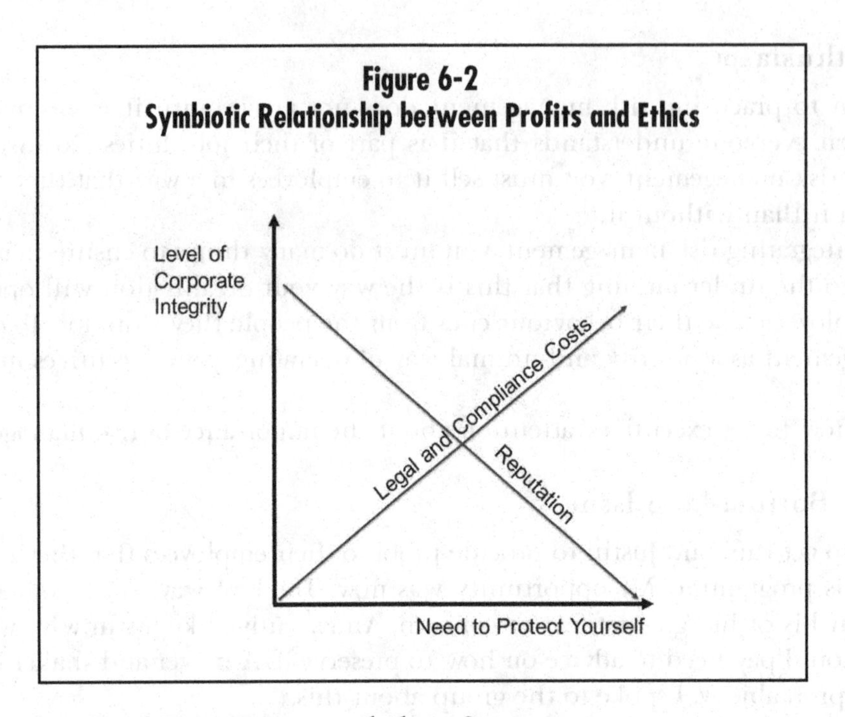

Risk Management Tool Ten– Responsibility Statement

A specific way enables you and other leaders to get employees to see that formal risk management is now part of their responsibilities. This simple and impactful tool is a statement that needs to be placed in every employee's job description:

Every employee plays a critical role in this organisation's risk management process. Proactively preventing unnecessary, unwarranted or improper risk is expected from everyone.

You are responsible for

- seeking out where we waste company resources.
- offering suggestions to save both money and time.
- watching for hidden opportunities to create new revenue or income.
- suggesting ways to make your work more productive.
- offering ideas that make you more effective.
- thoughtfully expending company resources.
- making smart decisions.
- identifying problems and ways to overcome them.
- regularly asking, "What is the downside of my action or decision?"

Whenever you see areas where we put ourselves and each other at risk, your responsibility is to proactively fix the problem or implement a solution. If you are unable to do so, then please consult with your team, supervisor or another manager about the issue, so they can support you in fixing the problem.

Teach Managers about Risk Management

The most valuable stewardship activity for an executive is teaching managers at all levels how to make intelligent decisions about risk. As you understand by now from the information about culture, senior leaders play a huge role in the acceptance and integration of ERM in their organisation. A senior leader's responsibility is four-fold:

1. Deeply learn about risk management.
2. Adjust your attitude about the need to formally manage risk.
3. Use the process in your executive decisions and choices.
4. Ensure that everyone in the organisation embraces and practises risk management.

Murphy's Law of Risky Ideas

Innovative leaders create the biggest problems and then ask a linear-minded person to fix them.

Five ERM Actions for Immediate Implementation

For many directors and management teams, this heightened focus on risk is new and somewhat daunting. Most likely your organisation may not have the resources, such as people, money and time, to implement every aspect of an ERM programme. You can obtain the immediate benefits of the ERM structure within the limitations of your resources in numerous ways. Here are four risk management actions you can immediately implement:

1. *Examine all your goals to ensure they are realistic.* The task of identifying, quantifying and managing all the risks that your company could face is compelling but daunting. For any risk management programme to be effective, your organisation must clearly define its goals, make them realistic and identify their intended results. The end results will both adequately protect the organisation and allow you to identify opportunities to grow, expand and gain shareholder value.
2. *Examine your strategies for profitability and potential risks.* The entry point of a strategic risk assessment is designed to identify your organisation's strategic risks. If they exist, develop specific action plans to address those risks. Because it would be nearly impossible for the company to quantify every risk it faces, risk identification starts at the 10,000-metre level. Later you can empower employees to deal with risks at the closer-to-the-ground 100-metre level.
3. *Use process improvement to seek out risks.* Companies usually can address their risks through a combination of insurance and internal process improvements. Many continuous quality methods exist that match risk appetite without spending so much that it breaks your organisation. Improving your processes also adds to increased profits because it decreases cost and removes waste. Your organisation can address many of its risks through a combination of insurance and process improvements. Many innovative practices exist today that allow you to determine how much to spend in order to match your risk appetite with your resource limitations.
4. *Put structures into your culture that support balance.* If your culture fails to create an equal emphasis on risk taking with risk reduction, one side will override the other. You cannot afford to let that happen. A healthy risk-balanced culture has structures to enforce both sides. Here are some you can easily implement:
   a. Put risk management into all your planning.
   b. Instil open and ongoing communication and feedback.
   c. Create employee councils, panels, focus groups or sounding boards at all levels of your organisation.

d. Implement and enforce a one-person rule that states that every key decision must be made by a team, not just one person.

e. Foster and reward openness to new ideas.

f. Foster a learning environment.

g. Create the awareness that danger is opportunity.

h. Foster an atmosphere of empowerment.

i. Allow employees the freedom to make mistakes.

j. Ensure there is accountability when things go wrong, but put the focus on solution instead of blame.

k. Get rid of outdated and bureaucratic policies.

5. Conduct an annual SLOT analysis as described in Risk Management Tool Eleven below.

Risk Management Tool Eleven–SLOT Analysis

You can easily create risk awareness by annually conducting a SLOT analysis, keeping it updated and then turning it into specific action plans.

A SLOT analysis is a diagnostic tool for analysing and understanding your organisation's current situation or status. This self-evaluation takes a balanced approach and highlights both positives and detriments, so this honesty can be used to spark transformation. The SLOT analysis is a four-part tool for creating an honest baseline and foundation in order to generate and measure forward progress.

Structurally, the SLOT analysis looks like what is shown in Figure 6-3. A detailed SLOT analysis contains

- *Strengths.* Things your organisation does well.
- *Limitations.* Things that hold back your organisation.
- *Opportunities.* Things that could benefit your organisation.
- *Threats.* Things that could undermine your organisation's success.

Figure 6-3
SLOT Analysis

Strengths	Limitations
Opportunities	Threats

The outcome of the SLOT analysis is an honest self-assessment of where your organisation is today. A bonus is that a SLOT analysis is used to assess the firm's risks. You need to annually perform a SLOT analysis of every aspect of your company. Smart leaders then use these in-depth analyses to hone their company's strategic plan. This insight becomes part of your annual risk management programme.

SLOT Versus SWOT

You may have encountered the strengths, weaknesses, opportunities and threats (SWOT) analysis before. The SWOT analysis has only one difference from the SLOT analysis, and that is the replacement of the word *weaknesses* with *limitations.* I prefer the limitations aspect because many people have fragile sensitivities about their leadership abilities and may be hesitant to talk about them, and others suffer from hubris regarding their limited skills. I have found from experience that leaders dislike the word *weakness* because it implies something terrible and irreversible. By using the term *limitations,* I find people switch their thinking from gloom to optimism. A rosier outlook in a business plan is better than a fatalistic one.

Think about what each of these two words imply. Many people recognise their weaknesses yet shy away from doing anything about them. On the other hand people recognise their limitations and create ways to get past them, and the SLOT analysis is designed to spur action, not denial. Use the word that is appropriate for your situation.

Your External Threats and Risk Management

The SLOT analysis will define one or more things coming at you from outside the organisation that could undermine your plans. The threats can be things you fear, anticipate or want to completely avoid. Here are a few examples:

- *Environmental perils or threats.* An earthquake, damage to the local supplier of utilities, storms, flooding, excessive snow, prolonged drought or deadly pollution.
- *Financial perils or threats.* Extended recession; bank failure;or an unexpected obligation, such as losing a lawsuit, losing insurance coverage or embezzlement.
- *Competitive perils or threats.* Nationalisation of an entire industry, a product being banned, the high cost of complying with new regulations, losing a major customer or supplier, losing a production facility, bankruptcy of an outsourcing partner or involuntary condemnation of a building.

Your Opportunities and Risk Management

The SLOT analysis will define one or more things that could benefit your organisation if you pursued them. The opportunities could come from internal sources or be externally generated. Here are a few examples:

- *Competitive opportunities or possibilities.* A new or emerging market, the surprising demand of a feature not on an existing product, bankruptcy of a major competitor, rapid expansion by a customer or prospect, or an inquiry from a competing organisation that is interested in a joint venture.
- *Internal opportunities or possibilities.* The expansion of an existing product line, doubling of capacity, improved efficiency or productivity, dramatic automation, and outsourcing or insourcing.
- *Brand or reputational opportunities or possibilities.* Being ranked first in the industry, receiving positive worldwide press coverage, survey results showing consumers think of your products first, positive results from a marketing survey or winning a prestigious award.
- *Intellectual capital opportunities or possibilities.* The recent hire of a nationally recognised expert; franchising; leasing the name to others (eg, Trump Towers); finalisation of a patent or trademark; or a request to consult on your unique expertise or process.

As you can readily see, there is a fantastic upside to having a SLOT analysis regularly completed because, in the mindset of risk management, your entire leadership team is armed with invaluable knowledge about onerous potentialities to mitigate and numerous possibilities to exploit.

Onward

To end the day I gave the managers a pop quiz to determine the depth of their understanding about the role they must play in the successful implementation of risk awareness in their culture. In their small groups I asked them to discuss and then agree as a group on one answer to this question: Why would knowing how your culture is built help you in analysing your firm's ability to handle business risks?

It took quite a while for them to arrive at a consensus on a single statement. Their answers subsequently shown let me know they were comprehending the concept:

- I would know if I should be concerned.
- I could determine who most likely would follow through and who wouldn't.
- I could change the reward system to reward more risk taking.
- We could evaluate the risky goals and get better feedback to determine if we're on track or should worry.
- I believe that if employees are behind us, then we will more likely be successful, but if employees are against us, then our risk becomes greater.
- I could trust that my people were on top of things.
- I could put more of my attention on my leadership job because I have the confidence that employees are doing their job.

"Your assignment is to complete the SLOT analysis for your team or business unit. Next session we will discover the ways the SLOT guides your risk management activities. Here is another pearl of wisdom on managing risk."

I summarised what they experienced that day. When risk management is forced on the employees without the senior leaders providing the context about the need for it, it will get crushed. Employees will feel that and not support the effort. The lesson today has been that taking time to identify the ideal culture that balances risk taking and risk exposure is something a leader must do. Employees understand culture, and the context you must provide is that tomorrow's culture will feel so much better than the one that is in place now.

"Just because you know better doesn't stop you from doing it.
This is your biggest battle and risk." Ron Rael

Your Action Plan

Step One
Complete the culture assessment on your organisation. What does this tell you about the firm's ability to survive a major risk? List any aspects of your cultural norms that could be a problem. List any aspects of your cultural norms that aid or benefit wise risk taking.

Step Two

Where does your organisation fit on the culture balance? Does it lean too far to one side or the other? If you are not sure complete the "Assessment of a Balanced Culture" tool.

Step Three

List real obstacles that would be faced if or when formal risk management is introduced to your organisation. What are the causes or sources of the obstacles? Do you have an over abundance of employees who are risk takers, risk averse, custodians or indifferent?

Step Four

Think about what would happen if every employee in your organisation had the responsibility statement in their job description. Would it be beneficial or cause problems? Why?

7

WHO Needs to Be Involved?

"We all were part of the problem. Yes, we made a severe error in judgement, but our real sin was not communicating with one another." Mason P.

Everyone fears a wildfire, but it is of greatest concern for people who live in a desert environment. The fire's fuel—trees and plants—are the perfect fodder because of the dryness. Desert winds can turn a small fire into a disaster because of its ability to quickly spread out of control. The worse the fire, the greater the risk.

The air in Phoenix, Arizona, that day was so pungent my nose hurt. The sun was hidden by a hazy greyness because of a wildfire burning many kilometres away that was currently under control. Despite the smell and artificial darkness, I now had another analogy to explain enterprise risk management (ERM), which I used to start the session.

"Do any of you recall the Smokey the Bear public service announcements?" Several hands went up. For those who were not familiar with the Smokey the Bear PSAs, I explained that the long-running ad campaign in the United States features the iconic, hat-wearing Smokey Bear. He advocates for the prevention of wildfires through personal responsibility and the slogan, "Remember ...only YOU can prevent forest fires."

As a child I did not understand Smokey's message. I wondered how I could prevent something beyond my control. That's the fireman's job. With more wisdom I understood his real message. Smokey was reminding me that I needed to do things to ensure that I did not start a fire or contribute to one getting out of control. Smokey's advice applied to me when using fire on a camping trip and when performing activities that could spark a fire, like using a chainsaw or riding a motorcycle.

Smokey's advice and caution is what risk management must do: remind employees that each of them has a responsibility to lessen or avoid the high cost of unnecessary or unwarranted risk.

As a child I thought only fire professionals were accountable for preventing forest fires. Similarly most of your employees currently believe the leaders are the ones accountable to preventing risk. In ERM every employee is accountable for preventing wildfires. Your company's motto, clearly communicated to every employee, is only you can prevent costly or harmful risk.

As before I will share with you a story of a client, "Mason," whose wildfire relates to what you will experience today.

Charlie, Ollie and Mason believe they have the perfect partnership: inCOM Solutions. As consultants to the software development industry, each partner plays a specific role in the organisation. Charlie is the nuts and bolts planner because he has the ability to get past the distracting code and develop or find the appropriate driver for their clients' products.

Ollie is the visual expert of the team. Because many technology solutions are using visual devices, such as the smartphone and portable tablet, their clients needed an easy-to-use and very colourful interface. He knows how to make the hidden code turn into a powerful interface that relies on Charlie's driver.

Mason is the visionary of the team. He can listen to the client's very complex problem and, within a few hours or days, create a crystal clear one-page recap of what the software is supposed to accomplish. Mason can quickly see past the fog of data and hone in on one salient area that would become the focal point for the client's software objective.

With rapid growth over the last seven years, each partner got busier and busier, leading many diverse project teams, as well as preparing proposals and wooing potential clients. Despite their record of achievement and client list made up of the who's who in technology, their perfect partnership severely stumbled. It all started when inCOM hired employee "K." They needed a code writer and systems tester immediately, and this urgency caused them to shortcut their normal hiring process. These two skills are difficult to locate in one person, so there was not a large pool of qualified candidates. Once the word got out, an out-of-town recruiter contacted Mason and described K's qualifications. Because of their desperate need, Mason conducted the first two interviews: one over the phone and the second using Skype.

Because he is a big-picture person, Mason did not delve into K's background and qualifications, assuming that Charlie or Ollie would do that. The candidate seemed to be who they needed, so Mason scheduled K to fly in for an interview with Charlie and Ollie. It was very difficult to find an opening in their hectic schedules, so Ollie and Charlie separately met with K. In their haste neither one took the time to check K's portfolio and background or communicate with Mason. During the rushed interviews with K, each one spent most of the time extolling inCOM's accomplishments and successful projects. Before K returned home Mason made K an offer that K accepted the next day.

Although there were specific warnings signs that K was not working out, no one noticed. The three partners rarely took the time to meet and discuss the big picture of their firm.

Mason was the first to learn of the problem when a long-term client cancelled its ongoing retainer engagement. Next Charlie was fired by another long-term client who complained, "You guys have lost your way. Your quality isn't what it used to be." Ollie was dismayed when one of his clients threatened to sue if inCOM did not refund fees already paid on a very large project.

One Saturday morning, when they found themselves together in the office, each owner started to complain about his client problems. After tossing this problem about, they looked for common factors and ended up with only one: K. The three projects in jeopardy were ones they handed over to K without any oversight. Needing to get to the heart of the matter, Charlie (the detail guy) spent the next three days finding out what K had or had not done and obtaining client comments and concerns..

By Thursday of that week, Charlie presented his findings to the partners. According to multiple sources K was

- verbally abusing the client's employees.
- arrogantly ignoring the client's advice and feedback.
- unskilled in many of the areas in which he claimed to be knowledgeable.
- blaming client personnel for his own obvious mistakes.

K was terminated the next day, but it would take some time to repair the damage to inCOM's reputation because word spreads fast in the networked community of software development.

Mason asked me during a coaching session right after he fired this employee, "What did I miss? Why did we get into this mess?"

I responded, "Each of you saw only a small aspect of the whole within the scope of your very narrow roles. In risk management everyone must play a key and interdependent role. When you as a company chose to seize an opportunity in the form of hiring K, an unknown quantity, you and your company incurred a normal-sized risk that quickly grew out of control. Each of you was unaware of the abnormal risk and its consequences because you were focused on your work and desperate for help. As a result you missed or ignored the warning signs that K was not the solution you wished for."

Risk Management Is a Team Effort

Your mom probably warned you, "Don't put your nose where it doesn't belong." That quaint adage does not apply to managing risk. As the story about Mason's problem employee showed, when it comes to detecting and then managing a potential problem, it requires many noses. Risk is everywhere and arises from all around you. Because you are not omnipotent or omnipresent, you need other responsible, trained people to poke their noses into the visible and invisible potholes and pitfalls.

> **Murphy's Law of Risk Accountability**
>
> The more people involved in solving the problem, the worse the outcome. The fewer people involved in solving the problem, the longer it takes to create a solution.

ERM establishes a suggested structure of specific risk managers who report to the ERM executive (chief risk officer [CRO]) and provide risk-based information to the ERM committee. As previously discussed a horizontal view of risk is not available with the traditional "silo" approach in which you rely on specialists and insurance to address your daily risks. You need many noses sniffing for risk because typically

- internal audit employees only deal with control risks.
- finance employees only look after accounting-related risks.
- operational employees only deal with day-to-day business risks.
- asset managers are only concerned with property risks.
- executives mostly deal with strategy risks.
- sales management only looks at market and customer risks.
- quality employees only watch over product risks.
- treasury employees solely handle monetary risks.

This specialist method of addressing risk separates accountability from solution, and it also hampers open dialogue about risk, the sharing of best practices and spotting broad trends.

Yet someone in your organisation needs to have the ultimate responsibility for ERM, with a team of employees supporting him or her. This vital role is your CRO who reports to both the CEO and board.

> The CRO is the senior-level employee who is in charge of the risk management team and focuses on risks that could affect the bottom line and firm's future existence. The CRO's team is empowered with deciding what is and is not risky.

The ERM committee is an employee group who seeks out areas where the payoffs for risk are overstated or the costs of risk are understated. They examine documentation, test transactions and review specific decisions. They also highlight external areas of concern. The CRO, though the work of the ERM committee, gives the CEO assurance that risk is being managed and that the firm's checks and balances are working, so the CEO can sleep well at night.

Throughout the entire risk management process, your organisation must retain a strategic focus, and although a senior-level executive must be the champion of your risk management efforts, other groups of people can be established to support ERM.

How many employees in your organisation have a 10,000-metre view of risk?

According to Henry Ristuccia, a partner with Deloitte & Touche and U.S. leader of its governance and risk management practice, "While more companies are now appointing chief risk officers, many don't have that position, and therefore responsibility for risk management ends up with the board and the CFO."

Justin asked, "What is the best way to oversee the management of risk? Who needs to be part of the risk management team?"

I answered, "There are two approaches: one for big organisations and another for small ones. The requirements of each one are the same, and this will be where I start to answer this question."

CRO

Experts in risk management agree that organisations need to shift the focus of their risk assessment efforts away from specialists to a broader base of employees who are led by a high-level person, such as a senior executive who is accountable for global risk oversight. This person needs a much broader field of vision if he or she hopes to successfully see what's raining down upon the organisation in the form of unforeseen risk. This is hard for the executive who specialises in one discipline, such as sales, production, marketing or research; therefore, choosing the right individual is crucial to the success of your ERM programme.

Companies That Understand the Importance of Risk Management

These organisations recently created a new position of CRO: AXIS Capital Holdings; Eutelsat Communications; Navistar International Corporation; Pepco Holdings, Inc.; State Street Corporation; Synovus; Walgreens; and Webster.

Arcelor Mittal, the world's largest steelmaker, recently announced it added a risk committee to its board.

CalPERS, the largest pension fund in the United States, formed an ad hoc board-level risk committee.

Every risk management programme, regardless of whether it is based on ERM, requires an executive-level champion who must be able to assemble a multidisciplinary or cross-functional team that can effectively discuss the risk and its related business issues your organisation faces and then share his or her findings with the entire organisation. Your designated champion and his or her team must understand why your company has succeeded in the past and is currently succeeding or not succeeding.

Risk Management Team

The risk management team takes a 360° perspective that broadens the typical "I don't want to worry" focus to include less tangible assets, specific exposures and the links among them. By understanding the broad risks facing your firm and how they are interrelated, you are able to better manage them and create a sustainable strategic advantage and, hopefully, the firm's value.

ERM requires that all members of the risk management oversight group (ERM committee) work together to pinpoint and measure the critical risks confronting your organisation and then develop a systematic approach to manage the risk portfolio.

As shown in the risk management oversight chart in Figure 7-1, there are many participants. This team's membership consists of the controller and key decision makers (DMs) from every part of your organisation, from human resources to sales and from operations to treasury. The team's centre point is the CRO.

I recommend that the CFO not be a member of the ERM committee as a way to strengthen the checks and balances that the CFO is accountable for.

The members of this team, other than your controller and director of internal audit, need to be responsible DMs charged with accountability for the quality of decisions and processes within the department they represent. However in larger organisations, this responsibility could be assigned to someone other than the manager as a way of building the competence and confidence of future leaders.

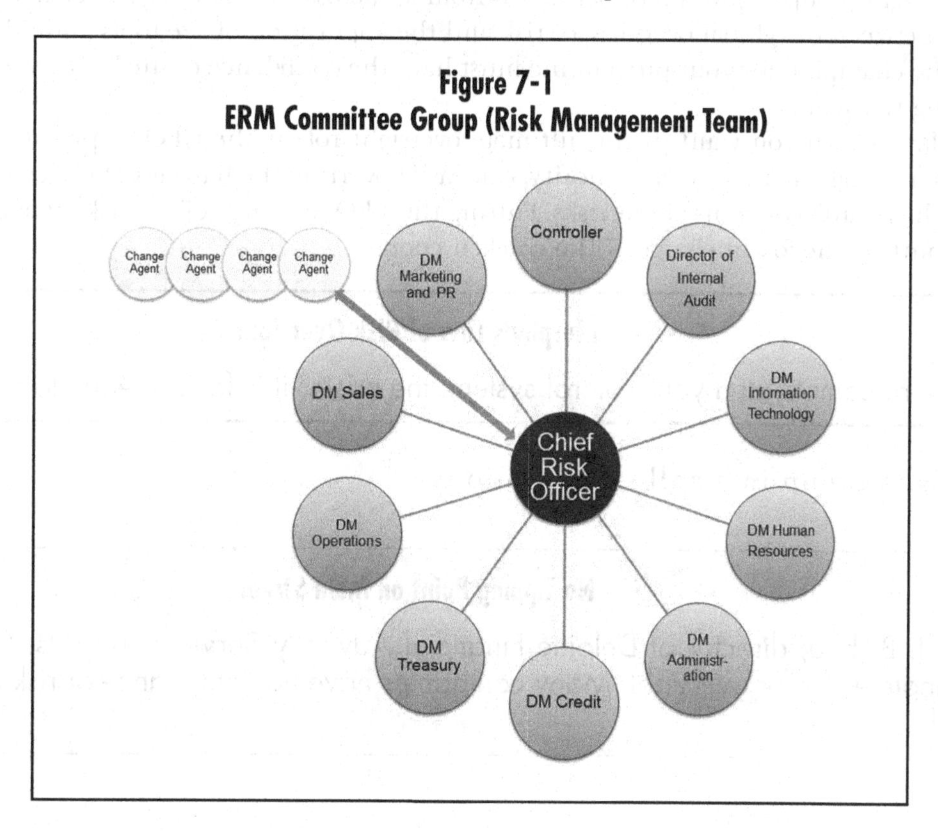

Figure 7-1
ERM Committee Group (Risk Management Team)

The employees who the CRO directly supervises can be described as change agents because that title reflects more of their ultimate goal, rather than their responsibilities. The change agents in your oversight group

- delve into certain areas that are or will be affected by risk taking.
- assist in implementing the changes that the oversight group recommends.
- train employees on how to use the risk management tools.
- report to management using a balanced set of risk-oriented metrics.

You could assign different titles to these change agents, but giving the employee a title, such as analyst, auditor or risk assessor, does not communicate to others how the employee is benefiting the organisation and could be confusing if you have other employees with similar titles.

The Tipping Point on Wall Street

James Lam, president of James Lam & Associates, a risk management consulting firm, recently commented about what he is seeing in large organisations. Almost 90% of global organisations with more than $1 billion in revenue are either putting ERM into place or have an ERM programme up and running. Of the S&P 500 companies his firm studied, 58% said their audit committees were responsible for risk management.

Board of Directors

Of course risk management efforts must have the support of your board of directors because your risk oversight group requires representation from all across the company. They need to create stronger ties between the global overview of risk and the application of the tools and mitigation of those risks. The champion for your programme must have the confidence of the board and be comfortable reporting to them.

The last person you want in this ultimate oversight role is the CEO or president who, through his or her automatic mantle of authority, can easily override the findings of the oversight group and ignore the board's concerns about risks. Putting the CEO in charge of the risk management function is like putting the fox in charge of the chicken coop.

Murphy's Law of Risk Oversight

The more complicated your control system, the easier it is for someone to circumvent it.

Oversight Group in Small Organisations

No Tipping Point on Main Street

Toby J. Bishop, director of Deloitte Financial Advisory Services, reports, "There's often no single entity for oversight. Many companies have no compliance or risk management at all."

In smaller organisations, usually, not enough decisions makers are available for them to devote large amounts of time to the discussion and analysis of risk. Therefore it becomes the responsibility of your line managers and a few administrative managers to identify, classify, monitor and control operational risks. They form the oversight group who reports to a senior executive. Holistic analysis of risk requires cross-functional participation.

In this simplified structure you expand every manager's job scope to include identifying these everyday risks and preparing for them if the perils worsen. This identification duty applies to opportunities your managers should already be attuned to. In the scope of their daily work, your managers face many other sorts of risks that are less visible and that unfortunately get ignored. Yet these risks also need to be monitored, measured and managed. It is an extension of your supervisor's or manager's vital role, not a duty or task you add on.

The managers who comprise the oversight team need to learn how to take risks, as well as watch for them. These two intentions can be seen as contradictory, even though they aren't. The thought process for taking risks and managing risks is the same. To effectively take risks, your manager needs to anticipate the possible and probable impacts of their actions and then make a conscious effort in deciding to

- move forward.
- not move forward.
- move forward in a way that reduces any negative consequences.

When your managers learn to take risks, they automatically become more conscious about the risk management requirement of their job. As each decision maker improves his or her ability to identify then mitigate a potential business risk, he or she gains confidence when taking innovative and creative leaps of faith.

Every manager who makes critical decisions for your organisation needs to be trained on risk management, so that it becomes part of his or her daily activity. This qualifies the manager to be the de facto member of the oversight team. In this hands-on training, you help each manager understand the concepts, principles, tools and techniques for considering and managing uncertainty. This training optimises their abilities to achieve both individual and corporate goals.

Without a formal risk management programme, most small organisations assign the risk management role to either a contracted professional risk manager or their CFO. Either choice leads to the "silo" approach of risk management. Finally the role that is often neglected or under emphasised in small organisations is that of the primary risk executive or CRO. This person still needs access to, and authority over, employees who have a responsibility to do the follow-up work necessary after a solution has been put into action. In a smaller organisation the team's change agent who supports your risk executive could be a department head or supervisor or technical expert.

Your executive team, consulting with the board, must decide who best in your organisation can take on this role. He or she is given the authority and budget to form your firm's risk oversight group. The structure for the smaller organisation is shown in Figure 7-2:

Figure 7-2
Risk Management Oversight Team

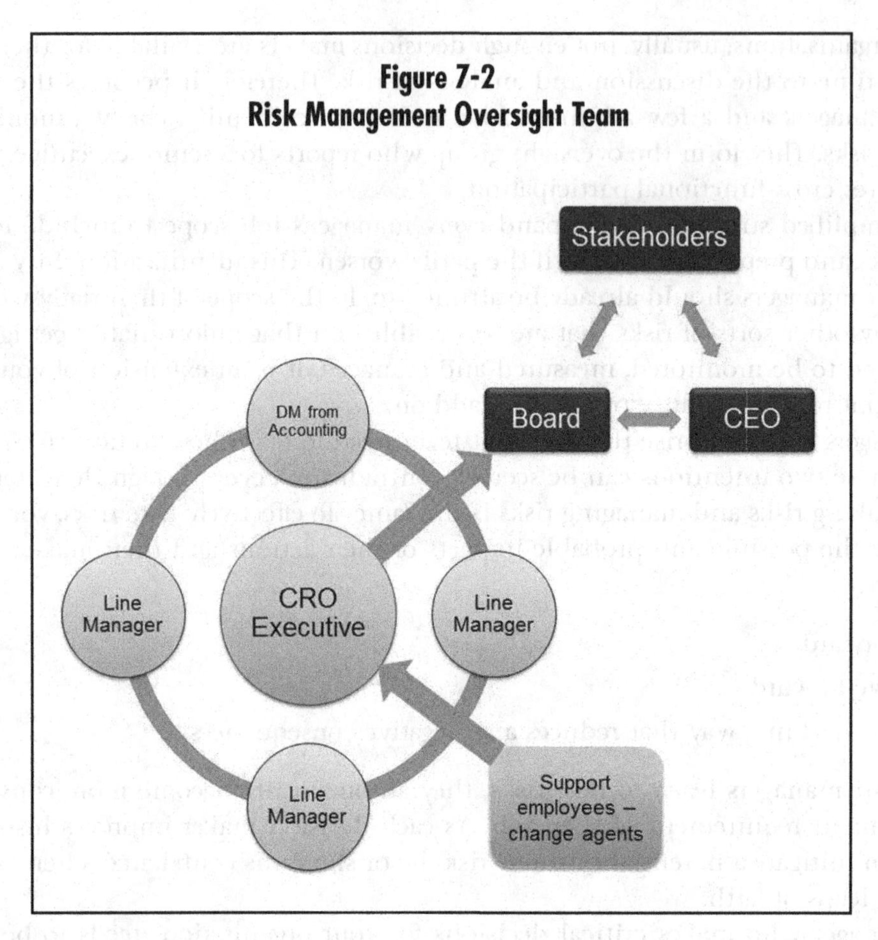

Finance's Role in ERM

The organisation's finance team is the group best equipped to support and assist the organisation's leaders in their efforts to globally manage risks, but taking the lead on risk management is not your finance department's responsibility. Your accounting employees play a pivotal role in management of risk in several areas.

Selecting Metrics

ERM requires that the oversight group have access to a set of metrics known as key performance indicators (KPIs) and leading indicators. Finance, which has access to a wide variety of pulse points, can assist the ERM team in determining the methods of tracking and the meaning of each measurement. It can also assist in defining, measuring and monitoring key risk indicators (KRIs) that serve as early warning signals about impending problems.

Providing Feedback

Your risk management programme requires a reporting mechanism for it to work as designed: to decrease rash or unwarranted risk taking. In ERM this consists of a dashboard of the KRIs and KPIs made available to the risk committee and executives. Because ERM suggests the development of alternative financial plans and forecasts using different selected scenarios, finance is in a position to provide information on the status of those plans in its reports.

Recommending Policy Updates

Because finance usually serves as the "sheriff" for errors, omissions and unethical conduct, it can advise leaders on where policies need updating or strengthening.

Testing Transparency
ERM requires that leaders display transparency in their decisions, goals and actions. Through their reports finance can serve as the ones who analyse and test the efforts for transparency. Because leaders of the effort must ensure transparency in the risk management process, finance has an obligation to connect the risk management programme to the organisation's system of internal controls.

Scenario Planning
With its skills in analysis, finance can project the financial implications of alternative strategies and test the sensitivity of key assumptions, financial measures and variables under different scenarios.

Process Improvement
Although not a primary source of hidden risk, all operational processes can contribute to the creation of rash or irrational decisions and the acceptance of unwarranted risk. Complex processes are often used to cover up fraud, embezzlement and waste. Finance can be the group that leads the plan to improve all major processes, with the intention of reducing waste, improving decision making and removing hidden agendas.

Return on Risk Measurements
As shown earlier in this chapter, the acceptance of ERM hinges on proving the programme pays for itself. Although cost avoidance can lower overall risk, finance can assist the oversight team in creating a scorecard that compares the implementation costs to the benefits received. This will require agreement on a complete set of assumptions on how the organisation and its stakeholders benefit when employees are actively detecting and mitigating risk.

You will discover more ways that your finance employees are able to make your ERM programme a success, as long as they are considered assets to the process but are not the group burdened with implementing or overseeing it.

CFOs Weigh In

CFO Research Services and Liberty Mutual Insurance Company reported in June 2010 the results of a survey of senior financial executives on the state of risk management in their organisations. The report started, "Although research suggests that many companies would benefit from a more-forward looking approach to managing risk, 25% of the financial executives say that systematically identifying risk exposure is 'very challenging' at their companies." However they added that justifying an investment in risk management is a challenge because of the difficulty in determining a viable return on risk management spending.

Source: http://www.cfo.com/article.cfm/14509202/c_14509253

Insurance's Role in Risk Management

Buying insurance serves to provide your firm with funds whenever a covered risk costs you money, such as a fire, lawsuit or currency exchange loss. Insurance coverage is a commodity that has to be purchased to protect the financial resources of your organisation. Your leaders cannot fall into the trap of only looking at the cost of the insurance for the cost of running a risk management programme. Buying insurance is only one exposure reduction tactic and must not be your firm's entire risk management programme, a philosophy used by many small and mid-sized organisations. In ERM, not insurance acquisition, is where you get to examine the scope of the risk vulnerability of the entire enterprise.

Insurance Does Not Always Reduce Exposure

In an attempt to manage their risks, both large and small companies mostly focus on insurable risks and ignore such things as operational and strategic risks. In the event that a risk needs insurance coverage, your company needs to take a fresh approach. When adopting specialised insurance coverage your organisation still needs to create long-term mitigation solutions. For example a risk to your firm's brand might be easily mitigated through insurance coverage today, but in the long run it could have a significant negative impact on future sales and profits if the causes of your exposure go unaddressed. Brand risk is an example of an exposure that may not be covered by your current insurance coverage. This is why your creative exposure reduction efforts are critical to the successful implementation of ERM.

The balance between insuring yourself and managing risk without expensive coverage will depend on your firm's risk management philosophy. A smaller company has a desire to protect itself and yet can have a large risk appetite. However that philosophy is risky because, quite often, the company lacks the infrastructure or leadership to support good risk management practices and, therefore, over-relies on costly specialised insurance to reduce its exposure. A more profitable philosophy would be to spend the same amount of money implementing aspects of ERM, which can reduce losses and operating costs.

Jeff Burchill, the CFO of FM Global, a commercial property insurer warns, "I think a lot of [executives] think of insurance as a commodity that they buy, and that all insurance is created equal. It's not until you have an event that you find out that it is not created equal" (http://www.cfo.com/article.cfm/14570123/2/c_2984346?f=archives). The most common mistake companies make when purchasing insurance is that "once you've transferred the risk you don't have to manage it. That's not true at all."

Insurance's Inadequacy

One area where your organisation has tremendous exposure is in its use of technology and the Internet for e-commerce. Yet you cannot always rely on insurance coverage to protect your exposures. The insurance industry is only now beginning to address and work with its clients to deal with the risks in today's electronic world. Every day insurers are finding different exposures that they have not encountered before. The first deficiency with insurers is the lack of historical data because they use history to determine both the size of the risk and its statistical probability. From this data the insurer sets a rate to charge its clients. This information must be reliable yet always arrives years after the risk is identified. The phenomenal growth in electronic business, or e-commerce, is another major and hard-to-quantify risk in business today. Although awareness to this risk is rising, the second deficiency is that some insurance companies still have a hard time getting their senior insurance executives to recognise that this exposure requires a new strategy or approach.

In today's e-commerce a lot of risks are unquantifiable. For example your business model requires a heavy dependency on a contract manufacturer. You are unaware that the contract manufacturer also consults with your competitor, thus causing your business harm. The contract manufacturer failed to disclose this relationship to you. You now have to find and engage another contractor. You ask your insurance company for compensation, and it asks you, "What are your economic losses?" You are unable to show specific out-of-pocket costs, other than some travel and legal fees. You demand compensation for the damage to your reputation, for the work to quickly find an alternative supplier and for lost future earnings. Because this is a contractual relationship and one not addressed in your policy, the chances are high that your insurance company will only reimburse for your out-of-pocket costs.

This example demonstrates a modern risk faced by every business that relies on strategic partnerships. In a panel discussion with top insurance experts sponsored by the Risk and Insurance Management Society, this specific shortcoming came up. Both the representatives from the insurance industry and their clients expressed concerns that the insurance industry has been slow to see the need to assess and underwrite risk differently from its traditional methods.

As exposures grow in our global, around-the-clock, interconnected and outsourced world, I predict that the major insurance companies will require their clients to provide proof that they have a risk management protocol in place in order for them to receive affordable coverage.

ERM Step Four: Minimise Exposure to Risk

There are two relationships regarding risk in a culture. The first is the one you know well: the symbiotic relationship between risk and reward. The second one is of equal importance: the symbiotic relationship between risk and awareness. What undermines a company is not necessarily the risk itself but the ignorance about the potential consequences of each viable risk. If managers are aware of the risk, along with the source, nature and magnitude, they can take appropriate steps to avoid or mitigate the hidden pitfalls. This ability is critical in the operational areas or front lines of an organisation. The more your people know where and why risk hides in the organisation, the quicker they can respond and react.

This is why Step four is necessary. Although most organisations that currently use ERM initially identify 50–100 or more specific risks, the key is to pare the list down to the top five or 10 risks that are significant enough to warrant quantifying and analysing. Once a company has identified its key risks among those top 10, it has to quantify the magnitude of those risks. Quantification helps the leaders decide whether to control, prevent, finance, ensure or avoid the risk altogether. One person alone cannot stay on top of that many risks.

The essence of Step four is to minimise your organisation's risk exposure or, better yet, inspire actions to lower the cost of failure. The biggest challenge of a risk management programme is to bring your organisation to a point where it can

- identify the risks that are the greatest threat to its continued growth and success.
- quantify the size of those risks.
- finally take steps to manage or mitigate them.

Once you have convinced people in your organisation that multiple threats need to be taken seriously, Step four starts you moving towards taking action and placing tools in the hands of employees, so they make smarter decisions and manage the perils. An old saying is, "Fully warned is fully armed."

Rarely do executives identify a particular operational risk because they are tuned into strategic risk or faulty assumptions in the business plan. It is almost always an employee doing the work and dealing with the situation who recognises a cost you cannot afford and is willing to find one or two solutions. As leader your job is to help the employees at the lowest levels define the seriousness of the problems, so they can take action. The rest of this chapter provides insight into where to look for your vulnerabilities, along with the methods and tools to minimise your exposure.

Look for Risk during Times of Success

First Paradox of Business Success

Enjoy and capitalise on the good times, and in the good times you must look for impending dangers.

In the good times it is easy to forget about risk, yet it is during the upswings when you are most vulnerable and when your executives need to be most watchful for the signs of impending danger. In aggressive "can do" or "grow at all cost" strategies when bold initiatives are underway, and customers are streaming in the door, it is quite common to silence or shoot the messenger who carries bad news or concerns.

Success and limitless opportunity should make leaders nervous because those conditions identify an increase in the level of internal risk exposure. As you know not every risk is bad, and in order to survive and make progress today, you must take risks. Yet those of you at the top of the organisation are less aware of risk exposure than those closer to the trenches. Likewise your people closer to the operations are aware of the risks that affect their area but are blind to, or underestimate the exposure impact on, other parts of the organisation. Therefore understanding the positive conditions, such as upswings and fast growth, that create unnecessary levels of risk allows you to prevent exposures while taking advantage of opportunities.

A business cannot survive over the long term or prosper without entrepreneurial risk taking that leads to innovation and creativity. However success can give some risk takers, especially CEOs, so much confidence that they harm the company's assets and reputation, all in the pursuit of greater gains. This is an irresistible urge in organisations experiencing meteoric success. Often, in a successful firm that has never experienced a loss, employees accept excessively risky deals, forge alliances with others who do not have the ability to honour their contracts or make promises to customers that are impossible to fulfil. The catalyst for this type of behaviour usually is the rewards and incentives built into your cultural norms. Rewards can be overt or hidden. As your incentives for entrepreneurial behaviour grow, so does your risk exposure. As a leader you must also reward rational decision making using risk evaluation and mitigation.

Banking's Weakness Continues

A 2009 report from the Senior Supervisors Group, made up of financial regulators in seven countries, explained that despite some recent progress, financial institutions continue to overestimate the quality of their risk management systems.

Source: http://www.newyorkfed.org/newsevents/news/banking/2009/SSG_report.pdf

Look for Risk in Your Vulnerable and Hidden Areas

For an executive the scariest aspect of managing is not knowing; therefore, ERM is designed to make the invisible visible. The process of risk management allows you to fly over the organisation and regularly dialogue with the employees on the ground about problems and opportunities. Very soon there will be little that escapes your attention.

ERM creates an awareness of where your plans and dreams are vulnerable through tools like the strengths, limitations, opportunities and threats analysis and culture assessment. Both the risk oversight team and executives monitor those areas using metrics and feedback and through ongoing communications with the employee who is responsible for managing the vulnerability.

Look for Risk in Your Timelines

In the hubbub of activity that goes on each day in your company, it is easy to take on too much, thus adding to the chaos. Because you will regularly be flying over things at 10,000 metres, you will be encouraged to pay attention to the timelines of your various action plans and goals. The employees involved with them will become more vocal when they see conflicts about the timing and deliverables you expect from them. Because timeline or deadline conflict creates vulnerability that leads to more risk, ERM is designed to prevent this or create awareness that your managers notice these conflicts in scheduling and promises.

Integrate ERM Goals into Existing Infrastructure

As you implement the infrastructure for risk management, expect to invest plenty of time and effort for its creation because it is not something that can be accomplished in one week or even one month. A large investment of time will be in taking your existing management systems and instilling an aspect of ERM into each one. Your most vital processes that you integrate first are the

- budgeting process.
- reporting and feedback process.
- goals and measurements system.
- prioritisation process.
- project development and funding process.

Budgeting Process

As you discovered in a prior chapter, your budget is an integral part of your risk management programme. Reason one is that taking risks affects aspects of your budget, such as increased sales, larger investments in assets, acquiring lines of business, expanding operations and hiring talent. Reason two is because the mitigation and prevention of risk requires resources to accomplish. As you implement your ERM processes, you will see the need to revise your insurance coverage, train employees and hire experts. Each of these will consume precious resources and must be reflected in your organisation's three budgets for insurance, training and consultants.

This is why an immediate integration of your current budget methodology into the rollout of your risk management programme is a priority.

Reporting and Feedback Process

In order for your executives and the risk oversight group to know if their efforts are paying off, they need feedback in the form of specific metrics, improved scorecards and tailored reports. As a direct result your organisation will need to immediately examine its existing reporting processes, methods and tools and then integrate them into the ERM programme. This is also a top priority during ERM implementation.

In the same way that a shift in cultural norms can help foster the attitude of risk awareness, a modest improvement in your firm's information system can provide an improvement to risk management efforts. You simply integrate risk management reporting into your regular reports, so that you foster increased awareness about what everyone is doing or supposed to be doing.

Goals and Measurements System

As you begin implementing ERM you do not start over with new goals. Instead, as each goal is examined during your normal progress reviews, you begin to fold aspects of risk management into your action plans.

If you have a formal goal-setting protocol in your organisation, you already require the person responsible for achieving the goal to provide information about its progress and obstacles. Because this is an important aspect of ERM, integrating these existing goals into your risk management programme will be easy to accomplish.

However there may be some inherent risk or unnecessary peril in your current goals. Therefore one way you can test for risk in a goal is to ask a series of questions about the goal to determine if you should be concerned about it:

- Do the employees involved see a difference between a stretch goal and an unrealistic goal?
- Are the employees involved required to explain the means used to achieve each goal?
- Are the employees accomplishing this goal held accountable for how they achieve their goals or just for achieving them?

Prioritisation Process

A challenge every large and small organisation faces is that there are more priorities than time and money available. As you implement your ERM protocols you will need to pay close attention to what are deemed your top priorities, both as an organisation and within each business unit and administrative department. Because ERM is designed to help you detect risks and perils in both high-level and operational goals, the holistic approach to managing the organisation will automatically bring to the forefront priorities that are causing problems or consuming more resources than expected.

As you integrate ERM into what you are doing, be sure to pay special attention to, and keep track of, everyone's top priorities for the month, quarter and year. Apply some of the risk management tools when you notice a conflict in priorities.

Project Development and Funding Process

Similar to goals, throughout your organisation, employees are working on specific projects. As you conduct a budget and progress review of each project, it is in your best interest to start analysing the pitfalls and downsides in each one. Then have the project's champion determine what additional action items must be included in the project tasks in order to reduce any inherent risk.

Your monthly review of projects in process will be a good place for your executives to sit down with the project's managers to discuss what they need to do differently or improve to reduce any exposures inherent in the scope of their project.

Minimise Internal Risk of Unethical Employee Behaviour

We like to blame Mr Murphy when things go wrong. Yes, randomness and chaos exist around us, but the truth is many of your risks are instigated by the people around you. Understanding the human element or X factor will enable you to reduce exposure or the cost you cannot afford. Your lesson starts with the allure of the path of least resistance (POLR).

Risk and POLR

POLR is the principle that energy moves where it is easiest for it to go. It is reality that a person will almost always take the course that is the most convenient or least painful.

To address the human side of ERM, start by understanding the POLR principle. To detect vulnerabilities study employee behaviours and be on constant watch for places where POLR exists. By discovering the path that leads to undesirable behaviours that create unwarranted risk for your organisation, you can easily shape employee's behaviours. Here are a few truisms about POLR:

> **Twelfth, Thirteenth, and Fourteenth Principles of Risk Management:**
>
> When I display a behaviour that increases risk, it is usually because my behaviour is the path of least resistance. There is some sort of payoff for my actions.
>
> Temptations to take the path of least resistance come in many forms, most of which you are not aware of.
>
> If you choose to shape someone's behaviour, you must alter the existing path of least resistance.

Setting the Expectation for Ethical Behaviours

Organisations keep chaos at bay by adopting rules and standards that derive from your corporate values. Yet even in these rules and standards you run a risk for unethical behaviours. Once the standards are established you set the expectation that everyone must live up to the standards. Without this expectation anyone can find reasons for not living up to the standards. To have an ERM programme based on ethical practices, your standards and expectations must be

- defined.
- based upon positive outcomes.
- beneficial to all stakeholders.
- clarified.
- measurable.
- promulgated.
- visible.
- practised.
- rewarded.

In risk management, as in leadership, there needs to be some flexibility and discretion in your policies and rules. Rules and laws cannot cover every situation. Because you want your employees to use good judgement and think for themselves, your high expectations are really their guide for what is and is not appropriate. That is why the standards you establish, clarify and widely communicate become the touchstones of behaviour you want employees to display in your risk management efforts.

Temptations for your employees to take POLR exist all the time, and the only thing that prevents them from succumbing to the urge to be less ethical is not the fear of getting caught or the desire to do the right thing. When your employee believes he or she is respected, treated fairly and has influence, he or she will resist POLR. When employees take the high road your risks go down.

That is why culture is such a key cornerstone of your ERM programme. If your culture story lifts employees' spirits through trust, empowerment and enrichment, they will stay aware of risks and do their best to reduce your exposure.

Let us explore how your policies, expectations and rewards increase exposure to risk because of POLR.

Unreasonable Policies Increase Ethics Risk

The risk of leading a culture without a commitment to high ethics is not just dangerous for the company, it makes you as a leader personally vulnerable. We now live in a society and environment where any business owner or executive can be sued for pretty much anything.

Yet you often teach your employees to cheat or embezzle based upon your company policies because the rules and their enforcement can drive employee behaviour in ways you never expected. According to the POLR principle, your employees' tendency to take advantage of you by accepting unwarranted risk or defrauding you can be described on a normal distribution curve:

- Your employees will never do anything unethical or undesirable (5–10%).
- Your employees are always looking for ways to take advantage of you (5–10%).
- Your employees will commit situational fraud or take unwarranted risk when it is to their advantage (80–90%).

James works really hard, putting in extra time, including weekends, to meet an impossible deadline you gave him. James completes the project for you on time and asks for a couple days off to recuperate and replace the time he missed with his family. You point out to James that your firm's policy reads, "Employees can only have paid time off work for illness, maternity leave, vacation, jury duty or a death in the immediate family." If you were in James's shoes what would you do? Get mad? Suck it up? Get back to work?

Guess what James and approximately 80% of your employees would do? James will either take time off, claiming he is sick (even though he isn't), or he will come to the office but not get much accomplished for several days, leaving early and arriving late.

You probably believe that James should be fired for this unprofessional behaviour, but remember this: because you chose to stay rigid on your policy and not give James any consideration for the extraordinary effort he put into your project, you placed James in a no-win situation in which he chooses to default to his own ethical values.

Unfortunately you cannot expect ethical behaviour from your employees unless you and all the leaders display ethical behaviour. Each of you must walk the walk and talk the talk in fairness, equity and equality every day. Unless you all live up to the highest levels of professionalism that are demanded from your employees, you will be unable to expect this behaviour of anyone else.

Unreasonable Expectations Increase Ethics Risk

Managing risks to your organisation's reputation requires a sustained dialogue with each stakeholder, including employees. All too often executives set goals and expectations based upon what they want or what is demanded by stakeholders, such as specific earnings per share. Because they are not the ones doing the work, executives fail to see the goal is impractical or impossible.

You tell your sales employee, Marcus, "You need to increase your sales by 10% before the end of the year." So he aggressively markets and issues a proposal to a potential customer who is choosing between your company and a competitor.

Your sales personnel are empowered to set terms, provided the gross margin is above 20%. Marcus gets the new client to sign a long-term contract that states if the clients buys all it promises to buy, your company will pay the client a 5% incentive. Your company lacks a clear policy on contract rebates or special incentives.

Marcus presents you with the agreement, which you approve. Before the order is entered your CFO, who must signoff on all new clients and all special terms, nixes the deal. She refuses to accept the order and issues you a memo that reads, "The special incentive, when exercised, reduces the contract's gross margin to under our 20% standard."

However if you don't include Marcus's order in this quarter, you miss your team's quota, get called on the carpet and lose your performance bonus. You inform Marcus that he must get his prospect to agree to new terms. He responds, "Unless they receive the terms they requested, they will buy from our competition." You remind him, "Your job is to get that order, so make it happen!"

You just nudged Marcus towards POLR with your unreasonable expectation. An employee not committed to high ethical standards my take an action that creates risk for your company, and the risk arises from two naturally occurring conditions that exist in most organisations:

- Rules are often vague and written without clear behaviour standards.
- Rules often conflict with the goals and self-interests of both the individual and organisation.

The overall solution for reducing your risk for unethical behaviours and practices is for you to use reasonable expectations in order to alter POLR. These truisms point out you must also set the expectation for ethical conduct and not just say, "Read the policy."

Incentives Increase Ethics Risk

Rewards as Incentives

The behaviours and decisions that leaders reward tell employees what is most important. People pay attention to who is rewarded and why. If employees are rewarded for the wrong behaviours, other people see this and model those same behaviours. If a negative or risky behaviour is displayed by an employee, and the action is either ignored or condoned, other employees see this and model the behaviour.

Risk in Your Static Rewards

Behaviour never remains static. As a leader you must be willing to alter your invisible and visible rewards and compensation system whenever employees show behaviours that put your organisation at risk. Change your compensation system, and employees automatically will change their behaviour. Your job is to drive desired behaviour by establishing the right rewards for the right reasons.

To seek out the perils in your existing and proposed incentives, use these questions as your guide:

- Why do we have or need this particular reward?
- What behaviour is the employee being rewarded for?
- What form do our formal rewards take?
- What form do our informal or invisible rewards take?
- What sorts of messages do the formal rewards send?
- How are our positive-aimed rewards being subverted?

Internal Pressures Increase Ethics Risk

Pressure has the same impact on taking risks as rewards. Your employees are almost always under some pressure to perform or produce, which is normal. The greater the urgency for your firm to take risks and the higher the reward you set for being innovative, the greater the likelihood that undue pressure will be placed on employees to achieve certain results. This is where your vulnerability hides.

There is a delicate balance between the incentive to achieve something and the pressure to perform. Applying pressure on someone to achieve can be a positive thing, yet it is often misused or subverted.

Your CEO requests that the sales group provide her with stretch numbers for the sales forecast. Ignoring their data she sets a target much higher than what they believe is possible. She promises your sales team incentives in the form of cash rewards and a vacation in Hawaii if they can reach her high number, but this incentive creates exposure when intense pressure is placed on them to achieve the unrealistic target. What is worse is your employees are not given the tools or means to achieve the higher target. Employees are put at a disadvantage when she penalises them for achieving the original target, the one based on what they knew was possible. To earn their incentive some of your employees may take POLR.

Here are some questions to ask yourself as you look for inherent risk around pressures to produce targets and goals:

- Could someone who is in a position of power get away with a detrimental behaviour by exerting undue influence?
- Where do pressures to perform or achieve a specific result come from, and why do they exist?
- How do our employees normally respond to performance pressures?
- How do our employees respond if the pressure is excessive or if the goal is unrealistic?
- How do we want our employees to respond?

Risk from Fraud and Employee Abuses

The overall loss from fraud is estimated to be over $660 billion, or 6% of turnover. Fraud and abuse of employer assets translate into $9 per day per employee. How many employees work in your organisation? Multiply that number by $9 then by 365. This figure will give you a compelling reason to be concerned about your exposure to fraud! Two of the most common forms of fraud are kickbacks and conflicts of interest involving employees and others. Other forms of business fraud include

- fraudulent disbursements.
- skimming (cash stolen before the company has recorded it).
- larceny (cash stolen after the company has recorded it).
- fraudulent billings to fictitious companies or for fictitious goods or services.
- employees making false claims for compensation.
- employees requesting reimbursement for fictitious or inflated expenses.

White-collar fraud continues to grow. The 2010 Report to the Nations on Occupational Fraud and Abuse from the Association of Certified Fraud Examiners (ACFE) provided an estimate that the highest losses from fraud—31%—occur in businesses of fewer than 100 employees. These are the businesses that are less likely to have audits or strong cultures of ethics. Fraud is a crime based on concealment, and many organisations do not know they are being victimised. Occupational fraud ranges from simple stealing of company assets to complex financial manipulation. Most frauds are either never detected or go on for years before they are discovered.

More ACFE findings were

- tips are from an anonymous source (13%).
- all cash frauds come in the form of fraudulent disbursements (66%).
- fraud was caught by the firm's internal controls (14%).
- fraud in small business involves a billing scheme (29%).
- fraud involves cheque alteration (13%).
- most fraud cases were asset misappropriation schemes (90%).

The ACFE study reported that for the small businesses included in the study, only 30% had any form of internal audit or fraud examination department.

The 2010 findings show a slight improvement over the 2008 study, but survey participants estimate that the typical organisation loses 5% of its annual revenue to fraud.

Although ERM is designed to detect or deter fraud, small businesses are more vulnerable to unethical employee behaviours due to four factors:

1. They are less likely to require an audit.
2. They do not have a hotline for employees to report suspicious activities.
3. They rarely have adequate internal controls.
4. They are less likely to do any formal risk management on employee behaviours.

The Sarbanes-Oxley Act of 2002 (SOX) requires audit committees of publicly traded companies to establish procedures for "the confidential, anonymous submission by employees of the issuer of concerns regarding questionable accounting or auditing matters." These companies install a hotline run by an independent organisation for people to use if they see questionable or dangerous activity. Unfortunately small businesses, which are not subject to SOX, fail to see the value or importance of this tool to detect fraud or abuse.

When employees and customers have access to a hotline and know their comments and concerns are taken seriously, they are more likely to use it. Each call to a hotline is a potential exposure. Hotlines will not always detect frauds, but they do create a reporting mechanism for employees that allows for the collection of tips on possible wrong doing. Firms that use such a hotline are more likely to be aware of potential fraud with employees but also with customers, vendors and third parties. Firms that utilise employee hotlines or some sort of anonymous and safe reporting mechanism show the greatest decrease in fraud incidents. A key element in almost every discovered fraud is a dishonest employee who had the opportunity to commit the infraction.

Re-read the statistics about employees' attitudes regarding opportunity in the "Risk and POLR" section.

> **Murphy's Law of Risk and Ethics**
>
> The person with the loudest voice who knows the least and is the most unethical is always put in charge.

Situations for Exposure to Unethical Behaviours

- Employees who are being downsized.
- Employees who are bored and looking for excitement.
- Employees who find a hole in the company's internal controls, benefit from it and fail to report the lapse.
- Employees who enjoy bending the rules.
- Employees who are under personal stress.
- Employees who experience personal financial problems or setbacks.
- Employees with addictions, such as alcohol or gambling.
- Employees who need to be the centre of attention.

Two Tools to Analyse and Reduce Exposure to Ethics Risk

Risk Management Tool Twelve– The Five Whys

This tool, known as the "Five Whys," allows you to find the root causes of risks that can lead to high exposures. The contributor to the downside of risk taking is rarely in physical things, such as bricks, mortar, technology or tools. Most of the time your operational and strategic perils are generated or caused by the way people think and act or use your assets.

Case Study: The Risk of Special Favours

To understand how this tool works I used an example from PJI's history in which an empowered employee in the travel department contracted with a major hotel chain to provide rooms at a set price. The Director of Events, Carmen, described a termination that took place a few weeks ago.

"PJI's culture emphasises to all our employees that they need to use their best judgement when dealing with the vendors, when making purchasing decisions and when obligating the company to contracts. We trust our employees and empower them, so they almost always had the final say. I thought we had clearly defined policies and controls in place but found out that this was a false assumption. One of my employees obligated us for a guaranteed rate that was higher than similar hotels. By contract PJI agreed to use this hotel for a fixed set of nights, and if we did not we had to pay a penalty. I was so mad when I found this out. The employee who I terminated claimed he received several bids, which he showed me, and theirs was the lowest. I have been unable to determine what led to his behaviour."

"Carmen, I can show you why the employee created this exposure if you allow me to take you through the steps of this tool."

The "Five Whys" tool has four simple steps, but do not get fooled by its simplicity. It is the questions you keep asking after you obtain your initial answers that generate its power. As a manager or an executive your task is to find the root cause of a problem, which I refer to as a fire. Yet you often waste time on finding and removing the smoke, and you never get to the cause of your fire. This tool allows you to discover what caused the fire, so that we can prevent the fire from starting again.

How to Apply the Five Whys

Step One: State the risk as a problem.

Step Two: Ask: "Why is this happening?" or "Why did this happen?"

Step Three: Continue to ask why until you get to a root cause that you can do something about and, when reduced or eliminated, will change the situation for the better.

Step Four: Summarise your findings, and form a recommendation for change.

Using the "Five Whys" tool, Carmen, who had time to prepare for this, will demonstrate how to find the root causes of the problem that created exposure.

Step One: Statement of problem.

An empowered travel agent obligated us to a service that was not competitive, and we could not cancel.

Step Two: Now that the problem is defined, ask the first question:

1. Why did this happen?

   The employee did not adhere to our policy for contracted services.

   Carmen: "I discovered through investigation that the employee did not follow the policy that states, 'A travel agent may not recommend a service provider whose rates are not competitive.' And another policy states, 'A travel agent may not enter into a services contract that is non-cancellable or contains a penalty clause for non-performance on our part.'"

   Normally most of us would stop at the first why and fire the employee for violating a policy, as Carmen did. If you only do that, however, all you have accomplished is dealing with the smoke. You failed to search for the cause of the fire. Because you are committed to risk management, you want to prevent the fire or risk from recurring. You keep drilling down into the problem.

Step Three: I asked Carmen again:

2. Why did this happen?

   The employee wanted to impress the hotel's sales employee.

   Carmen: "My ex-employee is a young single man who has a problem finding dates. The hotel's sales employee is a very beautiful young lady with a friendly personality. I think our agent agreed to this contract based on the personality of the vendor. Maybe she promised him a date, or maybe she appealed to his ego."

   I asked Carmen again:

3. Why did this happen?

   The agent seemed to want something special from this vendor, a perk that he wanted.

   Carmen: "I found several instances in my research that this employee has done this before: asking for special conditions in his initial dealings with new vendors. In this instance he was allowed to stay at their hotel in Hawaii at a highly discounted rate."

   I will pause to review the ethical implications and risks of this situation. As someone who is concerned with the ethical attitude of your employees, you would jump up and down and demand that any employee who did this be fired, but how do you know if this situation is an isolated incident, a trend or a normal practice? I asked Carmen again

4. Why did this happen?

The employee wanted to earn his large incentive bonus.

Carmen: "I know my employee really wanted to get his large semi-annual bonus. He bragged to co-workers that he had his heart set on a new car."

We are starting to get to the root cause. By regularly using this "Five Whys" tool, you will find that the root cause is often based around human issues, such as power, emotion, drive, greed or lust. Some human frailty is involved with lingering problems, especially those related to unwarranted risk taking and ethical breaches. I asked Carmen again

5. Why did this happen? Concentrate your answer on the incentive.

The incentive rewards the employees for holding the line on costs by entering into fixed long-term service contracts.

Carmen: "Unfortunately for us our incentive programme for all travel agents was designed by accounting to convert a variable cost travel into a fixed one. If we know how many rooms we are obligated for, we can coordinate other travel plans, like air fare, so that our travel budget is more manageable. The incentive contains no penalty or downside for when we pay more than the going rate. Whoever designed the incentive wanted to control costs."

I could stop the why questions here, but intuition tells me there could be another cause for Carmen's fire. You do not have to stop at five whys. You can persist in asking why as many times as needed to find all the possible sources of your fire. I asked Carmen again

6. Why did this happen? Focus your answer on the approval of contracts and verification of contractual rates.

The employee knew how to game the system. He worked here long enough to know that no one would check up on him.

Carmen: "This employee knew that no one reviewed service contacts under $10,000. He also knew that no one in my group would notice that the bids from other hotels were different. He had them bid on a higher level of service—bigger room—and selected smaller cities where our employees rarely travel. That is why he had on paper proof that the hotel he wanted us to do business with had the lowest rates."

"I also found that, contrary to our procedures, contracts for my department go directly to accounting, and we do not retain a copy in our files. Once they are signed by the vendor, we assume the employee will verify the rate charged is the contractual one. No one else on my team is involved in the verification process."

Step Four: Conclusion and recommendation

Carmen told us, "I can see now that we have several areas that caused the problem. First how we handle contracts and the bidding process created the situation. Second is the way we have split the responsibility for budgeting travels costs between accounting and my department. Third the incentive is skewed, and fourth, even though I trust my employees, I have no way to ensure they are not playing games because our vendors are in a position to offer our agents some nice perks. I need to fix these internal weaknesses ASAP and then, with accounting's help, verify that no one else is doing what he did."

Tool's Lesson

What we discovered in using the "Five Whys" tool is that you split the authority with responsibility. You also created an incentive in the form of a bonus that did not shape the behaviour you wanted. It's no surprise that this employee followed POLR to get his bonus in whatever way he could. The lesson from this tool is that once you find the root cause for your exposures, you can take quick action to reduce the negative impacts and find solutions to prevent more exposure.

Risk Management Tool Thirteen– Establish Contingency Funds

We will return to your exposure from the recent acquisition of the oil and gas company in Columbia, which was discussed in chapter 2, "The WHAT of Risk Management." For the next year, as you work to make the company more productive and profitable, you include in your current year's budget a contingency fund of $500,000. This money can only be spent under three scenarios, should one or more occur:

1. If the raw crude produced by this drilling company fails to reach the target you set
2. If the production employees there go on strike or stage a slowdown
3. If the antiquated equipment there breaks down and slows production.

Only when one of these conditions occurs can some of the funds be expended to upgrade the equipment, pay the employees more, add extra shifts to speed up production or use whatever tactics the general manager needs to use to make the company profitable and productive. This contingency fund cannot be used for any other purposes, such as the general manager awarding himself a bonus, giving pay rises to the supervisors, throwing a party or adding staff to overhead, because if these activities were not planned in the budget, they are not approved.

If these Murphy's Law events covered by the contingency fund do not happen in the current year, then you carry the fund over to next year. Each year you can maintain or modify the conditions under which the dollars can be spent.

After a certain point of time, when the company meets all its targets–return on investment, production and profitability—the funds can then be returned by reversing the contingency expense, thus adding to the current year's profits because of good management. This is how to properly handle a contingency fund.

When you take the time to look for pitfalls and then develop contingency plans in advance, you grow in confidence in your ability to face or accept more risk. Better yet you reduce exposure in both the short and long term.

Back to PJI

I gave PJI's managers another assignment to complete before our next session.

You need to objectively look at the people you supervise, and answer these questions:

- Why does POLR show up in your department, company or group?
- How does POLR arise when there are no rules or guidelines for your employees regarding risk taking or risks faced?
- How does POLR arise when there are specific written rules or guidelines for your employees regarding risk taking or risks faced?
- What sort of POLR do employees take that leads to a lingering problem?

Onward

You just experienced the ways you can reduce exposure because you know things never go as planned, and the unexpected happens. Step four creates momentum for taking action and empowering employees with confidence and tools, so they make smarter decisions. ERM makes every decision maker's job easier because, with the scope of their responsibilities, they are acutely aware of where risk occurs.

I closed with a pearl of wisdom regarding risk management.

"A ship is safe in harbour, but that's not what ships are for." William Shedd

Your Action Plan

Step One

If your organisation did implement a risk management programme, who do you think would be the people to serve on the risk committee? List their names or initials, and think about each person's overall attitude towards risk (using the four categories in chapter 6, "WHERE Do Our Efforts Need to Be?": risk taking, risk averse, custodian or indifferent).

Step Two

Are expectations placed upon you and your co-workers to be ethical? Are they communicated in the manner described in the "Setting the Expectation for Ethical Behaviours" section? If the expectations are clearly defined, what impact does this have on employee behaviours? If the expectations are not clearly defined, what impact does this have on employee behaviours?

Step Three

Answer the questions posed previously about POLR within your organisation:

- Why does POLR show up in your department, company or group?
- How does POLR arise when there are no rules or guidelines for your employees regarding risk taking or risks faced?
- How does POLR arise when there are specific written rules or guidelines for your employees regarding risk taking or risks faced?
- What sort of POLR do employees take that leads to a lingering problem?

Step Four

Think of a lingering problem you or your organisation faces. Use the "Five Whys" tool to discern the real causes. Remember it takes practice to effectively use this tool because it is easy to get lost in the superficial reasons and forget the deeply ingrained ones or those issues no one wants to discuss.

8

HOW Do We Conduct Enterprise Risk Management?

"The more you practise risk management in your day-to-day decisions, the stronger your programme becomes." Chrystal V.

I felt a sense of urgency within Justin as we held the remaining training sessions at PJ Investment's (PJI'S) offices. The intention of the move to the office was threefold: (*a*) get more employees enrolled in their risk management programme, (*b*) allow their employees to practise using risk management tools and (*c*) uncover what was bothering the partners.

On the first day, even though it was tight, we crammed 90 people into a meeting room designed for approximately 65 people. Employees were sitting on the floor, on tables and leaning against the wall. The non-management employees joining us that day were already briefed on PJI's risk management programme.

After welcoming them and making a few jokes about the lack of elbow room, I posed this question to them, "Who is a big fan of the *Star Trek* series?"

Several people raised hands, one of whom was Mateo.

"Mateo, do you recall the episode in The Next Generation where Capt. Picard gives a visitor a tour of the starship? He points out her planet through a window. She asks about the size of glass it takes to stand up to the pressure of space. Picard surprises her when he says, 'It is not glass. It is a force field. A field of energy that separate us from the uninhabitable environment of space.' He informs that this powerful energy keeps people alive."

Mateo responded, "Yes. I remember that scene because I always assumed those were glass or plastic windows, and it blew me away that it was just a field of energy."

"Thanks, Mateo. I too was amazed by that 'fact' and developed a new respect for the dreamers behind the Star Trek saga. For those who did not see this show, please imagine there is a wall of energy that keeps oxygen in and the deadly gamma rays of space out. This energy field, when working properly, keeps people living inside safe, and when it fails causes instant death.

"Now imagine that we had a similar field of energy protecting PJI's people, assets and buildings, and there are several force fields instead of one. One layer of protection surrounds you keeping you safe. Another envelopes this room keeping us all safe. A third force field serves as a protection around this building while a fourth provides a protective bubble around this neighbourhood."

I pointed to Martha, an analyst. "Martha, imagine that these force fields are designed to protect you from bad luck, bad weather, bad food, bad people and unexpected things like a falling tree, a runaway car, even the flu bug. Would you feel safe?"

"Yes. Of course I would."

"How would a feeling of security that someone or something has your back affect you personally and professionally?"

"I'm a cautious person, so I get nervous when driving at night, trying out new foods or meeting new people. Personally I think my concern to feel safe would be lessened, but I would need to trust the people who put up the shields before I would let my guard down." The room broke out in laughter. (My guess is Martha had a reputation for caution.) She continued as if no one laughed, "Professionally speaking at work, I might be willing to stick my neck out more." More laughter. Martha covered her face with her hands.

"Thanks for your honesty, Martha. I have a quotation for you that you might use to remind yourself that opportunity is always out there for you."

"Fear of failure must never be a reason not to try something." Frederick Smith

In a formal risk management programme, these force fields actually exist because you create them. One is created and managed by employees as they seek out needless risk that might exist within the scope of their jobs. A second force field is created and managed by the team as they study unwarranted or unprotected risk in their collective goals. A larger force field exists around each business unit created and managed by those making critical decisions that requires them to analyse risks and ensure their actions are congruent with the unit's mission. Finally a larger force field is created and managed by your senior leaders who examine the business as a whole and look for potential harm emanating from inside the organisation, via strategies and tactics, and approaching from outside, such as the environment or marketplace.

When people see this protection exists and trust those who create the protection, employees will invest more energy and attention into their work and lessen their desire to protect themselves or be cautious. It does not mean you can be rash and heedless within this protection. In a working enterprise risk management (ERM) programme, employees feel safe enough to be creative and innovative, share ideas, and learn new things.

From Top to Bottom

A survey sponsored by CFO magazine and conducted by Towers Perrin, found that companies are more interested in systematic solutions to risk management than they have been in the past. Nearly half the respondents expect to implement broad changes to their risk management policies and practices that will affect both the shop floor and board.

Source: http://www.cfo.com/pressreleases/pressrelease.cfm/12343938

Fifteenth Principle of Risk Management

The more a person practises risk management, the more risks he or she is willing to take due to a feeling of security. Similarly the more an organisation practises risk management, the greater its risk appetite.

When it comes to taking risk in a business setting, some people feel confident because they are unaware of, or blind to, the perils and potholes ahead. Other people feel confident because they know how to deal with those perils and potholes. In ERM the programme builds confidence to take risks, which comes from knowing as opposed to not knowing. In fact pretending that risk is always beneficial or denying that risk does not exist can lead to the failure of an enterprise faster than any risk.

Process for the Leadership Body to Implement Risk Management

Most people can see a picture and quickly grasp its meaning. To assist you and others to fully understand the responsibility that leaders own in your how-to of risk management, I give you the next graphic, Figure 8-1:

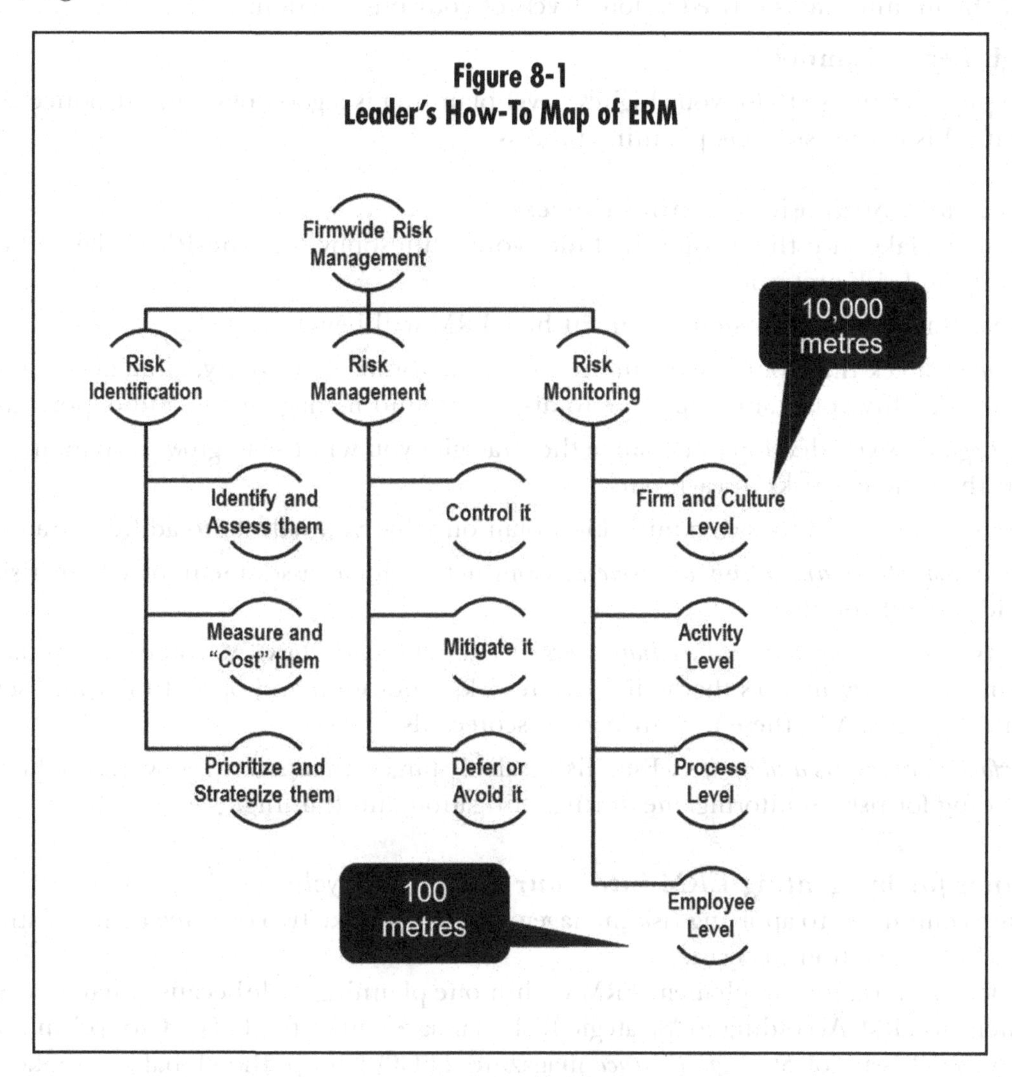

Each organisation has its own way to implement risk management. You have already read about places to start the integration, such as incorporating it into your budget, reporting and decision making processes. This section gives you a checklist approach to implementation.

Checklist for Implementing Risk Management

☐ **Protocol 1: Risk Identification**

Your key decision makers—risk owners—identify risks, assess their scope and size, use tools to measure their cost or impact, then with tools and guidance place them in a priority queue so they can be managed and reduced.

☐ **Protocol 2: Risk Management**

Building on the information and momentum of the first ingredient, the owners of risk proactively develop their action plan on what to do about the peril or pothole. They have numerous options that include controlling it, mitigating it, deferring it and avoiding it, in any combination that makes sense.

☐ **Protocol 3: Risk Monitoring**

Continuing on with their plan, risk owners then monitor the problem or opportunity. Notice that the monitoring is carried at four levels of your organisation.

☐ **High-Level Planning**

The process you use to for your highest level planning is a good place to introduce risk management. This is your strategic planning process.

Elements of a Strategic Planning Process

- *Mission.* Make sure the mission includes your philosophy for a healthy balance between risk taking and risk protection.
- *Vision.* Include in the vision statement how ERM will benefit you.
- *Values.* Check that your core values reflect the amount of creativity, awareness, autonomy and accountability you want employees to display around managing risk and opportunity.
- *Strategies.* As you develop or enhance the strategies you will use to grow, sustain and profit, seek out the inherent risks in each one.
- *Strategic goals.* Add to each a mitigation plan on what you will do to address strategy risk.
- *Environmental scan or risk assessment.* Conduct a global assessment of where risk currently resides in all you do.
- *Measurements (key performance indicators and key risk indicators).* As you establish targets for the year, select a few metrics that will measure risk, innovation and opportunity and serve as early warning signs. Add these to your regular scorecards.
- *Performance targets and budgets.* Establish realistic targets that prevent unwarranted risks. Include funding for risk monitoring, measuring, mitigation and training.

Timelines for Integrating ERM into Your Planning Cycle

If you are committed to applying risk management, it will take two or three cycles of strategic planning for full integration to occur.

Very few organisations implement ERM within one planning cycle because there is a learn-as-you-go element to ERM. According to “Strategic Risk Management at the LEGO Group,” an article in the February 2012 issue of *Strategic Finance* magazine, LEGO Group, the global toy maker, employed ERM after experiencing several years of losses and accomplished ERM in stages, one risk area after another. Its leaders realised years later that a large risk, fostered by its aggressive growth strategy, was omitted from their ERM programme. In 2006 LEGO added strategic risk management to its ongoing ERM activities and appointed Hans Læssøe as the person to lead it. Two years later Hans added Monte Carlo simulation to the mix. Each year LEGO improves its ERM protocol as it uses it.

Although there is no official timetable, on average, it will take your organisation between two and five years for ERM to be completely ingrained and integrated, but the benefits start in the first year. Be patient, and remind everyone that you are transforming the culture, which can take as long as six years to accomplish.

☐ **Analysis of Risk Versus Reward**

The next step is for the leaders to discuss what risk looks like in terms of their global risk appetite or the cost they cannot afford. Not all risks are equal or of similar priority. Some perils you face are worth dealing with, but others are not. These discussions between the board and executives are critical because the employees who will implement ERM need specific guidelines on what the risk-to-reward ratio looks like and also the firm's acceptable risk appetite.

Continuing with the February 2012 article in *Strategic Finance* magazine, LEGO Group executives use the amount of "earnings the company is likely to lose compared to budget if the worst-case scenarios happen." LEGO's board sets a threshold of 5% worst-case loss as the upper limit. This means the cost they can afford goes as high as 5% of profits lost. "That guides management toward understanding and 'sizing' the risk exposure." Knowing this "has helped the LEGO Group take more risks and be more aggressive than it otherwise would have dared to be and grow faster than it otherwise could have done."

☐ **Resources Assignment**

"Put your money where your mouth is." You may have heard that expression, and it applies to implementing ERM because you will incur both hard and soft costs. Unless you approve and fund the programme, your implementation will stall. You will spend budget money on consultants and advisors, new technology, temporary employees, and tools. Employees' time will be diverted from their daily work to undergo training, learn how to use the tools, attend numerous meetings and analyse their work processes. You must plan for this necessary work for the first two years of implementation.

☐ **Tools in the Hands of Employees**

ERM's benefits will flow once employees use the tools they are trained on, but expect a long learning curve. Some employees who have experience or perform risk management in their current jobs will speed this up. It will be your employees who are new to risk management or resistive that will lengthen the learning curve. Be patient and plan to continually reinforce the new behaviours.

☐ **Process Goals**

Your implementation efforts are next directed towards your key processes. Your executives kick this off by answering this question: Is the level of risk we face in this process acceptable to managers and those we are accountable to in the dogged pursuit of the process objectives?

Each time the answer is "No," the process owner must examine the purpose or intent of the process to ensure its objectives include risk detection, prevention and balance.

☐ **Integrate into Existing Processes**

Each process needs to be evaluated and improved to add risk monitoring and measuring to it. Each major work process, in ERM, should detect risk if there is any. If the work does not involve any sort of peril, the process, at a minimum, should at least add to transparency of the key decisions made within it.

☐ **Responsibilities and Ownership**

The next step is to determine who serves as the chief risk officer and form the oversight group. You also establish every employee's accountability towards risk awareness and mitigation. You can accomplish this through risk management tool ten, discussed in chapter 6, "WHERE Do Our Efforts Need to Be?". A critical part of this work is to identify the owner of each risk category. Your sales executive owns all sales risk. Your operations executive owns all operational risk. The CEO owns all strategic risk. Ownership of risk cannot be delegated.

☐ **Make it a Priority**

All along the journey of implementation, your executives must make it clear that risk management takes priority over everything else. The message needs to be posed in a way that employees understand that they look at their work differently and put more thought into it. When employees do work in a rote manner, without thinking about what they are doing and why, they will overlook opportunity, miss undetected perils or not question actions and decisions that could put your firm at risk.

Minimum Elements to Establish Risk Awareness

Even if you decide not to implement a full-blown ERM but plan to institute the discipline of formal risk management, six foundation pieces need to be installed to ensure risk awareness gets embedded in your culture.

Feedback Loops

If you embark on a trip somewhere you haven't been before, you need to know where you are compared to where you are headed. This holds true for the major shift in thinking that ERM requires. You must create numerous feedback loops and place them in your regular reports, metrics, action plans, employee surveys, customer surveys, employee performance evaluations and other areas that you organisation uses to know where you are and where you are heading. Behaviours that are measured will get managed.

Quality Loops

Feedback on whether risk management is being practised is not enough. You also need feedback on the quality of decisions made and actions taken after risk management becomes the norm. Employees may be finding little vulnerabilities and miss the big one. Line managers may take so long sizing up a risk that they miss an opportunity.

Control and Support

Employees need to feel they are in control and supported in what you are asking them to do. The group with accountability to oversight also needs to believe they have say in what needs improving and that their hard work is valued and taken seriously.

Value of Risk Auditor

The risk auditor role is not for the faint of heart. You need mental toughness, a high Ethics Quotient and thick skin. Those who have served on a risk compliance team warn that dealing or working in risk compliance is not a job that wins friends and influences your fellow employees. It is a thankless job. Don't just take my word. Thomas Quilty, CEO of BD Consulting and Investigations, said, "The compliance officer is the most hated person in the company." When commenting on the risk compliance employee, Sam E. Antar, the former CFO of the now-defunct electronics chain Crazy Eddie, advises, "Companies often retaliate against them." Tracy L. Coenen, a fraud investigator and leader of Sequence, a forensic accounting firm, shares another opinion about the role. "Most fraud today is uncovered by whistle-blowers, or by accident—a tip, a rogue piece of mail, or by happenstance. Compliance staff frequently ends up pushing paper just so it looks like the company has tried to do the right thing in case there's an investigation. They're not effective."

Source: www.cfo.com/article.cfm/14557373/1/c_14557613

Communication

Risk management, if properly employed, should foster better and more frequent communications about opportunities and threats and what is being done about them. Your redesigned reports should clearly indicate the areas being monitored and the progress being made to lessen your vulnerability. All leaders need to look for indications that communications are taking place and appropriate.

Rigorous management of risk using an established framework allows managers to have some tough conversations that are beyond the limiting scope of their job duties because senior leaders task the next level with implementing changes and improvements. This onus contributes to risk exposure. In these open conversations about potential risks regarding size and impact, your managers address each risk as they simultaneously select those opportunities that are worth pursuing. This requires your managers to communicate with courage, conviction and credibility.

Accountability

Because you are asking line and administrative managers to own the risks inherent in their specialties, accountability must be extolled, honoured and rewarded. True accountability requires that solutions replace blame, truth and honesty replace filtered communications and hidden agendas, and real ownership replaces passing responsibility and excuses.

ERM provides a useful evaluation tool for leaders to stay informed about their employees' abilities to identify, prioritise and respond to apparent risk. This way everyone becomes informed of potential risks. Your framework requires managers to create an action plan in order to mitigate or address each risk. With such a structure, managers are able to understand and acknowledge all potential risk, thus increasing individual and collective accountability.

Rewards and Penalties

Behaviours that are rewarded will happen again. They best way for you to drive employees' behaviours towards adopting risk management in their daily activities is to reward them. You want to tell employees that you are serious about this way of operating, and one visible and impactful way to get their attention is with a reward.

The second best way you drive employees' behaviours is to visibly penalise the employee who does not take risk management seriously. You will most likely have to replace employees, managers and executives who refuse to embrace this new operating standard. This is why you add the behaviours you want from employees into your employee performance evaluation process. When employees who are on the fence about risk management learn that someone lost a bonus, was demoted or got fired because he or she did not adopt the new attitude, the fence sitters or resisters will either join the effort or quit. This is painful to hear and experience, yet it is necessary in any culture transformation.

Starting to Implement ERM

Murphy's Law of Risk Progression

The greater the urgency to get a control or security system in place, the faster someone can slow it down.

You cannot rush ERM implementation because it requires education and training. Integrating elements of risk management into existing ways of working is like trying to remodel your kitchen while using it. You can influence the speed of its adoption and acceptance through many of the activities you control:

- Training
- Action planning
- Rewards and performance evaluations

- Meeting agendas
- Employee scheduling
- Executive utilisation
- Executive communications

ERM Works as Risk Grows

In 2010, the Committee of Sponsoring Organisations of the Treadway Commission commissioned a formal survey regarding the state of ERM. The data were collected during June and July 2010 from different organisations. The individuals who were most likely involved in leading the ERM-related processes or knowledgeable about the efforts within the organisation were the study's target. The conclusion was, "Despite growing complexities in the risk environments of most organisations, the level of risk management sophistication in these organisations remains fairly immature."

Source: http://www.imanet.org/PDFs/Public/SF/2010_11/11_2010_beasley.pdf

Every organisation, not just yours, starts from scratch when adopting and implementing formal risk management. That is why this material was developed for you, so you know what to do and expect.

The good news in this is that there is no formula to follow because ERM is not a turnkey process. You design its structure around your needs. (Some readers may deem this as the bad news!) Even better news is a wealth of consultants are willing to help you create your own ERM methodology. Enter "risk management" in a search engine, and you will see software tools, consultants, books, magazines, conferences and even a risk management professional group. Assuming you have the money, time and interest, these resources prove that you will not need to feel alone when adopting ERM or a more simplified version of risk management.

ERM Step Five: Recover Quickly from the Negative Impacts of the Risk

Murphy's Law still exists despite your best planning, anticipating and analysis. There will always be things you cannot anticipate, your implementation will go awry, or you will make human errors in judgement. Yes, even smart, talented leaders can make mistakes. I believe every innovator, investor, business owner, CEO, COO and CFO should have the statement, "Risk happens," tattooed on their foreheads, so they can remind themselves each day.

You create an imperative within your risk management plan for your employees to have specific methodology for quickly recovering from a negative, costly or painful event. The key element in this fifth step is to make sure you hone employees' recovery skills on the small lapses. The reason is explained in this analogy.

Assume that you get the itch to run a marathon—42 kilometres. You are not a runner and have never run a marathon. Instead of going out and immediately trying to run 42 kilometres, health experts suggest you prepare by taking small steps. Your first task is walking and setting a milestone of being able to walk two hours without stopping. Next you alternate walking and jogging until you can go 2 kilometres without stopping. Your next task is to build up stamina until you can run 2 kilometres without walking. When you are comfortable with 2 kilometres, you extend it to 4 kilometres and then 6 kilometres. You continue with these smaller goals until you are able to run more than 42 kilometres in one outing. Can you be ready for a marathon in one day or even one month? Of course not!

Will you be able to reduce your exposures or increase your risk appetite from the first day? Of course not! That is why Step five is vital to a viable ERM programme. Think about getting prepared for "the big one" when getting ready for it is a group task. Like the investment you make in preparing your body for the rigorous marathon, you make a similar investment in preparing your employees. The first tollbooth you encounter on the path to empowering employees and the cost you face (before training) is asking employees to think for themselves.

Empower Employees to Act

This recently happened. I was leaving the next morning for an out-of-town consulting project, and I stopped at an office supply store to get some hard-to-find protective covers I use for documentation purposes. I found only one box containing 50, but it had been opened. I searched but could not find other boxes. I took my purchase to the counter, showed the clerk the torn box and asked her if she can locate another box. She checked the stock and said that was their last box. I expressed my concern that protectors could be missing, so she counted them and found only 49 sheets. At that point the sales clerk did not know what to do next. I was anxious to leave because I had several things to do before the end of the day. She was the only cashier, and now several customers were impatiently waiting behind me. Because the clerk was at a loss, I suggested she call for a manager. We waited and waited. I then suggested she just deduct $0.05 from the box price to cover the cost of the missing protector. She replied that she wasn't authorised to give any discounts. We waited and waited.

That evening the office supply store created much customer ill will, not over $0.05 but because its culture is one in which employees are discouraged from thinking for themselves.

Compare that experience to the Marriott Hotel group that has a policy for all its frontline employees that they can spend up to $2,000 to satisfy any customer problem. Marriott employees must mentally answer a test of five questions before they spend Marriott's money to solve a specific problem. The five-question test that empowers Marriot employees is as follows:

1. Will this action harm the reputation of the hotel?
2. Will this action cause a problem for another guest?
3. Will this action only defer a problem?
4. Will this action upset the guest even more?
5. Is this action illegal or unethical?

If the answers to all five questions are "No," the employees can take the action they deem necessary to satisfy a guest or customer. What Marriott has learned from its empowering policy is that it usually takes approximately $100 to satisfy the customer or solve the problem. It might be buying the guest a meal; paying for cab fare somewhere; paying one night's stay at another hotel; or providing a gift, such as a bottle of champagne or wine. Rarely has the entire $2,000 been spent.

I posed these questions to PJI's employees. "Contrast the two examples of the office supply store and Marriott. Which one wants its frontline employees to think for themselves? Which one uses empowering tools that allow employees to solve problems before they turn into risks or big issues?"

Several shouted out, "Marriott!"

I asked the next question of the managers in the room. "Do you trust in your employees enough that you would give each of them $2,000 of PJI's cash to only be used to save a customer relationship without coming to you for permission? Raise your hand."

By the number of hands in the air, their overall response rate was similar to those of most manager and supervisors. Fewer than 25% are comfortable empowering their employees this much. If you are among the 75% who feel uncomfortable, that is why employees either fail to notice risks and opportunities or, even worse, say nothing about them. The managers who did not raise their hands were looking at the ground in embarrassment. They were not able to look at their employees while admitting they did not trust them.

I selected specific managers and supervisors who, by not raising their hands, implied they did not trust their employees. I then posed this question, "Why do you hesitate to give your employees the key to the door? I am putting you on the spot because if you do not know the real reasons, we cannot improve the situation."

Their reasons were as follows:

- I don't know the extent of my own authority, so how can I define it for someone I delegate to?
- Each time I try to think for myself, my boss gets mad that I did not ask for her advice (an employee's comment).
- My employee asks too many questions, so I just make the decision because I don't have time to debate him.
- I try to let my employees work without intervention, but lately when one of them makes an error, my boss blames me.
- I have over 20 years of experience, and my employee has three years. I know more than she does.
- I got burnt in the past. Each time I gave money to my employees, they wasted it, and I had to explain to my boss why that happened. He was not happy with me.

Please notice from their comments that the reasons managers and supervisors fail to truly empower their employees can be summed up in three culturally embedded problems:

1. Unclear or undefined responsibilities that make it hard to equalise authority and responsibility
2. A preference for micromanaging the employee, which means the manager's employees are discouraged to think for themselves and quickly give up the desire
3. Employee performance problems are not addressed in a timely manner, which means the problem gets reclassified as, "I cannot trust my employee because he or she is not trustworthy."

The following risk management tool fourteen will solve the first problem of unclear responsibilities and improve the conditions for solving the second problem of micro management. The third problem must be fixed by your human resource and performance management process, and if you fail to fix the problem, it will increase your vulnerably to lawsuits and worse.

Match Authority with Responsibility

PJI, like many other organisations, lacks the commitment to equalise responsibility with authority. A culture in which employees are not empowered will undermine your ERM efforts.

Murphy's Law of Opportunity Empowerment
The person with the best understanding of the problem is never asked for his or her ideas.

An important aspect of your culture transformation plan to lower overall risk by recruiting your employees in the effort is to conduct an authority and responsibility analysis. An underlying intent of an effective ERM programme is to foster constant awareness by everyone throughout your organisation about large and small risks. Leaders all too often make a mistake that is detrimental to fostering awareness, and that is simply failing to give employees the authority or latitude to take action. In formal risk management, when you ask people to be accountable and empowered to reduce vulnerability or take advantage of opportunity, you must be 100% sure that you have given employees specific authority equal to their responsibility.

I did a session on this topic in Reno, Nevada, and one very wise woman summarised the importance of this need to equalise authority with responsibility. She told us, "If you make employees responsible for unlocking the door, give them the key!" In your organisation you are asking employees to monitor risk—asking them to unlock the door—but you may not be giving them the key—tools, knowledge or authority—to do something about the risk.

A risk management programme requires employees at every level who are making decisions and taking action to let you know when something is going wrong. Employees need to believe and trust that you will not punish them for blowing the whistle or waving the red flag. That is why you strive to match authority with responsibility, so that employees can and will think for themselves.

In Figure 8-2 you will see the two circles coming together. Your goal is to try to match them up as closely as possible. You will never get it to be a 100% match because the need for oversight affects unlimited empowerment and authority. However any checks and balances you require need to be perceived as empowering employees to take action, not impeding their ability to influence the outcome.

Figure 8-2
Matching Responsibility with Authority

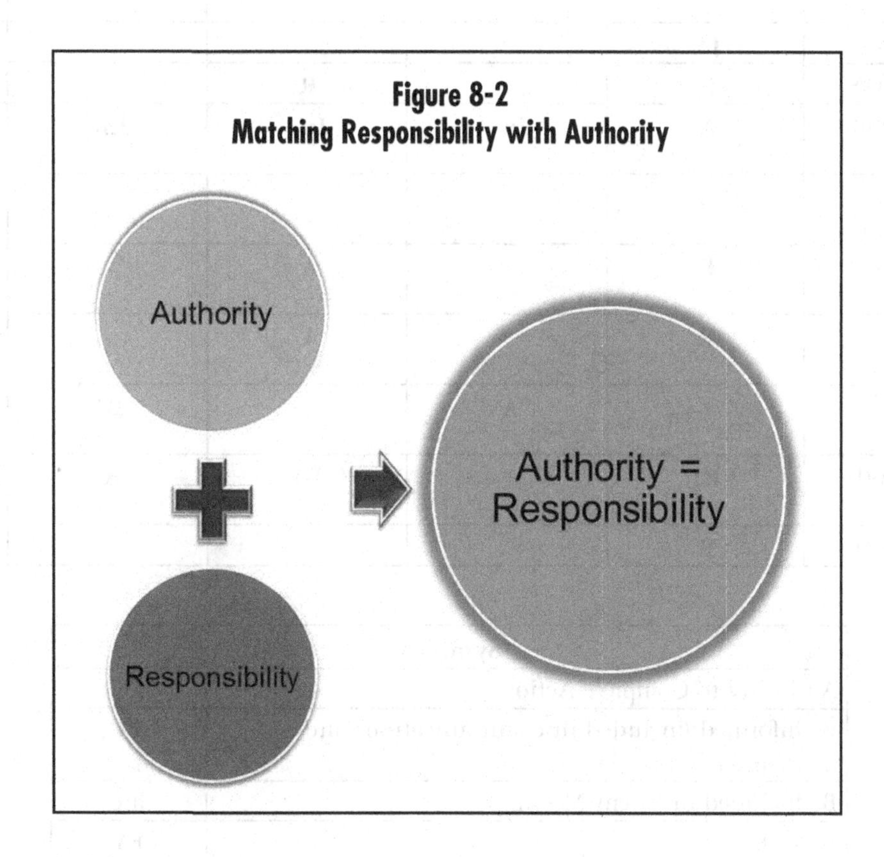

Five Tools to Help Clarify Accountability and Empower Employees to Act

Risk Management Tool Fourteen– Risk Authority and Responsibility Chart

A tool that will allow you to equalise responsibility with authority is called a risk authority and responsibility chart, examples of which are subsequently shown in Tables 8-1 and 8-2. You will notice that you can use this tool to easily highlight specific areas of concern, in this case actions oversight, approval decisions and asset protection.

Table 8-1 Risk Authority and Responsibility Tool

Client Quotation Issuance & Approval Process					
Action	**Project Manager**	**Research Assistant**	**Project Administrator**	**Credit Manager**	**Principal Consultant**
Process Quality Owner					✓
Process Risk Owner					✓
Prepare Proposal for Services	**A**				**Inc**
Conduct Research on Client's History	**R**	**A**	**R**		**R**
Establish Project Scope	**JD**				**JD**
Prepare Risk Plan	**A**		**R**		**R**
Obtain Client's Approval of Scope	**JA**				**JD**
Prepare Project Fees	**JA**				**JD**
Approve Project Fees	**R**		**R**		**A**
Contract Presentation to Client	**A**	**Inc**	**Inc**	**Inc**	**Inc**
Obtain Client's Approval of Contract	**A**				**FA**
Coordinate Project Scheduling	**R**		**A**		**BI**
Complete Project Staffing	**R**		**A**		**BI**
Verify Client Credit References		**A**		**BI**	
Approve Credit and Payment Terms	**BI**		**BI**	**A**	**BI**
Acceptance of Client	**R**				**A /FA**

Symbols	
Authority to Complete Action	A
Be Informed (included in communications and meetings)	BI
Be Included in Client Meetings	Inc
Risk Owner	FA
Recommend the Action	R
Joint Authority to Complete Action	JA

Table 8-2 Risk Authority and Responsibility Tool

Project and Jobsite Safety Process							
Action	**Safety Director**	**Jobsite Foreman**	**Director of Major Projects**	**Project Lead**	**Electrical Technician**	**Jobsite Manager**	**Customer Contact**
Process Quality Owner	✓		✓				
Process Risk Owner			✓				
Inspect Job Tools	**Inc**	**A**	**R**	**BI**		**R /FA**	**BI**
Inspect Job Site	**Inc**	**A**	**R**	**BI**		**R /FA**	**BI**
Inspect Electrical Connections	**Inc**	**R**		**R**	**R**	**R /FA**	**BI**
Train on Safety Procedures	**A**	**R**	**R**	**R**	**R**	**A**	**BI**
Develop Job Risk Assessment	**R**	**R**	**BI**	**R**	**R**	**R**	**BI**
Approve Job Risk Assessment	**BI**	**BI**	**FA**			**BI**	**BI**
Write up Site Inspection Report	**BI**	**JA**	**BI**	**BI**	**BI**	**JA**	**BI**
Raise Safety Concerns	**A**	**A**	**AF**	**A**	**A**	**A**	**A**
Address Unsafe Practices–Customer Caused	**BI**	**A**	**BI**	**BI**	**A**	**A**	**FA**
Address Unsafe Practices–Employee Caused	**BI**	**A**	**BI**	**BI**	**A**	**A**	**BI**

Symbols	
Authority to Complete Action	A
Be Informed (included in communications and meetings)	BI
Be Included in Client Meetings	Inc
Risk Owner	FA
Recommend the Action	R
Joint Authority to Complete Action	JA

The chart uses symbols signifying role, authority and ownership. "FA" means this person has the ultimate accountability for the process working as designed. "R" means this person has a responsibility to recommend or contribute to the action or decision. "A" and "JA" mean this person has the authority to take the action or decision. Because many decisions require other people's input, the chart uses symbols to clarify this. "BI" means this person is to be informed. "Inc" means this person is to be included in meetings. Remember, even though it is your job to keep the supervisor informed, it is the supervisor's job to stay informed. Communication is a dual responsibility. Because risk is ever present, the employee who owns the risk is designated "FA."

Notice in this process for issuing a proposal that the principal consultant (a senior leader) has ultimate responsibility for this yet has clearly delegated authority to the project manager and project administrator. The chart clarifies the authority of the employees who support the project team: the credit manager for approving credit terms and the research assistant for researching information about the prospect.

Look at the authority structure for the process to reduce safety risks on the job. The senior leader who owns the accountability is the director of major projects. Each employee who is involved in managing the project has his or her own authority based on expertise, such as the electrical technician and safety director. Notice also that the jobsite manager and jobsite foreman share in deciding what to put on the all-important inspection report. This joint authority deters one person from hiding a risk. One more thing to note is that everyone, including the client, has a responsibility to raise a concern on safety violations, which prevents someone from saying, "It wasn't my job to say anything."

This tool works in conjunction with both the responsibility statement and formalised action plan. When employees know exactly what is expected of them, they will meet or exceed the expectations over 90% of the time. This tool assists you in defining and communicating these expectations. It also serves to ensure that you provide authority with delegated responsibility in equal measure. It quickly rids your culture of the often given excuse of, "I didn't know I was supposed to do that. No one told me."

Risk Management Tool Fifteen–Formalised Action Plan

The tool that communicates what to do is the formalised action plan. An action plan is a visual definition or map of what it will take to make significant progress on a specific objective. The payoff from using formalised action plans is the ability to communicate accountability to people. The contents of an action plan include the following:

- Overall strategic goal
- Deliverables and due dates
- Major steps
- Detailed steps or tasks
- Individual responsibilities of participants
- Anticipated obstacles and challenges
- Performance metrics
- Risk assessment summary

Each action plan should define each level of change responsibility at the outset. Action plan participants include the

- sponsor, who is the person who has the ability to pay for the change and has ultimate accountability.
- advocate, who is the person who drives, wants or demands the change.
- customer, who is the person(s) who benefits from the change.
- agent of change, who is the person(s) who carries the responsibility for facilitating the change.
- accountability partner, who is the person who will help keep pressure on the change agent and is usually an executive the change agent regularly reports to about the progress (or lack of) made towards the plan's end state.

- risk owner, who is the person who serves in an oversight capacity to ensure that any risk is addressed and mitigated once it gets identified.

The action plan tool is for

- highlighting overall global or high-level objectives.
- showing expected or desired results.
- keeping track of actual results.
- holding employees to their authority.
- identifying risks in advance.
- allocating resources to something that needs to get accomplished.

Case Study: The Risk of Obsolete Stock

To demonstrate the power in this tool, I selected an important project that was currently underway at PJI. With the help of an investment manager, Roy, who was accountable for making his company profitable, I walked everyone through the action plan Roy and I jointly developed.

Roy told everyone the tale of woe.

"Two years ago we invested in an emerging electronic game company with the hope that their games could be turned into applications for the Apple iPad and Kindle Fire. Unfortunately the company's management was so focused on this effort they lost sight of an important thing: managing their existing stock of games. In the video games industry, if a game does not sell out within 60 days, it becomes harder to sell because something better comes out, but our client's company is starved for cash. So simply writing off the stock is not an option. They need to generate some amount of money to help pay for the game's development costs."

Exhibit 8-1 shows the action plan Roy will now use to make this problem go away, thus reducing Roy's client's risk and the risk to PJI's investment:

Exhibit 8-1
Strategic Action Plan

A Strategic Action Plan (Strategic Initiative)

Overall Strategic Goal: To profitably dispose of obsolete and dropped stockof games.

Connection to War Games' (WG's) Strategic Plan: Reduce WG's stock by 20%, and improve the turnover from four times to six times per year. (This is a measurable tactic of the strategic plan that WG's management team adopted for the year. This demonstrates that this action plan is aligned with what management is trying to accomplish at a high level.)

Connection to WG's Risk Management Programme: In the company's risk management plan we addressed the concern that, as a new company, we have not established sufficient processes and controls to deal with obsolete inventories. We acknowledged in the company's risk management plan that we currently are in the negative cash flow position and will be for the next 18 months. Therefore our inherent risk is that we may focus too much attention on managing cash, accounts receivable and accounts payable and not enough attention on the balance sheet items unrelated to immediate cash flows. Our operational risk is that the problem of existing stock will be of no value unless we are proactive in selling it faster.

(continued)

Exhibit 8-1
Strategic Action Plan (continued)

Major Action Steps:

1. Create and implement a process to dispose of all game inventories older than 45 days.
2. Create and implement a process to proactively identify game products that are not selling, and find a buyer who will purchase them in bulk before they become obsolete at 60 days.
3. Establish controls to ensure the old and obsolete products are sold for their highest value.
4. Establish an incentive programme for a sales employee to sell the old products without hurting the sales of current products.

Anticipated Obstacles and Challenges:

1. Assigning the responsibilities to sell and ship the products to an already overburdened staff.
2. Finding a cost-effective way to move stock from our Ohio warehouse to the buyer.
3. Protecting WG's reputation for innovative games while disposing of the obsolete games.
4. Paying adequate incentive compensation to employees who sell the stock because there will be no profit margin to WG.
5. Determining the negative financial impact of selling overstocked games and communicating this to the board and bank without creating alarm.
6. Maintaining the momentum or sense of urgency needed to fully dispose of all obsolete games.

Detailed Activities or Tasks (specific tasks already identified or under way):

1. Select the products for disposal (see separate games stock reduction plan).
2. Have the product manager provide an analysis of the saleability of all games over 40 days old.
3. Contact any companies that buy video games in bulk.
4. Hire a telemarketing person to handle the sale of smaller quantities.
5. Establish a commission or incentive plan for sales of obsolete games.
6. Determine the approval levels for authorising a discounted sale price.
7. Prepare weekly updates and the status of sales and negotiations with companies identified in step three.

Financial Resources Required:

(Intentionally omitted)

Due Dates and Deliverables:

(Intentionally omitted)

Economic or Financial Impact of the Plan:

The plan will increase sales by $50,000 in the first year and $135,000 in the second year.

The costs incurred to generate the sales and implement the new processes are estimated to be $27,600 in the first year and $55,000 in the second year. The costs include temporary personnel, one telemarketer full-time equivalent, shipping and incentives.

Action Team:

Change Agents–Paula P., Keith K. and Donovan D.

Sponsor–Junie Z. (WG CEO)

Champion–Roy R. (WG COO and PJI executive)

Tool's Lesson

After Roy explained his newly developed plan for solving the mess, I solicited questions about the tool from people in the room.

Q: This looks like it takes a long time to write. It is worth the time?

From experience the time it takes to write an action plan—between two and six hours—will pay for itself right away. Without it the employees involved in the effort could spend days trying to figure out what to do and who should do it. Better yet, by fostering both communication and coordination up front, you save the time and frustration normally devoted to those areas.

Q: Who writes this plan?

It is co-developed by the sponsor, lead change agent and champion. We assemble them together in one room and ask them to randomly throw out ideas that get entered on flipchart paper, on a white board or into a Word document. Later in the process the group organises these thoughts into a mind map and then into a logical linear plan.

Q: You mentioned this tool fosters greater accountability. Can you explain how that works?

Think about how often you have heard these excuses:

- I didn't know I was supposed to do that.
- I forgot.
- It wasn't a priority, so I didn't get to it.
- What did we decide to do?
- My notes from the meeting are different than that.

All these excuses show a lack of clarity and commitment to do what was expected. The formal action plan establishes expectations from the onset of the project or goal. It also specifies who is responsible for each task. No one can get away with those excuses.

The final way this tool raises accountability to produce a result or accomplish a goal is to raise the project's visibility, and this is accomplished through a related tool used for action plan reporting.

Risk Management Tool Sixteen– Formalised Action Plan Summary

To raise the visibility of the various action plans that are underway, the executive team needs a way to track them and stay informed of their current status. The action plan summary in Exhibit 8-2 is a tool that accomplishes that and more.

Quite frequently managers and others ask for resources to get something done and promise higher sales or lower costs as the rationale. Yet just as often, there is no verification if the promised financial benefits are ever achieved. This tool requires that the action plan's sponsor regularly report on the resources expended and the financial impact achieved as of the reporting period.

Think about that. If you ask for $500,000 to accomplish something, and you must undergo a monthly face-to-face check-in with the CEO to tell him or her what has been accomplished with the money you were granted, I will bet that you'd take this endeavour seriously. As a result, tracking the financial and budgetary aspects of each action plan really enhances accountability.

Exhibit 8-2
Action Plan Reporting Tool

Action Plans Summary with Financial Results

as of April 30, 20XX

Employees Involved	Action Plan Objective	Expected Financial Results: Increased Sales $$	Expected Financial Results: (Decreased) Expenses $$	Actual Financial Results: Increased Sales $$	Actual Financial Results: (Decreased) Expenses $$
Sponsor–Junie (CEO) Advocate–Board of Directors Customers–Purchasing, Sales Champion–Roy R. Agents–Paula, Keith, Donovan	Profitably disposed of obsolete and dropped game inventory	$50,000	$27,600	$0	$17,829
Sponsor– Advocate– Customers– Champion– Agent–					
Sponsor– Advocate– Customers– Champion– Agent–					

Definitions

Sponsor–The person with ultimate accountability who has the ability to pay for the change.

Advocate–The person who drives, wants, demands the change.

Customers–The recipients who benefit from the change.

Agents–The persons responsible for facilitating the change through to the end.

Champion–The person heading up the action plan's efforts.

Action without follow-up and reporting leads to weak accountability. Weak accountability leads to increased risk. In ERM you will have many employees taking actions designed to reduce risk or take advantage of opportunities. This tool requires that your employees be ready and able to account for their actions and resources on a regular basis. This transparency enhancement prevents employees from wasting time and resources.

> **Murphy's Law of Risk Simplicity**
>
> A simple solution will lead to a more complex problem. A complex solution will create numerous simple problems.

Risk Management Tool Seventeen–Pitfall Analysis

A recently hired supervisor at PJI raised his hand, "In a prior session you told us about scenario planning for potential problems that is done at a high level. I like to think about different scenarios when I have a problem that needs solving. Do you have a simple tool for me and my employees?"

"Of course I do, Charlie. Can you think of a problem that you face right now on which I can demonstrate the tool for pitfall planning?"

"Yes." he said.

"I work for Grace, our treasurer, and she asked me to investigate software that will enable me to manage our cash. Currently I have to look at four different screens daily. One to determine how much money to borrow, another to see how much was deposited, a third to see our cash position and another to manage our temporary investments. Where I worked previously we used a treasury work station, and I believe one would work here.

"The problem is that it will take about nine months to get the software up and running. My lone employee and I are already swamped with work, so how will I get the implementation done and still manage the company's cash? I have too many scenarios rattling around in my brain. What can you suggest?"

The tool for helping you quickly recover is a pitfall analysis. You may already think in terms of pitfalls and coming up with alternative plans. It is a way of life for many, but other people do not think like this. This tool works for both planners and people who normally spontaneously act. This tool forces the user to think of options. Using this decision making tool, you can create ways to lessen your risk exposure.

How to Conduct a Pitfall Analysis

Step One: List the possible pitfalls or obstacles of a particular course of action.

Step Two: Create a contingency action plan for each pitfall.

Step Three: Determine what would prevent implementing the solution.

Case Study: The Perils of Software Conversion

"We can understand this tool with a pitfall universally experienced and one fraught with exposure: implementing new software, like Charlie will soon be doing. Assume this is a major transformation. Assume that the cost of this real-time solution will be around $100,000. That's a lot of money to waste should Charlie be unable to make this transformation successful. For anyone who has done this, you know that this project is a minefield."

Our Exposure: Implementing new treasury software and a management system while managing cash daily.

"Charlie, as a lead on this project, please identify for us specific potential and common pitfalls based on your prior experience."

He told us, "My worries are

- Dana, my very knowledgeable and valuable employee, quits out of frustration or too much work.
- the conversion process takes longer than the estimated six months.
- Grace gave me a budget of $100,000 for software and hardware and consultants. What if I exceed that? Will the project be cancelled?
- we have eight years of historical data to enter, and I am concerned about losing that data during the conversion process.
- being so involved in the conversion, I might miss an investment opportunity, borrow unnecessarily or have too much cash on hand."

"Charlie, I can see why you have insomnia." He and others laughed. "The first thing to do is to list these pitfalls on the left side. Charlie, with Dana and Grace's help, will come up with a solution for each scenario while the rest of us are at lunch. Don't worry, there is a lunch waiting for them in the room where they will work."

When Charlie's team was finished, and everyone was in their seats, I showed them what the completed tool looked like (Table 8-3):

Table 8-3 Pitfall Analysis

Pitfall	Contingency Plan
Losing a key member of the conversion process–Dana.	Hire a qualified temporary employee for the conversion project to do Dana's regular work.
Suffering from burnout.	Hire a consultant with software conversion experience. Hire a second temporary employee to take on 40–60% of Charlie's routine duties.
Conversion process taking longer than the expected six months.	Spend more time planning up front with a formal action plan, and hold weekly status meetings with entire conversion team.
Cost of conversion exceeds the budget of $100,000.	Prepare an updated cost projection with help of conversion consultant.
Losing important historical data during the conversion process.	Store two complete copies of data: one onsite for quick access and one offsite.
Being unable to keep up with the daily management of cash.	Prioritise daily tasks. Then train and delegate these. Automate current methods of cash management to reduce amount of time spent. Devote first two hours of each day to high-priority tasks that only Charlie can do.

After we went through this tool, I asked Charlie to summarise what he learned from this. "How would this tool help you to minimise the negative effects of the exposure and recover quicker?"

He answered, "I can stop worrying. All these ideas were going through my head at all times of the day and night. Now that they are in the form of a plan, I can feel the tension leave my body. If Murphy's Law appears, as I know it will, this tool gives me and my team a disciplined way to articulate the challenge and then think rationally how to mitigate it. Oh yeah, I'll bet I sleep like a baby tonight, thanks to you!"

He pointed at me and grinned.

Tool's Lesson

When employees believe they have no options, they feel helpless or disempowered. This tool proves the numerous ways to lessen or mitigate a pitfall or pothole. The act may seem insignificant at first, but what the tool does is instil the confidence that you always have options and that Murphy's Law is rarely fatal.

We had time to learn one more tool.

Risk Management Tool Eighteen–Controllable, Negotiable and Given Analysis

Sometimes, despite your best plans, there are conditions in a risk, peril or challenge that you must accept and cannot change. I love sunshine, and I love living in Seattle, Washington, but one thing I accept about living in the northwest United States is that I won't experience as much sunshine as I would in the Bahamas, Dubai or Hawaii.

Yet in risk management you can always influence the outcome, which may lower your exposure or help you recover faster. The tool you can apply to show you how to influence your vulnerabilities is the controllable, negotiable and given analysis. This tool allows you to identify some of the specific actions you can take in order to minimise or mitigate a risk.

How to Complete the Analysis

Step One: Write out a clear description of the risk to be undertaken.

Step Two: Prepare a chart that describes the various aspects.

Step Three: List all the givens for the risk or problem.

A given is a condition you cannot change or do much about, such as accepting that the Islands of the Bahamas have hurricanes each year that destroy some homes and accepting that you cannot afford to move to Seattle (where we have less sun but no hurricanes).

Step Four: List as many negotiable conditions you can think of.

A negotiable is an aspect of the situation that allows you to influence the outcome by substitution, bargaining or some other action. Living in the Bahamas, your insurance company raises the rates for homeowners coverage. You cannot go without insurance, but maybe you can work with your agent to lower coverage on your overall policy, so that the premium increase is affordable.

Step Five: List as many controllable conditions you can think of.

An aspect of a risk is considered controllable if you can do something to lessen the impact of an unchangeable given.

You may not be able to control the weather in the Bahamas, but you could reinforce your house's foundation. You could install trees that block winds from hitting your house. You could invest in new designs of windows, doors and roof that are more resistant to high winds. As for personal protection you could store important papers, jewellery and other irreplaceable items in an underground storage facility.

Step Six: Turn the negotiable and controllable items you list into action steps.

Notice that, although you may not be able to avoid a hurricane, you can take steps to reduce your vulnerability while preparing to recover faster.

Case Study: The Opportunity to Save Purchasing Costs

To help you understand how the tool works, we will examine something that PJI is adopting: the use of purchasing cards. A number of companies are now using purchasing cards to replace costly purchase orders or the need for large quantities of petty cash. It is a major risk because it completely alters how you conduct purchases of many items. It makes you more vulnerable because some employees will try to abuse the system and use their purchasing card (P card) to pay for personal items. The P card is similar to a credit card issued by Visa or MasterCard, and the company that uses the P card is financially responsible for the charges.

Companies that use P cards warn others that you must go into this with your eyes wide open. It is not a simple solution nor is it easy to implement. Most importantly you must change or address traits within your organisation and culture that may hinder successful use of purchasing cards. Aaron is PJI's manager in charge of the purchasing function for PJI and some of the companies they invested in. Currently the company annually spends over $600,000 for purchases that average under $25. He calculated that the average cost to process each purchase order is $9.25, which means it costs PJI approximately $220,000 to make 24,000 purchase transactions. By paying for most of these 24,000 transactions with a P card, he saves the company over $200,000. Aaron convinced Paul and Justin of the need to switch to P cards, but Tracy's concern about the risk has put that decision on hold. She is worried that the internal controls for P cards will not be strong enough to prevent employee abuse or misuse. Tracy believes that the processing of P cards will create a workload burden in accounting, but Paul and Justin have made it clear she cannot hire any more staff for the next 12 months.

I asked both Aaron and Tracy to explain all this to us, so I could demonstrate the tool.

Step One: The risk

"We will soon institute purchasing cards for use by every manager and supervisor. Most of the users are not trained adequately to deal with the value-added tax and account code issues inherent in the P card. No extra resources will be available to handle the additional administration of purchasing cards. Without adequate controls P cards can easily be used for non-company purchases."

Step Two: With Aaron's and Tracy's help we completed the "Givens" section in Table 8-4:

Table 8-4 Given, Negotiable and Controllable Analysis

Givens **Aspects of the risk that we cannot control or that are unchangeable**	**Negotiables** **Aspects of the risk that we can influence by substitution or alteration**	**Controllables** **Aspects of the risk that can lessen the impact of the given**
We must use purchasing cards for all supplies and related buys under $5,000.		
We will be unable to work with some existing vendors who cannot accept the P card.		
We must be able to handle the administration of P cards with existing staffing.		
Verifying the account coding of each purchase can be time consuming but is an important internal control.		
The cards can contain only one account code in their memory.		
Verification about the correctness of each purchase is an important control.		
All managers will be issued a P card for use by their department.		
Companies that use centralised purchasing will be issued a P card.		

Steps Three and Four: I assigned groups of employees the task of brainstorming specific actions that could be taken that would mitigate or lessen the risk. I suggested they not be overly concerned with whether it was a negotiable or controllable item. They should just consider actions that would protect the company from fraud and unnecessary paperwork and be easy to administer.

Their Solutions

The groups amazed Tracy and Aaron with their creative ideas to mitigate this risk, which told me they understood the tool and its purpose. There were too many to list, but the ones that Tracy and Aaron selected for their action plan, which took care of Step Five were

- the user must attend training before he or she is issued a P card.
- accounting administers the training on the P card's use, proper coding and policies.
- the employee's immediate supervisor is accountable to ensure the appropriateness of the purchase and its coding. The supervisor is the first line of defence against misuse.
- employees will scan their own receipts for accounting's database.
- PJI will purchase P card software that checks for inappropriate use and makes the digital receipts easy to locate and access.

- update the policies for misuse of company resources by adding the proper use of P cards.
- any purchase of non-business items results in immediate termination, and the purchase will be deducted from the employee's pay packet.
- accounting will create a regular audit routine on P card usage to verify the process works as designed.
- Aaron will provide the management team statistics on the usage of P cards versus purchase orders and quarterly estimate the programme's savings.

Tool's Lesson

In this example notice that you have to accept certain things in every risk or opportunity. That does not mean you cannot lessen the perils. Parts of the risk that you can use to influence or minimise are called negotiables. These are things you ask for. Finally, when you proactively take control of the situation, you can reduce the danger or exposure of the risk. This tool empowers employees to act with purpose.

Onward

Today you discovered three important things. First you now have access to 18 unique tools that aid you in reducing the impact of Murphy's Law or dealing with unforeseen potholes. To ensure your employees will use them, you need engaged and knowledgeable employees who think for themselves and feel empowered. Finally you explored how ERM provides multiple levels of reassurance that people are scanning the horizon for perils, and this leads to employees feeling more comfortable taking risks.

By now you can clearly see how all the concepts of formal risk management fit together like a blanket of protection and warmth when it is storming outside. We end this training tomorrow by learning the final step of risk management.

Before I delivered my closing quotation, Chrystal raised her hand. When asked for her thoughts, like a bubble, she popped up and excitedly said, "I got it! I can see what you have been trying to tell us all this time. I go to a yoga class nearly every day. My yoga instructor says that yoga is practice. We experience the poses to get comfortable with them, and the more we practise them, the easier our bodies can assume the pose. Yoga is practice, not perfection. I see now that managing risk is like yoga. The more we practise risk management in our day-to-day decisions, the stronger our programme becomes."

"Risk! Risk anything! Care no more for the opinions of others, for those voices. Do the hardest thing on earth for you. Act for yourself. Face the truth." Katherine Mansfield

Your Action Plan

Step One

List any tools employees in your organisation have access to or use that aid them in addressing risk. How are the tools used? How do employees know to use them? Do the tools enable smarter decision making?

Step Two

Where in your organisation could your employees use the risk authority and responsibly chart? If you used the chart, what difference, if any, would it make? What could prevent the chart from being instituted to enhance accountability?

Step Three

Consider a major project you are working on or a major goal that must get done. Using the format in this chapter, prepare a draft version of a formalised action plan for the effort. Assuming one had already been written, what difference could or would it make to your project or goal?

Step Four

Think about an opportunity, a risk or a challenge you have in front of you, and apply either the pitfall analysis tool or the given, negotiable and controllable tool. How did either of these tools assist you in deciding actions you could take to affect the risk or opportunity?

9

What Happens NEXT?

"When people do not talk about their concerns and fears, the silence can destroy a perfectly good relationship." Teri W.

We met the next day at PJ Investments (PJI). Someone provided us with a mountain of doughnuts; cookies; small pastries; and, of course, coffee. Sweet smells filled that room today. Because this was the last session, I would miss the people but not the heat. It was 39° Celsius at 8.00 am.

Reconciling Different Views of Risk

All through the sessions I noticed that Paul and Justin always sat far away from one another. This was strange behaviour for peers who had built a successful and profitable business together. As I obtained a greater understanding about the inner workings of PJI, I came to realise why Justin hired me. Something placed a wedge between them, and Justin hoped I would remove it and rescue his company.

When we first met, Justin said, "I am in a quandary about what to do with a recent opportunity for my company," but he never spoke about it again. I broached the subject with Paul, who refused to say anything. Today I would attempt to define and maybe remove that wedge.

On this second day, while their employees worked on an assignment, I invited Justin and Paul to lunch at a nearby restaurant. After giving the waitress our orders I said, "I commend the two of you for getting this risk management programme implemented, but I guarantee that the programme will fail if the two of you do not support it, and I sense there is one risk that each of you want to talk about and do not want to talk about. Right now is a perfect opportunity to prove to me that you are committed to practising risk management."

While they ate, refusing to look at one another, I related a story about two friends.

Teri and Kris

Tears fell from Teri's eyes as she told me about how close she and Kris came to ending a lifelong friendship. Teri and her friend Kris are single professionals who love each other's company. People who meet this fun-loving duo for the first time think they are sisters; however, Teri is spontaneous and creative, but Kris is a methodical planner with a list for everything. They prove that opposites attract.

Now in their mid-30s, Kris and Teri have jobs that leave them less time for adventures and exotic vacations. Last spring they carved out two weeks from their hectic schedules to vacation in Curacao, a remote island in the Caribbean. Unfortunately this dream vacation nearly tore them apart.

Kris's dream vacation consisted of working through a long list of activities and explorations. Teri's new job was taking a toll on her, so her dream was to spend most of her time on the beach reading while sipping mojitos.

What started out as fun quickly turned into a disaster. First, just before leaving home, an unusual snowstorm delayed their flight for one day. While waiting at the airport, Teri spent the time napping or relaxing to music, but Kris frantically made calls to rearrange their itinerary. They landed the next day in Miami, Florida, to more bad news: they were bumped from their connecting flight to the island. Kris took this change personally and loudly argued with an airline representative to Teri's embarrassment. After waiting for nine hours in the Miami airport, the agent was able to get them on another flight. The only two seats available were middle seats at opposite ends of the jet.

When they finally arrived at their hotel two days later than planned, it was raining hard. The hotel clerk warned that a tropical storm was headed for the island and suggested that Kris and Teri return to the United States. "No, we are staying!" Teri screamed. Because of the high winds and drenching downpour, they were stuck in their hotel room for three straight days. Kris was fuming because many of the things on her list were cancelled. Meanwhile Teri felt miserable and achy, most likely a reaction to the stress.

Even the good news turned bad. The storm passed the island, and the sun returned, but the hotel lost power, so Kris and Teri spent the next two days without hot water or hot meals. It was too hot to be outside yet too humid and stuffy to be indoors. By this time they weren't on speaking terms, somehow blaming the other. They spent the remainder of the trip apart, each resenting the other for having "fun."

The only thing that eventually saved Teri's and Kris's friendship was a willingness to take a risk by apologising and ending the blame game. Teri and Kris each had to swallow their pride and embarrassment over their reactions under stress in order to reclaim their friendship.

Over coffee weeks later, Teri asked me, "What should I have done differently, so that the vacation might have turned out better? Do you think that what happened was inevitable?"

I gave Teri the same advice I will give the two of you.

"A big skirmish like yours was inevitable because you each approach life from a different place. Justin, you sweat the details, while Paul you do not. Paul, you like to act first and then decide what to do while Justin decides first and then acts. Neither way is right or wrong, but when you stop communicating about your concerns and fears, you tear apart what you have so carefully built. Your business could end up like Teri's and Kris' vacation.

"You need to see eye-to-eye again because today your stakes and risks are high, and other people are now impacted by your spontaneous or planned decisions. Neither of you seem to want to accept the other person's point of view regarding risk, assuming that the other needs to be more like you. The two of you must find common ground regarding the cost you are willing to pay with each risk you face or opportunities you chase."

Paul said, "You're right. For the last six months we have avoided talking about this, but we can't go on acting like the tension does not exist. Ron, here is the deal. In the past we have invested in land and buildings but always with the goal of finding the right property for a business unit, taking on very little risk."

Justin cut in, "I disagree! I think we do take on a lot of risk each time we buy a property." He glared at Paul who responded in kind.

I spoke up, "So this is what the two of you are in disagreement about: Paul feels the risk is predictable, and Justin feels it is unpredictable, right?" Both nodded in the affirmative.

Paul ploughed on, "About seven months ago a banker colleague approached me about helping with a distressed property. An out-of-town developer created a planned community nearby, and unfortunately both the contractor and developer went bankrupt. The community is nearly finished, and the banker wants to know if we would invest money in exchange for the rights to manage it while she puts together a consortium of lenders to complete the project. Our role would be to actually manage the retail and organisational part of this community.

"Up to this point in our history we would invest in a viable business that was established. In this situation we would need to establish businesses from scratch and attempt to recruit or operate 10–15 of them in this planned community. Even though we have never done something like this, I believe we can handle this, even if we have to hire the talent who can help us."

It was Justin's turn. "This is where I disagree with you, Paul. Taking this project moves us away from serving as adviser and landlord, a position where we limit or control our exposure. Managing a large-scale community means more of an investment, and I doubt we have the time and talent to take on a project of this size."

I could see both of them were armed to argue the point.

I said, "I can apply a risk management tool to address your overall concerns. Even if, based on the tool's analysis, you decide not to invest your money, you will be comfortable with using this tool, and I guarantee it will prevent the animosity I feel that is threatening your partnership."

Murphy's Law of Opportunistic Hindsight

After a major catastrophe everyone will say, "I saw it coming." No one thought to say anything. Everyone excuses their culpability by saying, "There was nothing that I could do."

Risk Management Tool Nineteen– Criteria Checkerboard

A tool called a criteria checkerboard allows you to analyse the exposure of a specific risk and then use the information to determine how to proceed. It is a key tool used by consultants for defining and matching the criteria for success with the possible alternatives. Using this information you can analyse your exposure to a risk and then use the data to decide the best solution or path to take.

How to Use the Criteria Checkerboard:

Step One: Describe the risk or problem.

Step Two: Select your criteria for a best decision.

Step Three: Brainstorm alternative solutions. Every alternative is acceptable and possible, and no idea is too outrageous. You write down every idea as it is presented. You stay open to the idea no matter the source or rationale for it. Later you go back and narrow the list down to the more reasonable or realistic alternatives.

Step Four: List the criteria and alternatives on a checkerboard tool.

Step Five: Check off, using symbols, how well each solution meets your criteria.

Step Six(A): Examine the original criteria to determine their validity or reasonableness.

Step Six(B): Alter or revise the criteria and retest.

Step Seven: Add or change the scenarios (solutions) to test how well they match up with your success criteria.

Step Eight: Answer these questions:

- How will this alternative or course of action reduce our exposure to the negative consequences of this risk?
- Which of these alternatives meets our need for a best solution?
- Why is it optimal?
- Is there any other criterion or alternative we have not considered?
- What will we do with this information?

Step Nine: Make your decision based upon which solution satisfies the most criteria.

Case Study: Opportunity to Find Common Ground

Step One: Describe the risk.

By investing in this planned community, we would go from managing land and buildings to managing a town. Managing the community would mean that we act like a government (eg, establish policies and regulations); manage infrastructure, such as roads, water, sewer and landscaping; recruit businesses to locate in the community; coordinate our efforts with the other community leaders; and operate small businesses instead of investing in them.

Step Two: Select your criteria for a best decision.

The next step of the tool is to select specific criteria for the best decision. This is what Paul and Justin listed, in no particular order:

Our criteria for a successful investment are

- quickly create a positive cash flow.
- invest in a property or an asset that can quickly and easily be sold.
- manage the investment without a lot of overhead.
- be the primary decision maker (eg, no joint ventures or partnerships).
- enhance our firm's reputation as a strategic investor.
- diversify our portfolio of investments to lessen overall risk.

Step Three: Brainstorm alternative solutions.

Normally we would brainstorm alternative solutions that could possibly work to solve the problem or lessen the risk. In this situation we used only one option.

Steps Four and Five: List the criteria and alternatives on the checkerboard tool, as shown in Table 9-1. Check off how well each solution meets your criteria.

The next action is to compare how well each solution or scenario meshes with the criteria.

At this point our checkerboard on Justin's whiteboard looked like this:

Table 9-1 Criteria Checkerboard

Proposed Solution →	**Serve as manager of a planned community**
Criterion for a Best Solution:↓	
Quickly create a positive cash flow.	X
Invest in an asset that can be quickly and easily sold.	X
Manage the investment without a lot of overhead.	X
Be the primary decision maker.	X
Enhance our firm's reputation as a strategic investor.	✓
Diversify our portfolio of investments.	✓
Symbols:	
✓: Satisfies the criteria.	
X: Does not satisfy the criteria.	
?: Lacking information–more research is required.	

"As you can easily see, the course of action that Paul wants only meets two of the six criteria for a low risk investment," I pointed out. As we proceeded through this powerful analysis, I could see both Paul and Justin relax.

Paul commented, "I did not fully think this investment through. There is a lot of managerial commitment we would need to make, and I do not have the time or interest to do that. In addition I do not feel comfortable putting my future in the hands of a lot of different people making different high-level decisions."

"That is what I have been trying to tell you," Justin said, with a little more anger than necessary.

Paul started to protest but then sat back. "I guess the excitement of the deal appealed to me, and my ego did not allow me to hear you. I feel this is not something we should do."

"But," I interjected, "you now have a sound basis for your decision instead of relying on your gut approach. That is how you often make decisions, Justin. Is that correct?"

"Yes," he admitted. "I sensed the amount of work we would be involved in, but I never analysed it fully. I guess that Paul may have put attention on last three criteria while I focused on the second and third."

I asked, "Is that true, Paul?"

"Yes," he replied.

I said, "The good news, besides the two of you now being in sync on this risk, you have a tool to use for further analysis. Use this tool to run through a few different scenarios before you tell the bank "Yes" or "No." For example assume that you relax your requirement about not partnering. Assume that you offer to just manage the land and buildings of those retail businesses. Assume that you found a project management company to invest in, and they are the entity to run the community. Those are alternatives that might help you turn someone's problem into an opportunity and a low risk."

Paul spoke up first, "No. You can skip steps six through eight. My decision, which I know Justin agrees with, is that we won't invest in this project. I finally see how this whole idea of risk management works. This particular thing that we just went through crystallised it for me. I really like this particular tool."

Tool's Lesson

Because every opportunity has a cost, it is important to use decision making tools to uncover these costs and analyse possible negative downsides, so you can quickly bring them under control. The criteria checkerboard can be used on small decisions, as well as major strategies. It may not always show you the best decision to make, but it will help you raise or lower your expectations and also decide your exit strategy.

ERM Makes You More Investor Worthy

Ernst & Young conducted a survey of 137 global institutional investors reading the impact of ERM in their investment decisions. The respondents reported that theywill pay a premium for companies that demonstrate successful risk management (82%).

- will not invest where there is evidence of poor risk management (61%).
- would withdraw investment when there is a perceived lack of appropriate risk management (41%).

Source: Investors on Risk. Ernst & Young, 2006.

ERM Step Five and One-Half: Learn Something (So You Can Accept Even More Risk with Confidence)

Murphy's Law of Risk and Progress

Just when you think you have all the answers, the question changes.

Normally I tell an audience a favourite quotation at the end of a session, but to set a tone for you to be open to this final step, I'll make an exception. The artist Michelangelo's advice applies both to the need for a balanced attitude between security and insecurity and always looking back to see how far you have come when making your leaps of faith.

> *"The greater danger for most of us lies not in setting our aim too high and falling short; but in setting our aim too low, and achieving our mark."*

This last step may seem like an afterthought, yet it is very crucial to the success of your risk-planning efforts. Even when you identify the pitfalls and establish recovery actions, as in step five, unless you and your employees actually implement the identified changes and improvements, you wasted the time spent in understanding the causes of risks and how to avoid them. Nearly every organisation that has effective risk management programmes, especially those that implemented ERM protocols, believes that risk management must become a natural part of their continuous improvement efforts.

Evaluating Your ERM Efforts

There will not be any firework display or ticker-tape parade that lets you know your risk management efforts are paying off. You will, however, specifically notice that you capture opportunities quicker, employees have a better attitude towards both risks and risk taking, people are prepared to both defend and critique an important decision, and everyone seems to make more intelligent decisions. Even when an organisation does have some type of risk management and governance programme, there is always a concern about its effectiveness.

"With risk comes reward." You have heard that adage many times. Here is the other side of that reminder: with opportunity (reward) comes risk. The world you live and work in is filled with opportunity, and you naturally desire to take advantage of it all. When applying ERM you have the discipline in place to do more and better risk taking. Organisations like the LEGO Group found their risk exposure goes down even as employees take more risks.

You want your people to make smarter, meaningful and intelligent decisions. When you see an increase in that behaviour, you know your ERM programme works. The improvement is evident because your employees use tools such as the criteria checkerboard, pitfall analysis or risk critical path in their thought process. The more ingrained the tools, the more they get used. Thus you end up with more disciplined and well-thought out decisions.

Still a Way to Go

Ernst & Young, in a 2010 survey of 567 companies across Europe, the Middle East, India and Africa, reported that two-thirds of the respondents acknowledge the need to enhance their risk management capabilities.

Source: Expectations on Governance, Risk and Compliance from the Management, Operational Leader and External Stakeholder Perspective. Ernst & Young, 2010.

I assume you are familiar with continuous improvement, which means you are constantly working to improve what you are doing. This dissatisfaction with the status quo attitude integrates well with ERM because of the learning nature of its dynamic protocols. Continuous improvement includes streamlining processes, rethinking work, re-evaluating goals, and eliminating unnecessary work and wastage, all activities designed to make things better and lower the cost of doing business. This cultural norm must be included in an effective risk management programme because when it is absent, your employees will continue to take the same needless risks again and again. Learning does not take place!

New or improved courses of action will naturally arise from your cross-functional team approach of examining risk. Your chief risk officer (CRO), or leader of your ERM effort, is the person responsible for ensuring that the risk owner commits to implementing the changes and improvements that have been identified and quantified.

Some large organisations have turned this CRO role over to the internal audit department. Whether you want risk management oversight to be a function of internal audit or the risk management team, both groups are chartered to constantly seek out improvements that could potentially lead to better risk evaluation techniques, more tools for employees to use, ending weaknesses in strategies, identifying metrics, establishing goals and instilling rewards. The CRO's team may be better able to monitor your firm's culture mosaic.

It is essential to make sure your overall plan emphasises and obtains commitments from employees responsible to be on the lookout for the conditions that lead to unnecessary or costly risk to avoid falling into the same pit. This commitment requires the desire and ability to learn.

Every human has the capacity to look back and learn from the recent past. This is a cultural norm that also serves your risk awareness efforts. ERM instils a protocol to look back at both opportunities and risk in order to do better next time.

Interpreting Results

At first it will seem difficult to evaluate the effectiveness of ERM. This is where specific measurements aid you in knowing how well ERM pays for itself many times over. You may not see more profits, cash or donations because each of those financial metrics is affected by many things besides risk and opportunity. You will identify benefits once you establish key performance indicators (KPIs), along with key risk indicators (KRIs), which serve as pulse points to determine if the risks are cropping up, or opportunity is losing out to any negative impact.

The right KPIs and KRIs will provide feedback on the effectiveness and usage of ERM protocol. Assume your company sells to small businesses and has been hurt by numerous business failures and bankruptcies. One of your KPIs is the aging percentages of your accounts receivables (customer IOUs) and the amount of bad debts compared to net sales. Before implementing ERM the amount of customers in the 90-day category was 6%, and your write-off ratio was 1% of sales. One of the first areas where you apply ERM is your sales process that includes customer selection, credit granting and collections. Within four months of applying the tools of risk management, these metrics drop. Ninety day is now at 4.7%, and write-offs fall to 0.7%. One year later these measurements are much lower: 90-day is 2.6%, and write-offs are now 0.4% of sales. Clearly ERM is working because your exposure of not getting paid has significantly dropped.

Selecting the right set of metrics as KPIs and KRIs for a scorecard is a learning function because you have to exactly know where the risk exists, what creates the risk, how to change behaviours and how to measure the results of better behaviours. ERM benefits you because you have a standard framework process that will provide continuous and ongoing feedback on employees' behaviour patterns and the firm's operational results.

Your historical KPIs and projected KRIs simultaneously support both governance and the ERM programme. Currently most organisations can readily access 60–80% of the data required to get a better overview of the metrics that measure or monitor the intangible costs of risk taking.

Tracking Process Output Versus Reality

You may experience this situation: employees telling you they have identified a risk and dealt with it, yet the situation blows up in your face (figuratively of course). That is why in risk management you establish process outcomes using qualitative measurements. Most likely your employees are not intentionally trying to deceive you about using the tools, but the reasons behind this undesirable behaviour are threefold. First you are asking the devil-may-care risk takers to think before acting. That is like asking them to hand their wallets and car keys over to you. Second you are asking the risk-averse turtles to stick out their necks. To them that may feel like you asked them to walk around the office naked. Third you are changing the culture of your firm, which to some is like asking them to change their allegiance. People often resist attempts to shift a culture because the one you have now, pre-ERM, is their comfort zone, and you know how you react when you are forced to leave yours.

This is why you will rely on process outcome metrics to let you know if employees are actually applying ERM. Larger organisations track their feedback metrics using a dashboard reporting system. In reporting on risk a dashboard that displays key data points will be on every manager's desktop or accessible using the firm's intranet. The dashboard reports capture, analyse and present the most vital information in summary or pictorial form.

Your investment in a risk management infrastructure must be viewed the same as making a strategic investment in new buildings and equipment. Once you know the rationale for the investment, you establish feedback measures to ensure the spending was beneficial and pays for itself.

Scenario Planning Again

Another aspect of learning and improving that pays huge dividends is the scenario planning done in the early stages of risk planning. A scenario is simply a mental rehearsal of alternatives if your original plan does not work out. Professional athletes adjust their diet to their workout schedule. During intense practices they consume one diet, and when taking time off they reduce their calorie and carbohydrate intake. Soon this becomes second nature.

Scenario planning in ERM becomes second nature, so when Murphy's Law attacks are larger and deeper than expected, you have specific or general plans on what to shift, add or subtract. Being able to comfortably do this adds to the backwards-looking and learning-as-you-go aspects of ERM.

Learning Lessons

Murphy's Law of Risk Wisdom

The person who knows the complexities of the situation is never put in charge. The person who is clueless is put in charge.

Organisations and people that are considered the winners in life and business have a common trait: they are always in the learning mode. They know they do not currently have all the answers, so they pursue fresh ideas and insights by incorporating a lessons-learned habit into their routine.

You learned that, in ERM, involving many people in the process creates better and lasting solutions. ERM takes the more brains involved the better concept and suggests that employees involved in ERM regularly pause and share what they have learned and what has and has not worked. They also cross-pollinate improvement ideas by sharing best practices, which are ideas and techniques that have worked well for someone else.

Risk Management Tool Twenty– Plus/ Delta Analysis

The plus/delta analysis shown in Figure 9-1 is an excellent learning tool for every aspect of risk management, especially looking back to learn from the recent past. The plus/delta analysis is a summary of actions worthy of repeating and that need improving. It spawns rapid improvements, shortens learning curves and increases accountability. The plus/delta analysis gives executives, managers, employees and the risk oversight team invaluable insight on what to continue doing and what to improve. You use this tool as you plan for each risky venture, as progress reports of an ongoing action plan and at the end of each opportunity taken. At every phase of your project or activity, the things that are working are identified as pluses, and the improvements, called deltas, are noted.

Figure 9-1
The Plus/Delta Tool

Pluses + (Things that worked and should be retained or repeated)	Deltas Δ (Things that need to change or be improved)

Compliance with the Sarbanes-Oxley Act of 2002 (SOX) in the US and similar legislation in Canada, Australia, Japan and the UK demands this sort of documentation because companies that got into trouble due to a high risk exposure were unable to prove the soundness of the reasons for taking the risk in the first place.

How to Use the Plus/Delta Analysis

Step One: In a normal or regular gathering of the participants, announce the purpose of the plus/delta analysis: to learn what works and gather suggestions for improvement.

Step Two: Spend adequate time gathering a list of conditions, activities and decisions that have worked well and list them on the "pluses" side.

Step Three: Spend time gathering a list of conditions, activities and decisions that people would like to see changed and list them on the "deltas" side. An idea for the delta column must be stated as an improvement, not a complaint. For example, "The room was too cold," is a complaint and not very actionable. "Someone appointed to monitor and adjust the room temperature," is a suggestion and recommends an action to be taken.

Step Four: Before the next committee meeting or stage of work, address the changes (deltas) that were recommended and accommodate those that cannot be changed. Remember there are many ways to pare an apple.

Step Five: Early in the next meeting review the most recently completed plus/delta analysis.

Step Six: Remind people in your group to continue to do what is working (pluses).

Step Seven: Inform the group of the changes that will happen as a result of their suggestions (deltas).

Step Eight: Explain those improvements that cannot be implemented, and brainstorm alternatives.

Step Nine: Continue to use the plus/delta tool at each meeting, event or gathering.

Step Ten: Notice and celebrate how quickly improvements are taking place.

Retain all your plus/delta analyses because it is good documentation to prove you are being pro-active in addressing risk to your boss, an insurance auditor, or your CA firm who may be checking for regulatory compliance.

To demonstrate the plus/delta tool's impact, we spend time preparing one for the series of sessions the employees and managers attended together. Figure 9-2 is what they came up with:

Figure 9-2
Completed Plus/Delta

Pluses + (Things that worked and should be retained or repeated)	**Deltas** Δ (Things that need to change or be improved)
Giving us a workbook to take notes in. Using hands-on learning of the tools. Using our problems and risks. Making risk management simple. Using analogies, stories and Murphy's Law. Providing us with food and many breaks. Having us sit with the executives and managers. Explaining how ERM pays for itself.	Every employee should take this training. The sessions need to be shorter and more frequent. Offer more examples and suggestions for things that every employee sees in the scope of his or her job. I want to be able to use my cell phone during the session.

I pointed out, "The pluses side of the tool helps me discover those things that were meaningful. The deltas are really suggestions for improvement that may or may not be valid, depending on the context, such as allowing employees to use their cell phones during the session. Every idea has merit, and when employees see their suggestions implemented, they get excited and are more enrolled in finding more improvements."

The Risk Audit

Effectively managing the risk of doing business is becoming a critical driver in many companies' success or failure. Periodically taking a comprehensive view of your risk management strategies through an audit or a formal review process is a good way to learn from your successes and misses. This risk management review (ie, audit) is an opportunity for your organisation to assess its ability to both handle risk and recover from its downside. The key element is to make sure you are actually learning something, so you see improvement over time. For example an acquisition, a merger or a significant change in corporate policy within the company can significantly change your organisation's risk strategy.

A risk audit will help you know if your risk management programme stays in alignment with your organisation's overall strategy and objectives. The goal is to make risk management review a part of your everyday business. You can use this review process to strengthen long-term relationships (and hopefully reduce premiums) with insurance brokers and underwriters.

As you gather information from your periodic risk audit, this information will be helpful in negotiating with underwriters. Resist the temptation to tie the timing of this review to the purchase of your insurance. The goal of the review is to identify the weaknesses in your system of controls regarding risk identification, oversight and mitigation. More than likely you will find in your review that your company has unintentionally retained a certain risk, either through benign neglect or a lack of internal communication.

Risk Audit Team

Your audit team consists of people throughout the organisation, including operations, accounting, IT, HR and any other service or support areas that are affected by risks, such as safety. It is critical that this cross-functional team communicate and relate well to each other because their charter is to ask one another, "What is keeping you awake at night beyond the normal risks?" This requires the team to creatively, organically and holistically think about the business. If properly applied the annual review will open employees' eyes to the impact that one risk could have on multiple departments or functions within the business.

This audit team must be headed by a senior executive who represents both the company's and shareholders' interests as they relate to risk management. The goal of the committee is to develop a customised audit risk checklist, so that individual managers—the actual risk takers—can assess the risk versus reward of their particular area of responsibility. The checklist asks managers to indicate their awareness and knowledge of the potential risks, define those risks and identify how they are being addressed on an everyday basis. The key question could be, "How many resources are being spent to address or mitigate this issue?" Don't forget to include resources such as people's time, extra paperwork, audit verifications and energy. Pay close attention to the time that could be spent in more productive endeavours.

Audit Findings

Once the risk review is complete, your company's next step is to use the information that it gathers to improve its overall risk management. By incorporating the review's findings into a specific plan for risk management, the company should be able to minimise the chance that the audit findings will gather dust on some executive's shelf. It makes sense that the leader of this audit team is the CRO and that part of the team's membership consists of members of the risk committee. In some larger organisations the risk oversight committee and risk audit team are the same.

Your risk audit will likely provide you with a great deal of knowledge about your current state of affairs as it relates to risk management and your overall state of risk taking or opportunity exploitation. Some of this knowledge will be beneficial and welcome, but other parts of it will be dreaded and unwelcome. In risk management, knowing the good with the bad makes the organisation stronger and better able to withstand serious and unanticipated risk. It may even give you a competitive advantage and build the confidence to risk more.

Lesson for Experience with ERM

In 2009 Ernst & Young sponsored a survey that was conducted by the Economist Intelligence Unit and that asked about experiences with ERM. Respondents

- have seven or more risk functions (73%).
- have overlapping coverage in two or more risk functions (67%).
- reported gaps in coverage between risk functions (50%).
- believe they can get better risk coverage for less money (62%).

Source: http://www.ey.com/Publication/vwLUAssets/The_future_of_risk_-_Protecting_and_enabling_performance/$FILE/EY_Future%20of%20risk_-_Protecting_and_enabling_performance.pdf

Ongoing Protection

Think of managing a risk and opportunity as protecting your personal computer from a virus. A virus can come through many different forms, so you establish a firewall to prevent viruses from coming through your ISP. Don't forget that viruses can be attached to documents in an e-mail, purchased software downloads and memory sticks or when someone accesses your computer system through his or her unprotected home terminal. Even worse someone could send you what seems to be a harmless e-card that contains a virus that is not detected by your firewall. Even if you have the best firewall available, you must regularly update it and run a daily check for new viruses to make sure the tool is doing its job.

The same holds true for your risk management programme. You could have strategies and tools in place, but that will not always prevent a costly risk from negatively impacting you, especially if it comes from an unexpected source, such as a disgruntled employee, foreign government or strategic partner. Just as you update your firewall often and run a daily protection scan, you must also regularly review your risk effort by updating your strategies, examining your plans, and conducting a risk audit or looking back at lessons learned.

Lessons Learned

Fast Company magazine published an illustrative example of lessons learned in the article "Make Smarter Mistakes." It lists six reality-tested ways to quickly learn from your mistakes that apply to the negative effects of risk taking:

1. *The cover-up is always worse than the crime.* The surest way to defuse a mistake is to quickly own up and face it.
2. *If it is your team, it is your mistake.* If something bad happens in your group or unit, you own the mistake and recovery plan. People forget the problem, but they remember your actions.
3. *Follow-up is as important as follow-through.* Little mistakes yield big insights.
4. *Seize the moment of truth.* Learn from the problem and its effects as quickly as possible.
5. *It pays to make mistakes.* Even when things are going well, we need to be shaken up and tested.
6. *Sometimes the best fix is a quick fix.* The quick solution can buy you time to learn and implement a lasting prevention.

Source: www.fastcompany.com/magazine/11/mistakes.html.

I asked the employees of PJI to share their lessons learned from taking risks, seizing opportunities or dealing with Murphy's Law. These are a few of their suggestions:

- If you wait until conditions are perfect, you will never act.
- Each time you take a risk, review what you did and celebrate it, even if you didn't achieve what you wanted.
- I never use the word *risk*. I call them opportunities.
- For a big risk, you can avoid drowning by going in the water one step at a time.
- Look before you leap. Then don't forget to leap.
- I used to think I never took risks, but when I really thought about it, I always do. I just never classified them as risks. I called it living.
- There are very few risks that you cannot recover from.

- I do something scary every day. Then when I am faced with a big deal, I know I can handle it.
- Start your day by eating a live worm. The rest of the day gets better.

From our experiences organisations are intensely aware of the need to transform their risk management capabilities to not only more effectively manage today's risks but to also sustain what they have now while improving business performance. Yet despite the pressure and desire to change, many company owners and organisation executives have yet to realise that a major reinvention of their risk management approach cannot be achieved using incremental improvements. What you need is a thoughtful holistic approach instead of merely dealing with your lack of a viable programme on a piecemeal basis.

Onward

Step five and one-half, a healthy evolution in a business, is maturity. In the prior steps we acknowledged that the downside of risk taking exists and is inevitable. Now that you have this realisation employees are given tools they can use to learn from successes and failures. As in the example about protecting your personal computer from viruses, a formal risk management programme provides a firewall that benefits the entire organisation.

There is an old saying about the job not being done until the paperwork is done. You can make the same case for ERM. The plan is not fully executed until you see employees incorporating it into their daily behaviours. This is why this final, never completed step, is the bookend to Step 1 in which we define risk at a global level. To ensure your firm's risk plan works, you must move it down to risk at the individual level. This last step is accomplished by holding people accountable to what they commit to doing regarding the awareness, analysis, measurement and management of risks undertaken.

After our meeting in Justin's office, I asked them both to tell their employees how much they believed in this new way of working. Justin went first, "I want you all to know that risk management is vital to our future. There should be no question in your mind about our adoption and usage of this. We are going to and we can. It will take us all a while to get used to this, but I have the utmost confidence that we can do this."

Although I was a little nervous about what he would say, Paul went next. "To be honest, at first, I was sceptical about this thing called ERM. Maybe you were, too, but I am 100% convinced that we want this and need this. You will see me practising risk management from now on, and I expect you to do the same. Let's learn how to do this together. I cannot wait for the day that it becomes second nature for all of us."

Employees actually clapped and cheered. I was pleasantly surprised.

End of the Line

After Paul and Justin sat down I told the employees of PJI, "I admire you for your courage and willingness to transform the culture to one where risk is faced bravely and boldly.

"I appreciate your honesty and willingness to share predicaments and challenges you face, so that I could use them as examples. Thanks for your hard work and ability to find the humour in a very serious topic. My grandfather used to say, 'If you aren't learning anything from your mistakes, don't make any!' There were a few chuckles and grins.

"To me his words highlight the importance of the step you took today. You will make mistakes, misjudgements and underestimate Murphy's Law, but each time you take a risk or go after an opportunity, it is vital to look back and learn something from your reward or pain and use that to improve your ability to face risk the next time. I will leave you with a quick digest of what this training was all about. It removes common misperceptions that exist about ERM. Share it with co-workers."

Five and One-Half Myths of ERM

Myth One: ERM is mostly about effective financial and operational internal controls.

Reality: ERM is about leadership, decision making and justifying the risks you undertake.

Myth Two: Auditors and accountants are mostly responsible for applying ERM.

Reality: Everyone in your firm is responsible for fostering and applying a risk management system.

Myth Three: If ERM works you will be assured that risks will not be costly or wasteful.

Reality: The failure of a risk could still be costly, but ERM allows you to quickly and confidently recover and know that the rewards exceeded the costs.

Myth Four: ERM mostly addresses external risks, such as market and regulatory.

Reality: Because risks can arise from anywhere and multiple sources, ERM requires both an internal and external focus and awareness.

Myth Five: The best measurement of ERM's effectiveness is lower insurance and compliance costs.

Reality: The primary measurement of ERM is adding value to the firm, as defined by the stakeholders.

Myth Five and One-Half: ERM only applies to big for-profit companies.

Reality: Every firm that faces risk can benefit from applying the fundamentals of ERM. It is necessary for survival.

"And the day came when the risk to remain tight in a bud was more painful than the risk it took to blossom." Anaïs Nin

ERM Tool Kit

Appendix A, "Roadmap" contains a recap of all the tools highlighted in this book. It is something to access whenever you are not sure what tool to use. You can also use it to teach others.

Your Action Plan

Step One
Think about something you are working on that has multiple options to it. Apply the criteria checker board to it. Be sure to write out your success criteria first.

Step Two
Think about an area where you could use the plus/delta analysis. Use it several times until you get the feel for it. Then use it in another area, and teach others how to use it.

Step Three
Reread the "Five and One-Half Myths of ERM" section. Which of these myths did you buy into before reading this book? Who else could benefit from improving his or her understanding of ERM?

Step Four
What will you do next? How and where can you apply what you learned about the proper way to manage risk?

10

Epilogue

"Risk is a part of God's game, alike for men and nations." Warren Buffett

Justin

He did his best to repair the hurt feelings between Paul and himself, but their different leadership philosophies towards risk became a sticking point. There was too much water under the bridge, and soon he and Paul jointly realised that they could no longer work as equal partners.

It took many meetings and lots of creative financing for them to agree to a reasonable "divorce." The risk they could not afford was to break up the company, so with that intent they were able to come up with a plan to make the company's continuity the priority. PJ Investments (PJI) spun off most of its land and buildings holdings to Justin's new company, and he received cash in exchange for his shares. His ownership dropped from 50% down to 15%, a position he believes will allow him to support as needed, yet not interfere with, Paul's dreams. Justin asked several employees who had been with him for years and preferred his more moderate approach to risk taking to work for his new company, and all of them agreed. We assisted with the implementation of enterprise risk management (ERM) in his new company.

It is somewhat ironic that Justin is now Paul's landlord.

Paul

Paul's pursuit of ever-larger risks worked for him but not for Justin. Paul prefers to manage the portfolio of companies they have invested in and was happy that Justin took over the land and buildings, which he always considered a royal pain.

Paul contacted and wooed a wealthy fraternity brother and former surfing champion to join the company. With the cash his friend contributed, Paul was able to buy most of Justin's shares. Paul's new partner, who now owns 25% of PJI, has a similar attitude towards risk, and this both pleases and worries him. Realising that he needed an executive team that could provide better balance when facing risk and opportunity, Paul decided to promote some employees. With our assistance he selected nine employees who were assertive, moderate risk takers and good leaders.

PJI International

The implementation of ERM went as planned and designed. Through the efforts of their managers, PJI employees quickly got on board and now use the tools. Not all their risks have gone as smoothly as desired, but each new investment opportunity gets handled with poise and discipline.

Due to the change in management structure, a number of employees left, a risk Paul knew would be inevitable. Finding their replacements is taking longer than expected and creates extra work for everyone who stayed. The unexpected challenge has been finding the right fit. They developed a profile of the ideal employee—a balanced risk taker—and they are finding it's an attitude that is difficult to find (Murphy's Law at work).

The employees who chose to stay with Paul support his vision and are excited about the new investment opportunities ahead.

> **Murphy's Law of the Golden Prize**
>
> A "golden opportunity" means that someone is attempting to hide the underlying risk.

The Future Is Bright

The future looks good for PJI and its employees and for Justin's company, as well. Both men continue to dream because it's in their DNA.

Justin plans to convert some of his company's buildings into manufacturing incubators, places where risk-taking entrepreneurs can design and build their products without having to invest in a costly manufacturing plant. In exchange for a reasonable rent and custom facilities, Justin will take an equity position in these start-ups. He is eager to coach these visionaries on how to take thoughtful, planned and balanced risks.

Paul has a similar dream. He plans to create an incubator institution for visionary entrepreneurs who are just getting started. For a reasonable management fee, PJI will take care of most of the back office logistics that prevent idea people from pursing their dreams. Paul wants to coach them on how to be visionary and still take thoughtful, planned and balanced risks.

Though their roads to success are now heading in separate directions, I foresee the paths merging again in the future. By combining resources they could help launch hundreds of new businesses before they retire. They would do it using their own versions of ERM to ensure these emerging companies achieve success faster and sooner than start-ups that do not practise risk management.

Both men deeply understand there will be potholes along the way and are committed to facing them with confidence and courage.

You and Your Organisation

You now fully understand that risk management is a holistic and comprehensive body of knowledge that has grown into a critical competency for the management of an organisation. ERM will aid you in being and staying successful, regardless of whether you define yourself as a visionary, a creator or simply a steward.

You can explain to peers and employees that your ERM programme must be a structured and disciplined approach that aligns your firm's strategy, processes, people, technology and intellectual capital with the purpose of evaluating and managing the uncertainties you face as your organisation moves into its desired future. It needs to become a truly holistic, integrated, forward-looking and transparent process approach to managing all key business risks and opportunities with the intent of maximising the value of your enterprise for the stakeholder.

You now know that developing a risk management programme alone does not decrease your risk or its negative consequences. Developing this programme and its structure is not something you can easily do. ERM is customised for your firm's unique needs. Although ERM considers every risk, your programme cannot be pre-packaged or a generic solution.

You now understand that managing risk cannot be sold as an idea or a theory. It must have substance, and with the help of your employees you use consensus to determine what the substance looks like. Each organisation must design its own unique approach to risk management by following current best practices, two of which are ERM and strategic risk management.

You now recognise that implementing an ERM capability provides greater value by building in you and your employees the confidence to take on risk rather than avoid it. By actively managing the right risks, especially the critical ones, you will soon have a timelier, more comprehensive and deeper understanding of the risk, which in turn facilitates better decision making. You will also gain greater confidence to take on new risks or accept higher levels of risk. Your risk tolerance or appetite will grow.

You now see that a wise investment in risk management in your own organisation will

- create a greater competitive advantage for you.
- reduce your cost of capital.
- make your organisation more valuable.

You now realise by this point that analogies work well to explain what risk management is all about. Here is my final one for you to share with employees, fellow managers and anyone who needs to understand ERM's importance and power:

Murphy's Law of Risk Trifecta

The conditions for the perfect storm are never known until the storm passes.

You already practise risk management and do not realise it. Let's walk through a situation as a demonstration of what you want your employees to do to prove you know the process.

Case Study: The Hornet's Nest

I am hosting a party in my backyard, and someone comments that the music is a little loud. Being a good host I decide to turn down the outside speaker's volume. The volume knob is located under a shelf near the grill. I notice a small wasps' nest next to the knob, so I cannot lower the volume outside. I go inside and lower the volume. Before I leave I verify that the nest is quiet, with no activity in or around it. I have a risk.

Although I could spend time worrying about the cause, doing that is a pointless waste of time because the risk is real. Not paying attention to its existence (I have not used the grill for months) is the only lesson I need to retain. My urgency is to remove the downside of this peril.

I have several choices for how to react:

- I could ignore the nest. Not a good decision! If I ignore it I put my guests in harm's way because Murphy's law exists, and the wasps could attack.
- I could remove the nest right now. Not a good decision!

- I could remove the nest later. Maybe this is the best way to handle the risk under the conditions, but that creates another peril. As I use the grill the heat and activity might stir up the wasps, but I have to use the grill, and I don't want to send my guests home early.

I have two more choices:

- I could say nothing. Not a good decision!
- I could warn the guests and ask them to avoid the area. A wise choice!

Before I do that I go through a few scenarios in my head:

- If I stay silent I expose anyone who goes near the area. Not a good decision!
- If I announce the nest some of the children in attendance could get curious and poke at it to get a reaction. Murphy's Law at work!

I create an action plan. I calmly inform my guests of the problem and suggest they stay away or remain indoors. I ask a family member, someone I trust, to assist me in keeping people and children away from the area. During the evening I frequently check the nest to ensure the wasps are quiet. Thankfully the evening passes without any mishaps.

I am not done because my risk is still there. The next day I know I have more choices:

- I could avoid my responsibility and develop intentional amnesia, knowing the peril will grow. Not a good decision!
- I could put off finding a solution, knowing the peril will grow. Not a good decision!
- I could remove the nest now, which may be the best way to handle the risk, but I have another peril. I am highly allergic to wasp venom, so by addressing one risk, I create another.

I develop a viable mitigation plan, and within one hour the wasps' nest is gone without incident; however, I am not done with the risk. I poke around the house and look for other nests because one nest usually leads to another. Sure enough I find three more small ones. Luckily the overall peril is in its early stage. Using the same mitigation plan I remove them all. I make a mental note to more frequently check for nests and recruit family members to assist me in that task. Awareness about the existence of wasps in my neighbourhood is now on my family's radar.

I suggest you walk through this story again, but substitute the wasps' nest with a risk your organisation now faces, and replace family with employees. You will notice the process makes perfect sense. Basically what I did was apply awareness (notice it); exposure assessment (conduct a location analysis); measurements (verify its size and amount of activity); monitoring (frequently check on it); empowerment and engagement (get others involved); scenario planning (foreseeing that children might disturb it); alternative identification; mitigation (use of smoke, pesticide and destruction of all nests); and increased diligence (family follow-up monitoring and greater awareness).

When you perform risk management you are doing the same thing: making choices, assessing and proactively removing the peril while looking for related perils. Compare my thought process to the map of a simple and effective risk management programme shown in Figure 10-1:

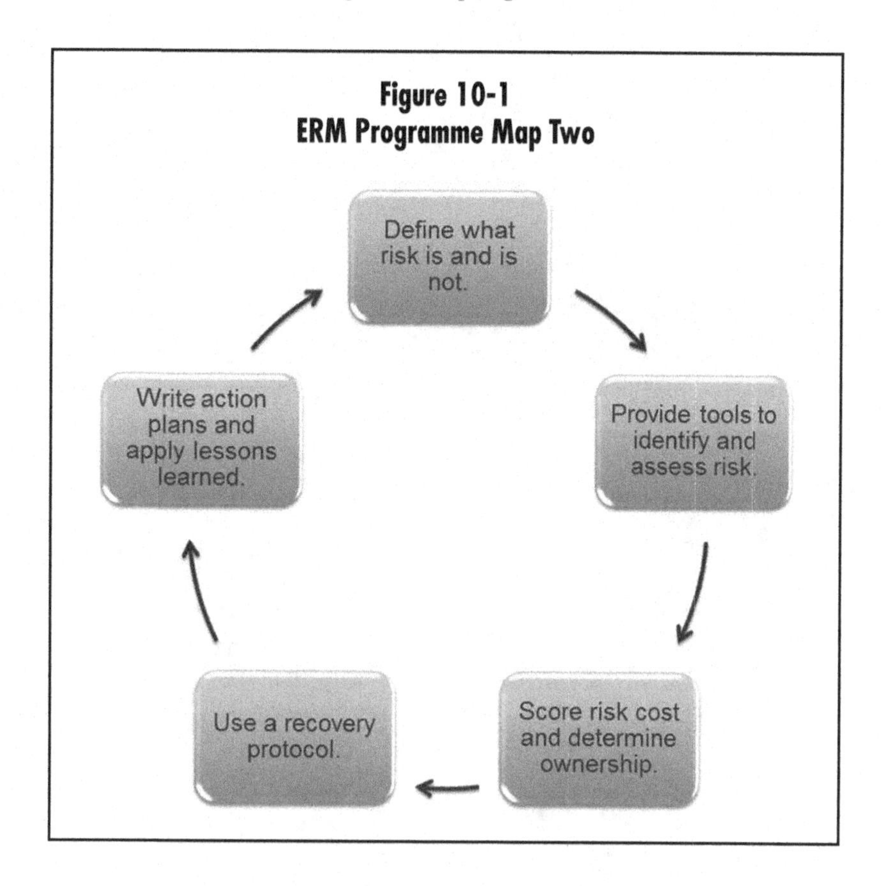
Define what risk is and is not.
Provide tools to identify and assess risk.
Score risk cost and determine ownership.
Use a recovery protocol.
Write action plans and apply lessons learned.

Figure 10-1
ERM Programme Map Two

Can you do it? Of course you can and so can your employees and fellow managers. That is the beauty of formal risk management. It is something a thoughtful, caring and concerned human like you do all the time.

Onward

Now that you know how to implement a firmwide risk management plan, I urge you to follow the advice of the fictional Capt. Picard of the USS *Enterprise*: "Make it so!"

"Courageous risks are life-giving they help you grow, make you brave, and better than you think you are." Joan L. Curcio

Appendix A

Roadmap

High Road Institute's Process for Implementing an Effective Risk Management Programme

Step One: Define risk.

Step Two: Examine your attitude towards risk.

Step Three: Analyse the ability of the organisation to handle risk.

Step Four: Minimise each risk's exposure or downside.

Step Five: Quickly recover from the negative impacts of the risk.

Step Five and One-Half: Learn something, so you can accept even greater risk with confidence.

Tools for Step One: Define Risk

Your goal in Step one is to get the leadership body to arrive at a consensus on a mutually acceptable definition for both risk and risk taking. A well-conceived consensus will almost always be a balanced view.

Risk Management Tool Two–Process for Gaining Consensus on What Risk Looks Like

This is done by the firm's leadership team consisting of all the executives and key decision makers in an atmosphere that is conducive to creative thoughtfulness and open, honest dialog.

How to Gain Consensus

Step One: Individually, write out the phrases or terminology each member of the group would use to define the word risk. In other words complete this sentence, "Risk is ..."

Step Two: Ask each person to read his or her definition out loud to the other members of the group. Set the rule that no one is allowed to criticise or comment on any person's definition. It is important to listen to the many versions in order to find common ground. I suggest taping each handwritten sheet to the room's walls.

Step Three: Ask everyone to walk around and study the various definitions that each person wrote down. Compare these definitions to your own response.

You will see some terminology or concepts that are similar and terminology that is different. On a separate sheet of paper or a flip-chart write down any similarities you note. When you compare all the individual answers, you will discover several trends in similar responses. It is important not to get hung up on the specific wording but instead to focus on the message behind the words.

Step Four: As a group, boil the essence of all the individual responses into one combined definition the entire group can agree on. Focus on the commonalities.

The more people you have involved the longer this step will take to complete properly. This takes patience. Your final product must be one that the entire group will support.

Outcome

Your primary objective is to craft a commonly accepted definition of risk that all employees will internalise and use in their daily decisions.

This vital exercise will demonstrate that there are a wide variety of ways for people of your organisation to see and define risk. The outcome of your hard work will jump-start the process of gaining consensus on a commonly acceptable definition of what is risky and what is the cost you cannot afford.

By going through this exercise of examining different employees' views of risk, you will discover the diversity of definitions, with opinions ranging from the optimistic to pessimistic. Some people will focus on the upside or payoff (worth the effort), and others will focus on the downside or pain (I could get hurt). Others will give you a balanced definition (something that has an upside and a downside). You will be amazed at how pessimistic some internal managers tend to be when discussing risk. Do not be surprised when externally focused managers and executives see risk as something necessary, inevitable and rewarding.

All humans want to be successful, but most do not take the risks that are necessary to achieve success. Why? The answer lies in how people view risk: something desirable or something to avoid.

When it comes to understanding how humans look at risk in two very different ways, the "Uncertainty Domino" helps. Every domino tile contains two numbers, either of which can be an option for play. Similarly people can look at risk in either of two ways: as a problem or an opportunity.

Figure 4-1
The Uncertainty Domino

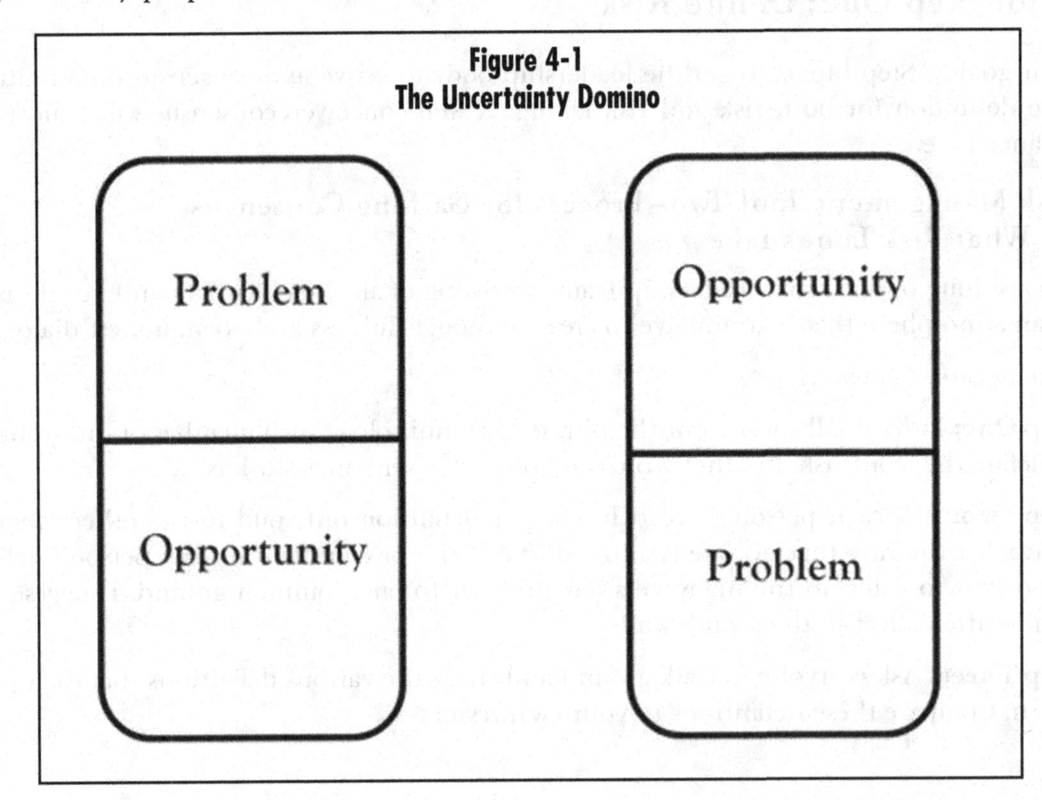

Some of your internal employees will see risk as a problem because they focus on the problem, know the dire implications of risk failure and let their fears come into play. Many employees see risk as a problem because that little voice in their brain says, "I don't think I should be doing this."

An equal number of people see risk taking as a great opportunity and would define the risky choice as a chance to try something new or a thrilling experience. For all employees to embrace risk with a common attitude, you need to adopt this truism:

Sixth Principle of Risk Management

Risk taking is in the eye of the beholder.

Risk Management Tool Eleven– SLOT Analysis

You can easily create risk awareness by annually conducting a SLOT analysis, keeping it updated and then turning it into specific formalised action plans.

A SLOT analysis is a diagnostic tool for analysing and understanding your organisation's current situation or status. This self-evaluation takes a balanced approach and highlights both positives and detriments, so this honesty can be used to spark transformation. The SLOT analysis is a four-part tool for creating an honest baseline and foundation in order to generate and measure forward progress.

Structurally, the SLOT analysis looks like what is shown in Figure 6-3. A detailed SLOT analysis contains

Strengths. Things your organisation does well.

Limitations. Things that hold back your organisation.

Opportunities. Things that could benefit your organisation.

Threats. Things that could undermine your organisation's success.

Figure 6-3
SLOT Analysis

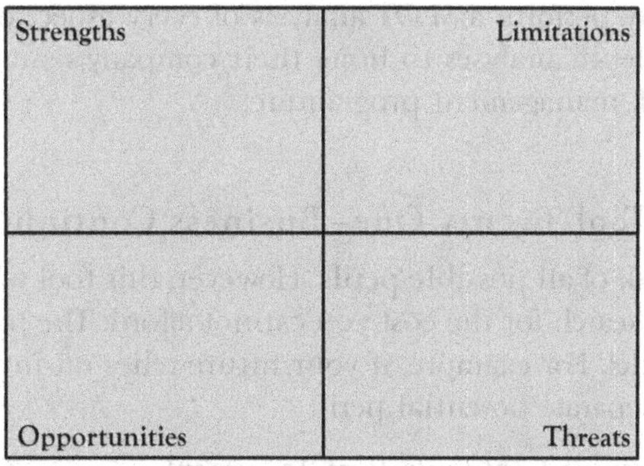

Strengths	Limitations
Opportunities	Threats

How to Complete the SLOT Analysis

Step One: Start with your strengths. Take as long as necessary. Look at all aspects of your organisation, from products or services, to people, from technology to brand or reputation, and from internal capabilities to market approaches.

Step Two: Next tackle your limitations. This can be hard because successful people dislike speaking out loud about what holds them (or their organisation) back. Yet it is important to strive for honesty because if you over emphasise your strengths and minimise your limitations, you will not have a truthful examination of potential risks.

You may need to appoint someone to play the devil's advocate here. Their job is to provoke honest analysis by voicing the concerns no one else wants to raise.

Step Three: List all of your organisation's opportunities. Again take as long as necessary.

You cannot have too many opportunities. You may experience some debate here because one person may see something as an opportunity while someone else does not. Stress to everyone that the point is not about being accurate. You are seeking out where risks could be hidden.

Step Four: List all the threats to your organisation, your business model, your people, your reputation, your technology, and your marketplace. You may want to create two lists—Internal Threats (those arising from within) and External Threats (those coming to you from outside).

In this step you may also need someone to serve as the devil's advocate or someone to referee. People will argue over whether something is a threat or not. This is valuable discussion as long as it does not distract from the tool's purpose.

Whenever a senior leader refuses to acknowledge that something is a threat, this is a clear indication that a risk does in fact exist. By denying the threat is real, you open the door for Murphy's Law.

Step Five: This last step will take a bit of time so plan for it. Using the entire list of strengths, limitations, opportunities, and threats you will clearly see real and potential risks. Make note of these.

Not all risks will show up in the threats section. Often your vulnerability lies in an opportunity that is never pursued or a strength that is not protected or a limitation that is ignored.

Outcome

The outcome of the SLOT analysis is an honest assessment of where your organisation is today. A bonus is that a SLOT analysis is used to assess the firm's risks. You now have a long list of vulnerabilities, potholes, or time bombs that will be winnowed down to a critical few. Later in your risk management plan, these will be measured and evaluated, mitigated or minimised, and monitored or managed.

You need to annually perform a SLOT analysis of every aspect of your company. Intelligent leaders then use these in-depth analyses to hone their company's strategic plan. This insight becomes part of your overall risk management programme.

Risk Management Tool Twenty One– Business Continuity Peril Assessment

There is no way to think of all possible perils. However, this tool will jog your leadership team's collective memory as you search for the cost you cannot afford. The potential perils can be renamed to suit your business model. For example, if your future relies on innovation or leading-edge technology, include that as a separate potential peril.

How to Complete the Business Continuity Peril Assessment

Rank the following business continuity risks based on their probability and its consequences on you according to the guidelines at the bottom.

Remember the rule of thumb regarding business continuity. For each day you cannot operate, the likelihood of you getting reorganised and continuing to stay in business drops by about 3%. So if a flood shuts you down and you cannot operate for 20 days, the likelihood that you will reopen drops to 40%.

Potential Perils	**Probability (see scale below)**	**Consequences (see scale below)**
Building Collapse/Failure		
Fire or Explosion		
Natural Gas Disruption		
Extended Power Outage		
Violent Storm		
Flood		
Wildfire		
Water Supply Disruption		
Sewer Disruption		
Earthquake		
Water Damage (rain or plumbing)		
Pandemic		
Terrorism		
Civil Disobedience or Riot		
Political Disruption (nationalisation or outlawing of business)		
Employee Fatality/Hospitalisations		
Food Contamination		
Vehicle Accident		
Robbery/Theft		
Key Employee(s) Loss		
Kidnap/Ransom		
Workplace Violence		
Fraud or Embezzlement		
Loss of Information		
Loss of Main Customer		
Loss of Major Supplier		
Technology Disruption		
Other:		

Probability: (Note 1)	Consequences: (Note 2)
0 – Impossible (almost never)	0 – Insignificant (less than $10,000)
1 – Highly unlikely (less often than every 10 years)	1 – Minor (up to $25,000)
2 – Possible (less often than every 5 years)	2 – Significant (up to $100,000)
3 – Probable (more often than every 5 years)	3 – Major (up to $500,000)
4 – Highly likely (every year)	4 – Catastrophic (more than $500,000)

Notes:

1. The team that completes this analysis must reach a consensus on the likelihood of each peril. If they fail to do that, some very dire risk may be minimised. The debate that leads to consensus is very enlightening.

2. The dollar amounts provided are guidelines. Your organisation will place in this section the amounts that represent your current risk appetite. If your organisation is small, the amounts will be too. If you are large and well-financed, the amounts will be larger. Remember to focus on the "cost you cannot afford" when setting the "major" and "catastrophic" categories.

Outcome

You now have an idea of your risk appetite and have commenced the process of measuring the size of your risks. This enables you to use the rest of the tools on each peril that you classified as Significant, Major and Catastrophic.

Tools for Step Two: Examine Your Attitude Towards Risk

Risk Management Tool One– Personal Risk Spectrum

There are many different flavours in the spectrum of individual risk taking. As a leader who is trying to build a culture that balances innovation with control and to develop employees who think for themselves, you must examine a risk through the eyes of your employees. The "Personal Risk Spectrum Tool," as shown in Figure 2-2, enables you to do that:

Figure 2-2
Personal Risk Spectrum or Risk Appetite

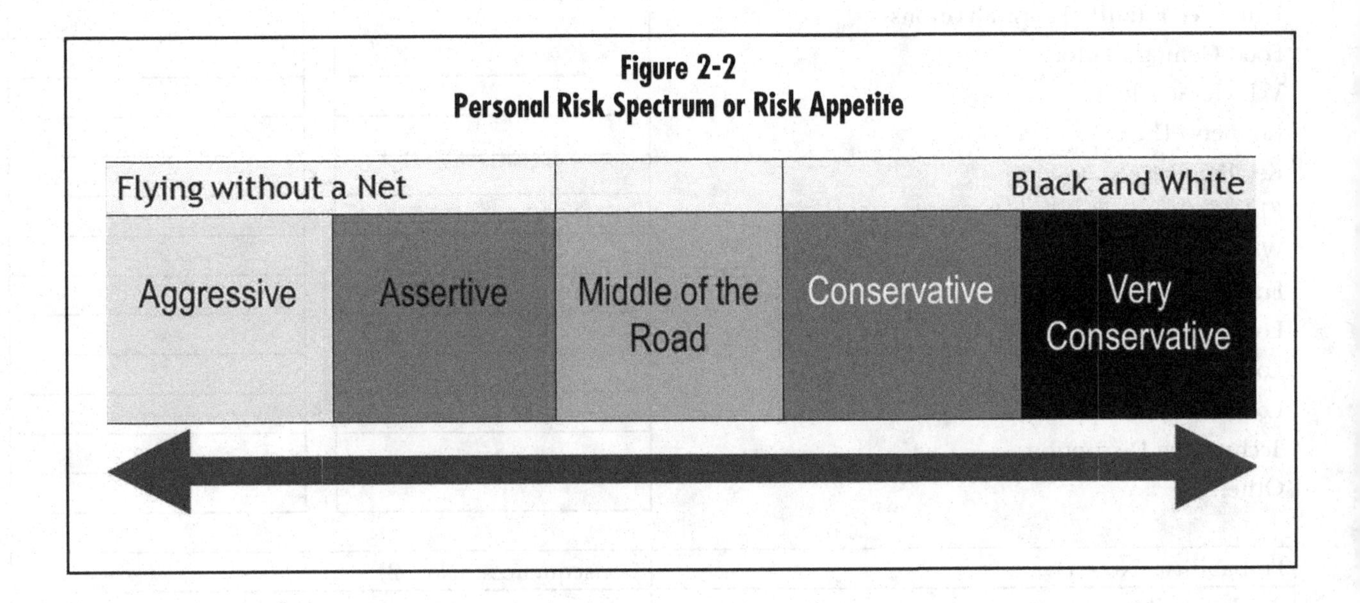

Each human being defines risk along this broad spectrum, depending on what we have at risk and the value we place upon it. Risk taking on the individual level is a range across a spectrum going from "flying without a net" on one end to "black and white" on the other. This tool demonstrates the wide diversity of the phenomenon referred to as risk appetite. Those who tend to stay on the right have a small appetite, and in comparison people who stay on the left have a larger appetite.

In addition to sliding across the spectrum, depending on what we hold as risky, people alter their views over time. I know many entrepreneurs who, in the early days, took all kinds of risks to get their businesses started. Then as they grew more successful and matured in their decision making, these risk takers became more cautious, conservative and even risk averse.

How to Use the Personal Risk Spectrum Tool
This tool is used by the either the leadership body or your risk management team, if you have appointed one.

Step One: Create a table that looks like this.

Risk Area	Person Managing (Accountable for) this Risk	Person's Attitude Toward Risk-taking
Examples:		
Sarbanes-Oxley compliance	Treasurer	Very conservative
New product development (from SLOT)	Director of R & D	Conservative
1.		
2.		
3.		
4.		
5.		

Step Two: List all the major areas where you discovered risk in step one in the first column. Do not attempt to prioritise or justify leaving any of them off.

Step Three: In the second column, list the name of the employee whose responsibility it is to manage this area.

Even if you have not named a specific individual yet, place the name of the employee who is accountable for taking care of it. For example, if you selected a flood as something that could put you out of business, name the employee who is currently responsible for not letting that happen, should a flood occur next week.

Step Four: In the column titled "Person's Attitude" write in the place where you feel this employee fits on the Personal Risk Spectrum.

You are not making a judgement about that employee's ability or capability. You are simply examining how this person approaches most risks. If you work with another person for a while you can easily identify their comfort level with risky activities or decisions. Think about how this person deals with change, new ideas or challenges.

Step Five: This is the hardest part because it takes seasoned judgement to do this well. You now must now answer this key question regarding this particular peril and the employee who has primary accountability for it: *Is the attitude of the person managing your risk area appropriate, too much or inadequate?*

Some risk requires a very conservative approach while another needs someone with a middle of the road approach. Of course there are risks where you want the manager to fly without a net.

Step Six: Now the leadership body or risk management team must answer these last important questions. Consider each of these carefully because if you are not honest and don't do the work necessary, your risk management programme will likely fail.

Is there a balanced view of risk in our organisation?

Do we have the right person managing the risk? Does the employee's overall attitude match the risk?

Outcome
You may find mismatches where a very conservative person is looking over an area where more risk-taking is required. Or you may have a person who eats risk for breakfast being responsible for a vulnerability that requires a more black and white approach.

If this tool is used properly, you will know whether or not you have a balanced approach toward risk-taking. You will also know where you may need to put the right person in charge of managing a particular risk. This is where the team doing this assessment needs the courage to take this important action.

Tools for Step Three: Analyse the Ability of the Organisation to Handle Risk

Risk Management Tool Eight– Culture Assessment

This tool consists of a self-rating format. It serves as an entry point for the third step of your risk management programme. It is to be prepared by the organisation's leadership body early in the implementation of the protocol. Each member of the team completes his or her own assessment form

How to Complete this Assessment

Step One: Read the following statement. Then check off any of the required attitudes that your fellow leaders currently have. Base your answer on what you experience, not what you feel.

We must believe in ourselves to take successful risks!

This requires us to have the

- ☐ courage to believe in abilities and talents.
- ☐ belief that we can take risk.
- ☐ belief that we should take risks.
- ☐ belief that we can be better than we are now.
- ☐ belief that our clients are the most important.
- ☐ belief that employees are as valuable as clients.
- ☐ belief that employees can think for themselves and be trusted.
- ☐ belief that by collaboratively working together we can grow our profits.

Step Two: use Table 6-1 to score your answers. The scale for this is: a 4 means you strongly believe the statement, 3 means you mostly believe it, 2 means it may or may not be true and 1 means you do not believe the statement.

Step Three: Answer this question: *What is your level of belief that this organisation can practise proactive risk management?*

Table 6-1

I believe we											
can follow an ERM plan.				will eventually embrace ERM.				are doomed to fail at ERM.			
4	3	2	1	4	3	2	1	4	3	2	1

Outcome

This assessment gives you that data regarding the level of cultural support, scepticism or resistance that exists in your culture. It gives you some idea about how hard or how easy it will be to get employees and managers to accept practicing risk management.

Risk Management Tool Nine–Employee Assessment of a Balanced Culture

This tool (Table 6-2) is designed for all or a majority of your employees to fill out. In the prior tool, your senior leaders gave their opinions about how balanced the culture is towards risk-taking and risk management. Now you need to know if your employees concur or disagree.

How to Conduct the Employee Assessment

Step One: Develop a master copy of this survey in paper or digital form. Give it to every employee (or at least 60% of them) and ask them to complete it.

Table 6-2 Assessment of a Balanced Culture

Instructions: For each trait below check off whether it exists.			
Culture Trait	**Does Exist**	**Does Not Exist**	**Do Not Know**
Accountability to standard and policies and goals			
Encouragement to raise concerns and issues			
Encouragement to take rational risks			
Encouragement to think before acting			
Honesty and openness			
Leaders setting the example			
Penalties for disregarding the rules			
Review of end results against the actions taken			
Rewards for innovation			
Sensitivity to the cost of risks			
Sensitivity to risk			
Sharing of information			
Team-based problem solving			

Step Two: To ensure they are comfortable in doing this, you must explain several things to them about why you want this information.

The purpose: This is part of your risk management programme.

Why you need the information: You really want their opinions about how the culture actually works. Since they see it in the context of their job, you want their insights.

How the information will be used: You will use it to determine where to start and what the organisation's global vulnerabilities are.

The confidentiality nature: The actual sources of the information will be confidential. You are looking for the overall view about the culture from their valuable perspective.

In this step, you must do everything you can to protect that confidentiality. If any employee sees that his or her opinion is used for any other purposes than you state, employees will either refuse to complete the assessment or not give you the truth.

Step Three: Give the employees a specific deadline in which to complete the survey. Remind them nicely of the due date several times, as they are busy and will not make doing it a priority.

Step Four: Collect the data and collate it by each question. You will receive answers that do not fit the norm. Some employees will use this survey to air out their dissatisfaction. Others will take the 'suck-up' approach and provide answers that they feel management wants. Focus on the norm.

I suggest that you put the results in graph form so everyone can understand it.

Step Five: Compare the employees' collective opinions about the culture's readiness to the one held by the senior leaders (prior tool).

Step Six: This step is critical so do not skip it or minimise it! The entire management team will examine the differences between the two assessments. The wider the gap, the bigger your acceptance and implementation problems will be.

Example: If the senior leaders believe they support the employees and the employees say that they are not supported this gap will severely hamper any efforts to foster both accountability and empowerment of managing everyday risks. The management team must then seek out the causes for this diverse range of opinions and fix any aspects of the culture.

Warning: There are two forbidden behaviours I see all the time at this point, which will be the kiss of death for your risk management programme and your leaders' credibility.

1. Senior management staying in denial about the reality of employees' opinions, ignoring the gaps and forging ahead with implementation anyway.
2. Management putting the entire blame for the gaps onto the employees and shaming them for their honest opinions.

Outcome

You will receive critical findings about your existing culture from two points of view—the top and bottom. The reality lies somewhere in-between. This tool can give you valuable enlightenment about why you need a risk management protocol in the first place. It is also designed to help your organisation's leaders lead better. Finally, it provides you insights into which aspects of your culture need fixing.

Risk Management Tool Three– Strategic Risk Assessment

The Institute of Internal Auditors (IIA) is a great resource for information and tools to deal with the downsides of risk. Although its primary mission is to support the internal audit community, internal auditors are valuable contributors to ERM.

One of the IIA's tools is the self-assessment presented in Exhibit 4-1 and designed for senior managers, executives and board members to create a global awareness regarding risk.

How to Complete the Strategic Risk Assessment

The organisation's board of directors or senior leadership team completes this assessment.

As you go through it, see how many of these you can honestly answer "Yes" to. Each "No" answer indicates an aspect of ERM that you need to be more concerned about.

Exhibit 4-1 Strategic Risk Assessment

Is there a process within the organisation responsible for assessing and monitoring risk?

Do I have assurance that controls are operating as planned?

Is there a thorough and an appropriate reporting mechanism within the organisation that allows for adequate checks and balances for fraud prevention and risk management?

Do I have assurance that financial and other information is correctly reported?

Are risk management, control and governance processes being evaluated and reviewed for efficiency and effectiveness on an ongoing basis?

Do I have a clear understanding of enterprisewide risk and the organisation's key areas of vulnerability?

Does the organisation have an operational system for managing risk?

Is there an internal process within the organisation for adding value to and improving operations?

Are the organisation's stakeholders provided with reliable assurances that their investments are protected?

If I were not a part of management or the board, would I be comfortable with the assurances provided to me as a stakeholder?

Am I able to sleep at night without worrying about risk in the organisation?

Am I comfortable that all risks have been appropriately addressed?

Source: The Institute of Internal Auditors. Altamonte Springs, Florida. www.itaudit.org.

Outcome

This assessment gives the group who has stewardship accountability over the entire enterprise assurance that the whole entity is committed to transparency. Where transparency exists, it is very hard for any employee to hide or cover up risky decisions and behaviours.

Risk Management Tool Four–Risk Tolerance Questionnaire

This tool, shown in exhibit 4-2, is a series of layered probing questions that will aid an individual employee or team in determining the tolerance level or risk appetite.

How to Complete the Risk Tolerance Questionnaire

Determine, before undertaking your next urgent strategic initiative or action plan, the full consequences of the failure to achieve the desired outcome. Compare the potential losses, including the softer, hard-to-measure ones, to the alleged or expected payoffs.

Exhibit 4-2 Risk Tolerance Questionnaire

Name the goal ______________________________

Why are we undertaking this goal?

What is the designed impact?

How is this goal connected to our mission?

What is the specific risk in this goal that we can afford to take?

What is the risk that we cannot afford to take?

At what point will the cost of completing this goal be considered too much to bear?

Outcome

Once this tool is completed it will be easier to determine if the goal, project, or initiative creates a risk that must be addressed while the work is being done. All too often we start doing the work and then later uncover the pothole in the road. That wastes resources and often the risk has grown larger or more costly.

Risk Management Tool Five–Critical Risk Questionnaire

The tool can be used by an individual employee or a team to identify the scope of a potential risk andconsists of specific questions that will help you look at risk differently. Exhibit 4-3 shows six very important questions that need to be asked before the risk is undertaken or opportunity pursued.

Complete this tool right after applying the previous tools. You will have identified specific risks inherent in your plans, goals, and business model. Use this for every risk categorised as significant, major, catastrophic and of course, the cost you cannot afford.

Exhibit 4-3 Critical Risk Questionnaire

Specific risk or vulnerability ____________________________________

What is the worst that can happen?

What is the best that can happen?

What is the most likely outcome?

What are the negative effects of the likely outcome?

How can we handle the negative effects?

How will we minimise or protect ourselves against the negative effects?

How to Complete the Critical Risk Questionnaire

Step One: Answer this question carefully: *What is the risk?*

You have already stated this in several other tools used before this one.

Step Two: Answer this question next: *What is the impact of doing this?*

This requires you to think both locally and globally. You do not want to focus on a small peril to the exclusion of a bigger one.

Step Three: Do some analysis and then answer this question: *What is the worst that could happen?*

This requires you to conduct serious scenario planning of a pessimistic nature. This is hard for some people to do. For them it is easier to upsides rather than downsides.

Step Four: Answer this question next: *What is the best that could happen?*

This step is fun for many and is necessary to arrive at the most likely outcome.

Step Five: Answer this question carefully: *What is the most likely outcome?*

Now you get to realism. Most likely the risk or opportunity will somewhere in between. It is easier to plan for risk when you have a sense of realism in your analysis.

Step Six: Answer this question carefully: *What are the negative impacts of the most likely outcome?*

You may need assistance to uncover all the possibilities to this question. When something is important to you, you can easily develop blinders.

Step Seven: Do some more analysis and then answer this question: *How would you handle the negative impacts?*

Again, using others to brainstorm this thoroughly could be helpful to inject realistic answers.

Step Eight: Finally, answer this question carefully: *How would you minimise these negative impacts?*

You have finally arrived at your mitigation path. This will enable you to handle the peril or opportunity appropriately and timely.

Outcome

You now have the outline of a risk mitigation plan for each risk. Even opportunities found in your SLOT analysis need a plan to exploit them. Since you will be involving employees, they need to know what you want them to do with the risk or opportunity.

This tool becomes your answers for them.

Risk Management Tool Fourteen–Risk Authority and Responsibility Chart

A tool that will allow you to equalise responsibility with authority is called a risk authority and responsibility chart, examples of which are subsequently shown in Tables 8-1 and 8-2. You will notice that you can use this tool to easily highlight specific areas of concern, in this case actions oversight, approval decisions and asset protection.

Table 8-1 Risk Authority and Responsibility Tool

Client Quotation Issuance & Approval Process					
Action	**Project Manager**	**Research Assistant**	**Project Administrator**	**Credit Manager**	**Principal Consultant**
Process Quality Owner					✓
Process Risk Owner					✓
Prepare Proposal for Services	**A**				**Inc**
Conduct Research on Client's History	**R**	**A**	**R**		**R**
Establish Project Scope	**JD**				**JD**
Prepare Risk Plan	**A**		**R**		**R**
Obtain Client's Approval of Scope	**JA**				**JD**
Prepare Project Fees	**JA**				**JD**
Approve Project Fees	**R**		**R**		**A**
Contract Presentation to Client	**A**	**Inc**	**Inc**	**Inc**	**Inc**
Obtain Client's Approval of Contract	**A**				**FA**
Coordinate Project Scheduling	**R**		**A**		**BI**
Complete Project Staffing	**R**		**A**		**BI**
Verify Client Credit References		**A**		**BI**	
Approve Credit and Payment Terms	**BI**		**BI**	**A**	**BI**
Acceptance of Client	**R**				**A /FA**

Table 8-1 Risk Authority and Responsibility Tool (continued)

Symbols	
Authority to Complete Action	A
Be Informed (included in communications and meetings)	BI
Be Included in Client Meetings	Inc
Risk Owner	FA
Recommend the Action	R
Joint Authority to Complete Action	JA

Table 8-2 Risk Authority and Responsibility Tool

Project and Jobsite Safety Process							
Action	**Safety Director**	**Jobsite Foreman**	**Director of Major Projects**	**Project Lead**	**Electrical Technician**	**Jobsite Manager**	**Customer Contact**
Process Quality Owner	✓		✓				
Process Risk Owner			✓				
Inspect Job Tools	**Inc**	**A**	**R**	**BI**		**R/FA**	**BI**
Inspect Job Site	**Inc**	**A**	**R**	**BI**		**R/FA**	**BI**
Inspect Electrical Connections	**Inc**	**R**		**R**	**R**	**R/FA**	**BI**
Train on Safety Procedures	**A**	**R**	**R**	**R**	**R**	**A**	**BI**
Develop Job Risk Assessment	**R**	**R**	**BI**	**R**	**R**	**R**	**BI**
Approve Job Risk Assessment	**BI**	**BI**	**FA**			**BI**	**BI**
Write up Site Inspection Report	**BI**	**JA**	**BI**	**BI**	**BI**	**JA**	**BI**
Raise Safety Concerns	**A**	**A**	**AF**	**A**	**A**	**A**	**A**
Address Unsafe Practices–Customer Caused	**BI**	**A**	**BI**	**BI**	**A**	**A**	**FA**
Address Unsafe Practices–Employee Caused	**BI**	**A**	**BI**	**BI**	**A**	**A**	**BI**

Symbols	
Authority to Complete Action	A
Be Informed (included in communications and meetings)	BI
Be Included in Client Meetings	Inc
Risk Owner	FA
Recommend the Action	R
Joint Authority to Complete Action	JA

How to Use the Risk Authority and Responsibility Chart

Step One: Select a process that is vital to proper proactive risk management.

Step Two: Fill in the chart with the people involved in it and the key decision to be made.

The chart uses symbols signifying role, authority and ownership. "FA" means this person has the ultimate accountability for the process working as designed. "R" means this person has a responsibility to recommend or contribute to the action or decision. "A" and "JA" mean this person has the authority to take the action or decision. Because many decisions require other people's input, the chart uses symbols to clarify this. "BI" means this person is to be informed. "Inc" means this person is to be included in meetings. Remember, even though it is your job to keep the supervisor informed, it is the supervisor's job to stay informed. Communication is a dual responsibility. Because risk is ever present, the employee who owns the risk is designated "FA."

In the example in the first chart: Notice in this process for issuing a proposal that the principal consultant (a senior leader) has ultimate responsibility for this yet has clearly delegated authority to the project manager and project administrator. Notice that the chart clarifies the authority of the employees who support the project team: the credit manager for approving credit terms and the research assistant for researching information about the prospect.

Step Three: Look at the authority structure for the process to reduce safety risks on the job. The senior leader who owns the accountability is the director of major projects.

In the example in the second chart: Notice that each employee who is involved in managing the project has his or her own authority based on expertise, such as the electrical technician and safety director. Notice also that the jobsite manager and jobsite foreman share in deciding what to put on the all-important inspection report. This joint authority deters one person from hiding a risk. One more thing to note is that everyone, including the client, has a responsibility to raise a concern on safety violations, which prevents someone from saying, "It wasn't my job to say anything."

Step Four: Make adjustments to individual and specific employee's duties and responsibilities. Make sure there is both adequate control and accountability assigned for risk mitigation to each process.

Step Five: Apply the tool another vital process where managing risk and opportunity is important.

Outcome

This tool works in conjunction with both the responsibility statement and formalised action plan. When employees know exactly what is expected of them, they will meet or exceed the expectations over 90% of the time.

This tool assists you in defining and communicating these expectations. It also serves to ensure that you provide authority with delegated responsibility in equal measure. It quickly rids your culture of the often given excuse, "I didn't know I was supposed to do that. No one told me."

Tools for Step Four: Minimise Each Risk's Exposure or Downside

Risk Management Tool Six– Critical Risk Path

This tool can be used to identify the implications of a decision to be made about an opportunity and a risk known as the critical risk path. Figure 4-2 shows the tool. Walking through this step-by-step process before the organisation takes a major risk will help you and others make smarter decisions. Please do not assume this tool is simplistic because its value lies in what comes after your initial decision. This tool can be used at any level for the employee to decide "should I or shouldn't I act?"

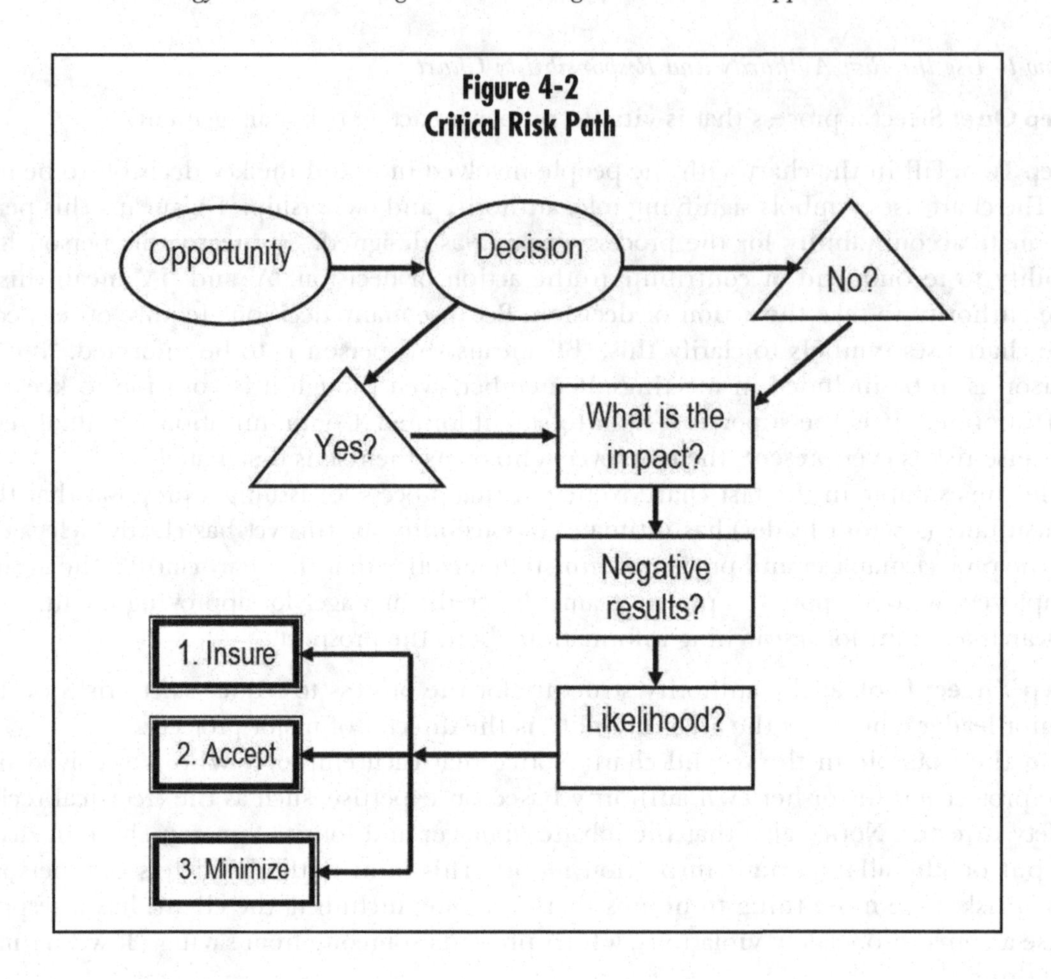

Figure 4-2
Critical Risk Path

How to Use the Critical Risk Path Tool

Step One: Clearly define the opportunity you see that will benefit your organisation.

Step Two: Assume that you will decide on a "no go" approach to the opportunity. Answer this question: *What are the impacts or negative results of saying "No"?* Continue until you cannot think of any more.

Step Three: Answer this question: *What is the likelihood that these negative results will take place if you say "No"?* It is appropriate to use percentages or odds of failure for your answers. Continue until you cannot think of any more.

Step Four: Answer this question: *How would you ensure that these effects will not be too costly or detrimental?* This takes work because you are doing serious what-if thinking.

Step Five: Answer this question: *How would you accept this risk?*

Step Six: Answer this question: *How would you minimise this risk?*

Step Seven: Now, change directions and assume that you will decide on a yes approach to the opportunity.Answer this question: *What are the impacts or negative results of saying "Yes"?* Continue until you cannot think of any more.

Step Eight: Answer this question: *What are the impacts or negative results of saying "Yes"?* Continue until you cannot think of any more.

Step Nine: Answer this question: *What could be the negative results of saying "Yes"?*

Step Ten: Answer this question: *What is the likelihood that these negative results will take place if you say "Yes"?* It is appropriate to use odds or percentages of failure for your answers.

Step Eleven: Answer this question: *How would you ensure that these effects will not be too costly or detrimental?* This also takes work because you are doing serious what-if thinking.

Step Twelve: Answer this question: *How would you accept this risk?*

Step Thirteen: Answer this question: *How would you minimise this risk?*

Notice how the questions in each step of the path are designed to get your employees to think for themselves.

Outcome

Once you have determined the likelihood of a risk occuring, you move to the choices you have to deal with the risk. One option is to accept it (knowing the cost cannot hurt you). Another option is to minimise the risk. There are plenty of actions to take before undertaking the risk to keep its impact or cost low. A third option is to insure, but that does not mean that insurance is your only option. Sharing the risk by partnering with another firm or putting a stop-loss through a limited investment of both time and money are ways to insure the risk. Best of all your three options are not mutually exclusive. For example, you could accept part of the risk, insure part of it and closely manage it, so that you minimise the potential downsides.

Your employee now has a mitigation strategy for lessening the impact of a likely risk. Mitigation does not mean the risk disappears. It still needs to be managed and regularly reassessed.

Risk Management Tool Seven– Risk and Opportunity Measurement Grid and Management Grid

The risk measurement and management grids are common matrices often used to assist decision makers in fostering intelligent decisions. It also applies to effective risk management.

This tool comes in three parts. The first, represented by Figure 5-4, is to help you determine the significance or impact of a particular risk. Each risk you analyse is defined by its probability or likelihood of occurring and its impact on your business or future. If a particular risk is both impactful and highly probable, it will be a high risk. If the risk is impactful but has a low probability of occurring, then it is a medium risk, as is a risk in which the likelihood is high, but its impact is low. Finally a low risk has a low probability and impact. Even small risks need to be analysed because they could grow, worsen or be underestimated.

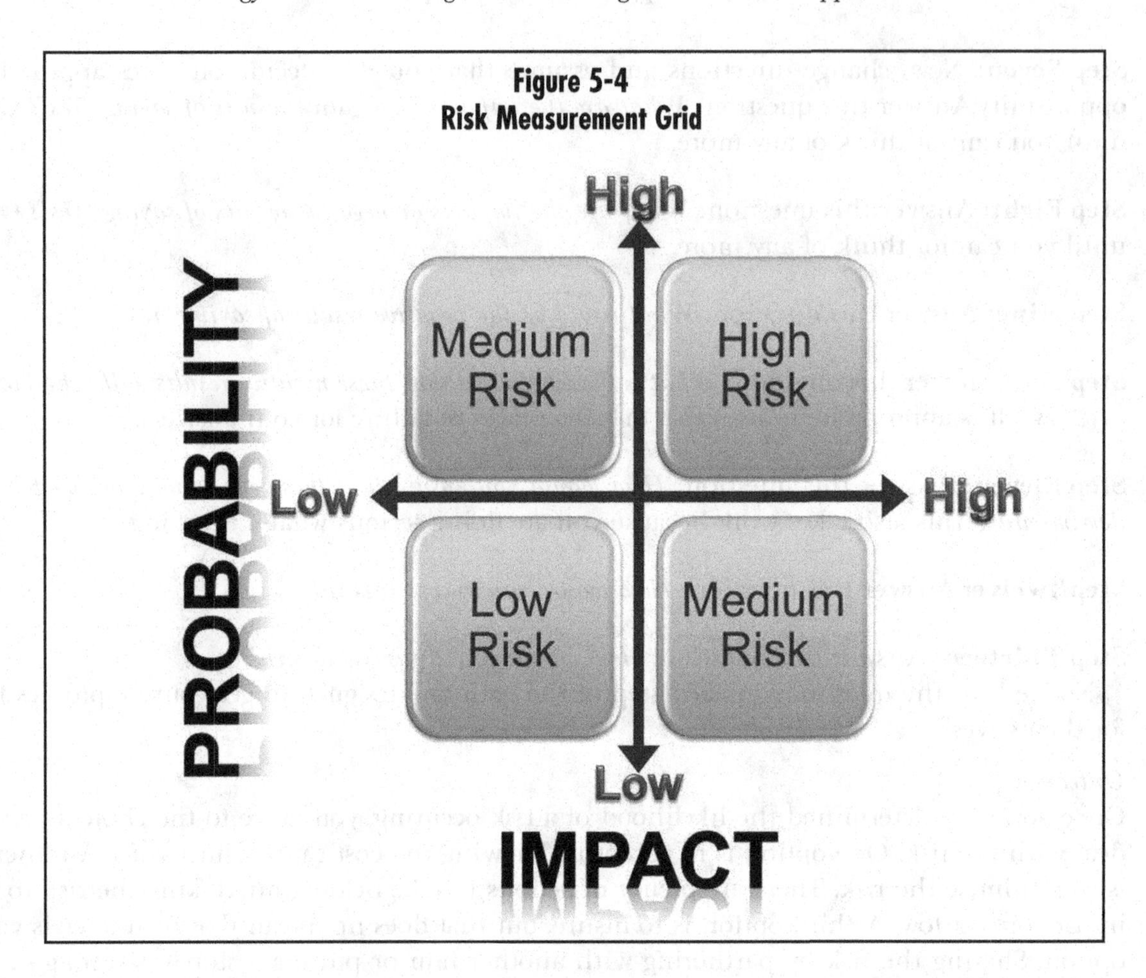

Part One–How to Use the Risk and Opportunity Measurement Grid

Step One: Identify the risk and/or opportunity. At times, they can be one and the same.

Example: Your organisation is seeking to obtain a long-term contract with a government agency for your products. You are one of two suppliers that submitted sealed bids. However, your competition is more experienced in this arena. The future of your company depends on winning this business. If you do not get the order, you will need to lay off employees and significantly cut spending.

Step Two: Estimate the upside for an opportunity or the downside for a risk.

Example: If you win this contract, it could mean about $50 million in new business.

Example: If you do not get awarded this contract, you will have to cut the operating budget by 20%.

Step Three(A): Determine the likelihood of the upside as a probability.

Your marketing director estimates that you have a 65% chance of being awarded the entire contract. However, the agency has the right to split the overall contract between your firm and the competition. The marketing director has no idea how much business you could get if the split happens.

Step Three(B): Determine the likelihood of the downside as a probability.

If you do not get any part of the order, there is a 90% chance you will need to cut spending immediately.

Step Four: Determine where the upside and downside risks will have their biggest impacts to your organisation. If there is more than one, you can apply this step to each area. The impact could be to something tangible such as sales (turnover), profits or cash. And it could impact things such as your brand, reputation, or viability.

Example: If you are awarded the full order, it will significantly improve the viability of your organisation. If you do not get any part of the order your cash balances will take a big hit.

Step Five: Use the grid to determine the size of your opportunity.

Example: Regarding winning the business, you think the probability is high (left side) and the impact will be high as well. Your opportunity falls into the "high risk" category, as shown in the upper right-hand quadrant.

Step Six: Use the grid to determine the size of your risk.

Example: Of course, if you do not win the business, you will be in dire straits. That can be slightly tempered in that you might be awarded part of it. Based upon thoughtful analysis, you think the probability of running out of cash is low and the impact on your business, should it happen, is high. Therefore, this risk falls into the "medium risk" category, as shown in the lower right-hand quadrant.

Step Seven: Next you turn to the second grid for your approach to managing the risk.

Part Two–How to Use the Risk and Opportunity Management Grid

The second part of this tool, in Figure 5-5, assigns each quadrant a number, which indicates a management strategy to use. This tool focuses mostly on the negative impact of both opportunities and risk. Remember, even upsides and windfalls have a cost attached to them that you may not be able to afford.

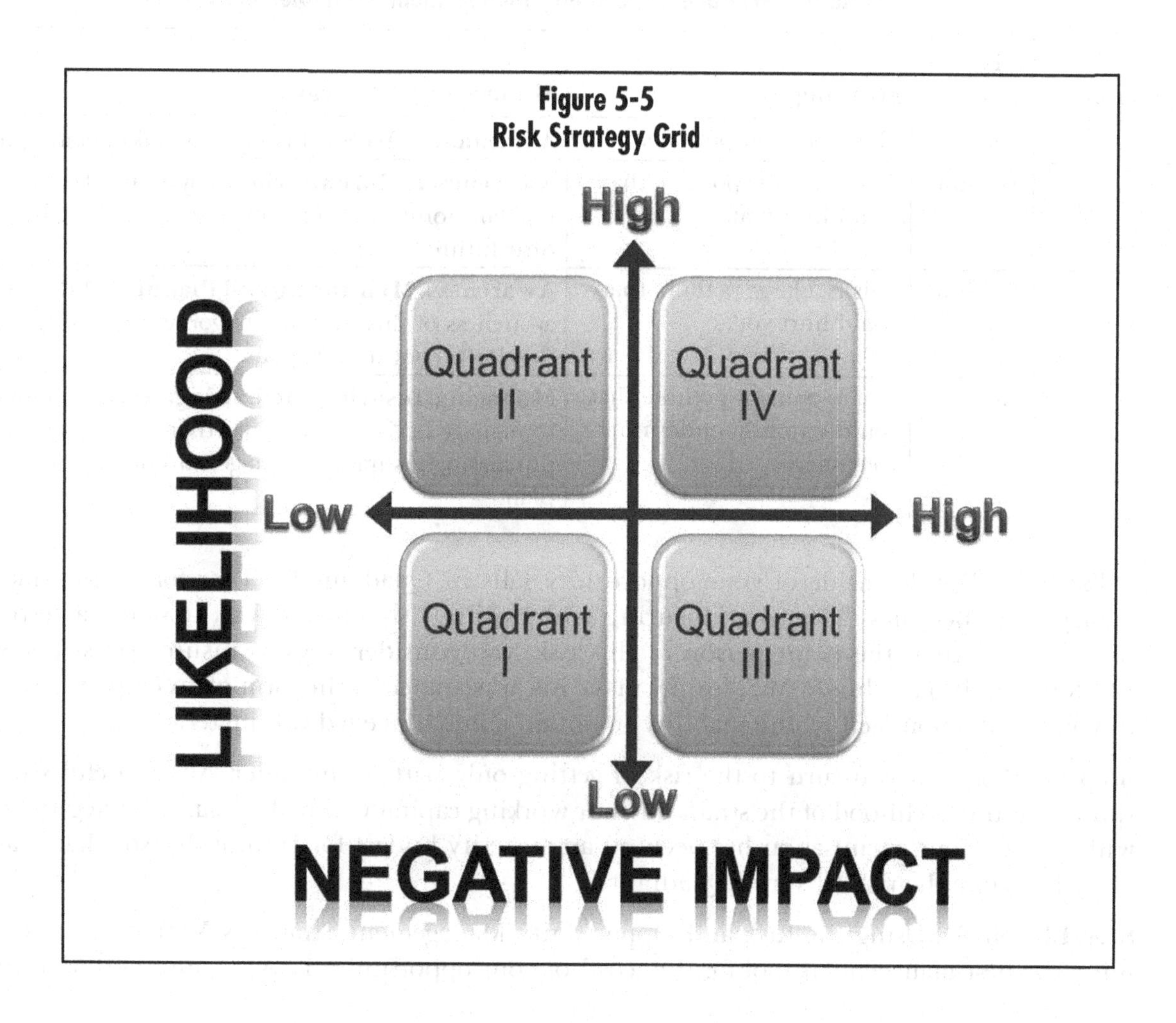

Step Eight: As before, go through the same thoughtful process for the opportunity. Focus on the potential negative impact of it.

Example: If you are awarded the entire contract, you will have to ramp up production quickly. Since there has been a hiring freeze for some time, getting your production facility up to speed will requiring hiring expensive temporaries, buying large quantities of materials and depleting your cash balances (and tapping lines of credit) until you get paid by the agency.

Step Nine: As before, go through the same thoughtful process for the risk.

Example: You are feeling some pessimism that you will get the full order and assume that your firm will be awarded about 20% or $10 million in new orders. This will mean no further layoffs but you will need to carefully watch cash balances and expenses carefully for the next year.

Step Ten (A): Use the risk management grid tool to determine how you will manage the risk inherent in this opportunity.

Example: Since you believe you have a 65% chance of being awarded the entire order you think that the likelihood of the drain on your cash will be high. You also think that the negative impact on your liquidity will be high as well. This means this opportunity falls in Quadrant IV (upper right hand quarter).

Step Eleven (A): Next, you turn to the Risk and Opportunity Management Strategies Matrix, in Table 5-1 to determine how to best manage the "cost" of your opportunity.

Table 5-1 Risk and Opportunity Management Strategies Matrix

Quadrant	Risk Level	Meaning	Management Strategy
I	Low	This is a small pothole.	**Acceptance:** Accept this as a normal operating reality.
II	Medium	This is a large pothole that could hurt you.	**Awareness and Monitoring:** Stay aware of this, conduct regular monitoring, and consider reassessing in the near future.
III	Medium	This is a large pothole that could hurt you.	**Awareness, Monitoring and Planning:** Increase awareness of this, conduct ongoing monitoring, and develop a contingency plan.
IV	High	This is a major pothole that could seriously undermine your success.	**Managing, Insuring and Exiting:** Appoint a manager to manage it, "insure" it by partnering, sharing or purchasing insurance coverage, and develop an exit plan.

Example: The downside of your opportunity falls in Quadrant IV. Therefore your strategy for managing it becomes "Managing, Insuring and Exiting." This means you appoint a responsible senior executive as the point person of this risk, you consider ways to insure yourself as well as develop an exit plan should Mr. Murphy make his appearance in the form of an employee strike, fire in your production facility, the inability to obtain a much needed raw material, etc.

Step Ten (B): Next you turn to the risk of getting only part of the order. After careful study, you think that the likelihood of the strain on your working capital will be high and the negative impact will be low. (Your organisation has been on an austerity budget for 16 months, so what is another 12?). Therefore the risk falls into Quadrant II.

Step Eleven (B): Using the Risk and Opportunity Management Strategies Matrix again you determine the best management tool for the "cost" of your opportunity is "Awareness and Monitoring."

Step Twelve: This last step is to move ahead with your plans. Should any conditions change significantly up or down, go through these steps again.

Part Three–How to Use the Matrix Values and Impact Zones Tables
Some organisation's leaders want a more statistical method for measuring their risk before deciding what to do. That is where the rest of this tool comes into play.

The third aspect of this tool, Tables 5-2, 5-3, and 5-4 are used to assign numerical rankings and management responsibility to particular risks and opportunities.

Step One: Define the risk or opportunity in as much detail as possible.

Step Two: Use the Risk and Opportunity Measurement Grid (Figure 5-4) to decide the level. First select the probability as either high or low. Be clear about how you define each of these terms. Then do the same for the impact or significance, as either high or low. Be clear about how you define those because you want to use consistent definitions as you examine a portfolio of similar risks.

Step Three: Use the Matrix Values from the Criteria Ranking Table (5-2) to assign your risk or peril a relational number from 1 to 9 with nine being the highest.

If you believe your risk is a level 10, then it needs to be treated as a crisis, eg, the explosion at the Japanese nuclear power station.

Table 5-2 Criteria Ranking Table

Area of Significance	Probability	Priorities	Ranking
Global or strategic or cultural (10,000 metres)	High	High	9
Global or strategic or cultural (10,000 metres)	Medium	High	8
Operational or capability or marketing (10,000 metres)	High	High	7
Global or strategic or cultural (10,000 metres)	Low	Medium	6
Operational or capability or marketing (10,000 metres)	Medium	Medium	5
Administrative or activity (100 metres)	High	Medium	4
Operational or capability or marketing (10,000 metres)	Low	Low	3
Administrative or activity (100 metres)	Medium	Low	2
Administrative or activity (100 metres)	Low	Low	1

The second table (5-3) is the Alternative Matrix Criteria Ranking Table. They both show the same numerical rankings. The first is more linear than the second. Use the one that is easier to explain to people.

Table 5-3 Alternative Matrix Criteria Ranking Table

Probability is...	Numerical Ranking		
High	6	8	9
Medium	3	5	7
Low	1	2	4
Significance	Low	Medium	High

Step Four: Define where the greatest impact of the risk or opportunity will be. You have three choices: 1) the Global or Strategic or Cultural (10,000 meter) level; 2) the Operational or Capability or Marketing (3,000 meter) level, and 3) the Activity or Administrative (100 meter) level.

Examples: A natural disaster will be detrimental to all three levels so it has global impact. A limited general strike could be detrimental to making or delivering your products so it is classified as having an operational or capability impact. A fatal car accident involving a key non-executive employee will likely have the lowest level impact, so you classify it as activity or administrative.

Step Five: Use the Risk or Opportunity Management Responsibilities Matrix (5-4) to define who would be responsible and accountable for both monitoring and managing the specific risk.

Table 5-4 Risk or Opportunity Management Responsibilities Matrix

Matrix Value	Area of Impact			Opportunity or Risk Managed by	
	Global	Operational	Activity	Primarily	Secondarily
7–9	✓			Senior executive	Manager or Director
4–6	✓			Manager or Director	Informed employee
1–3	✓			Informed employee	Informed employee
7–9		✓		Manager or Director	Informed employee
4–6		✓		Manager or Director	Senior executive
1–3		✓		Informed employee	Informed employee
7–9			✓	Manager or Director	Informed employee
4–6			✓	Informed employee	Informed employee
1–3			✓	Informed employee	Informed employee

Step Six: To communicate what your analysis looks like and support why you chose a specific way to handle it, use the next two views of this comprehensive tool, shown in Tables 5-5 and 5-6.

For an effective risk management programme it is wise to appoint a primary manager over the risk that is supported by a second employee. Here is what your final product or report will look like.

Table 5-5 Tool Report Part 1

Risk Examples	Probability	Significance	Matrix Value
1) Earthquake or other natural disaster	Low	High	7
2) Unauthorised entry into company database	Medium	High	8
3) Unexpected loss of CEO	Low	Medium	4
4) Vehicle accident	Medium	Low	2
5) Employee strike	Medium	Medium	5

Table 5-6 Tool Report Part 2

Risk Examples	Matrix Value	Managed by	Supported by
1) Earthquake or other natural disaster	7	Senior executive	Manager/Director
2) Unauthorised entry into company database	8	Senior executive	Manager/Director
3) Unexpected loss of CEO	4	Manager/Director	Informed employee
4) Vehicle accident	2	Informed employee	Informed employee
5) Employee strike	5	Manager/Director	Informed employee

Outcome

This comprehensive tool provides several solutions. It is a tool that a key employee, supervisor, and director can easily use and teach to others. It also quickly points out the optimal strategy to manage the opportunity or risk and then shows the most viable employee to take on that responsibility.

Regular use of this tool leads to quicker decision making once specific risks and opportunities are identified.

Risk Management Tool Eighteen–Controllable, Negotiable and Given Analysis

Sometimes, despite your best plans, there are conditions in a risk, peril or challenge that you must accept and cannot change. For example I love sunshine, and I love living in Seattle, Washington, but one thing I accept about living in the northwest United States is that I won't experience as much sunshine as I would in the Bahamas, Dubai or Hawaii.

Yet in risk management you can always influence the outcome, which may lower your exposure or help you recover faster. The tool you can apply to show you how to influence your vulnerabilities is the controllable, negotiable and given analysis. This tool allows you to identify some of the specific actions you can take in order to minimise or mitigate a risk.

Table 8-4 Given, Negotiable and Controllable Analysis

Givens **Aspects of the risk that we cannot control or that are unchangeable**	**Negotiables** **Aspects of the risk that we can influence by substitution or alteration**	**Controllables** **Aspects of the risk that can lessen the impact of the given**
We must use purchasing cards for all supplies and related buys under $5,000.		
We will be unable to work with some existing vendors who cannot accept the P card.		
We must be able to handle the administration of P cards with existing staffing.		
Verifying the account coding of each purchase can be time consuming but is an important internal control.		
The cards can contain only one account code in their memory.		
Verification about the correctness of each purchase is an important control.		
All managers will be issued a P card for use by their department.		
Companies that use centralised purchasing will be issued a P card.		

How to Complete the Controllable, Negotiable and Given Analysis

Step One: Write out a clear description of the risk to be undertaken.

Step Two: Prepare a chart that describes the various aspects.

Step Three: List all the givens for the risk or problem.

A given is a condition you cannot change or do much about, such as accepting that the Islands of the Bahamas have hurricanes each year that destroy some homes and accepting that you cannot afford to move to Seattle (where we have less sun but no hurricanes).

Step Four: List as many negotiable conditions you can think of.

A negotiable is an aspect of the situation that allows you to influence the outcome by substitution, bargaining or some other action. Living in the Bahamas, your insurance company raises the rates for homeowner's coverage. You cannot go without insurance, but maybe you can work with your agent to lower coverage on your overall policy, so that the premium increase is affordable.

Step Five: List as many controllable conditions you can think of.

An aspect of a risk is considered controllable if you can do something to lessen the impact of an unchangeable given.

You may not be able to control the weather in the Bahamas, but you could reinforce your house's foundation. You could install trees that block winds from hitting your house. You could invest in new designs of windows, doors and roof that are more resistant to high winds. As for personal protection you could store important papers, jewellery and other irreplaceable items in an underground storage facility.

Step Six: Turn the negotiable and controllable items you list into action steps.

Outcome

Notice that, although you may not be able to avoid a hurricane, you can take steps to reduce your vulnerability while preparing to recover faster.

In combination with the previous tool, you now have a concrete plan on how to both manage and mitigate the risk. Even if you never have to employ any of your predetermined tactics or actions, you will always have the confidence that you will be able to react quickly and wisely should Mr. Murphy make his untimely appearance as you and others execute on the goal.

Risk Management Tool Ten– Responsibility Statement

A specific way enables you and other leaders to get employees to see that formal risk management is now part of their responsibilities. This simple and impactful tool is a statement that describes how you want each employee to be both enrolled and engaged in your risk management programme.

How to Use the Responsibility Statement

Step One: Place this statement in every employee's job description.

"Every employee plays a critical role in this organisation's risk management process. Proactively preventing unnecessary, unwarranted or improper risk is expected from everyone.

You are responsible for:

- seeking out where we waste company resources.
- offering suggestions to save both money and time.
- watching for hidden opportunities to create new revenue or income.
- suggesting ways to make your work more productive.

- offering ideas that make you more effective.
- thoughtfully expending company resources.
- making smart decisions.
- identifying problems and ways to overcome them.
- regularly asking, "What is the downside of my action or decision?"

Whenever you see areas where we put ourselves and each other at risk, your responsibility is to proactively fix the problem or implement a solution. If you are unable to do so, then please consult with your team, supervisor or another manager about the issue, so they can support you in fixing the problem."

Step Two: Treat this directive as you do with the rest of the employee's job responsibilities. Require that the supervisor ask and answer questions about how the employee carries this out within the scope of their regular duties. At first your employees will not know what you want. This is why regular training and reviews of these duties are important. Your leads, supervisors, and managers are the key to getting all employees enrolled and engaged the right way.

Step Three: Add these responsibilities to each employee's performance evaluation. Once the employees know that retaining their job depends in part on seeking out and doing something about risk, they will take this responsibility seriously. You can also use this to coach the employees who are reluctant or unwilling to do their part in managing risk. Remember, on-the-job risk management just like on-the-job safety. If an employee refuses to do his or her part in promoting safety it becomes a cause for termination. Hopefully, it will never come to that. But if one of employee refuses to support risk management, they do not belong in your organisation.

Step Four: Design and implement rewards and recognition for employees who openly live up to this responsibility.

Outcome
With this tool, you have a formal notification to all employees that your organisation takes risk management seriously. This tool starts to embed it in your cultural norms. When you also include this accountability and empowerment into your performance evaluations and rewards those who practice it, the attitude of risk awareness becomes a permanent part of your culture's DNA.

Risk Management Tool Fifteen–Formalised Action Plan

The tool that communicates what to do is the formalised action plan. An action plan is a visual definition or map of what it will take to make significant progress on a specific objective. The payoff from using formalised action plans is the ability to communicate accountability to people.

The contents of an action plan include the following:

- Overall strategic goal
- Deliverables and due dates
- Major steps
- Detailed steps or tasks
- Individual responsibilities of participants
- Anticipated obstacles and challenges
- Performance metrics
- Risk assessment summary

Each action plan should define each level of change responsibility at the outset. Action plan participants include the

- sponsor, who is the person who has the ability to pay for the change and has ultimate accountability.
- advocate, who is the person who drives, wants or demands the change.
- customer, who is the person(s) who benefits from the change.
- agent of change, who is the person(s) who carries the responsibility for facilitating the change.
- accountability partner, who is the person who will help keep pressure on the change agent and is usually an executive the change agent regularly reports to about the progress (or lack of) made towards the plan's end state.
- risk owner, who is the person who serves in an oversight capacity to ensure that any risk is addressed and mitigated once it gets identified.

The action plan tool is for

- highlighting overall global or high-level objectives.
- showing expected or desired results.
- keeping track of actual results.
- holding employees to their authority.
- identifying risks in advance.
- allocating resources to something that needs to get accomplished.

How to Use the Formalised Action Plan

Step One: Define the overall strategic intent of the action plan (initiative). This is the big picture about the work being proposed.

Step Two: Connect the goal to the organisation's annual or strategic plan. This ties the specific activity to the 34,000 foot view of the company. If the person proposing the activity cannot find a connection, they must answer this question to senior management:

Why do you want to divert our precious and limited resources for this, since it is not considered a current priority of the organisation?

Step Three: Explain how the activity connects to the risk management programme. There may or may not be connections. However, this proposed goal or activity was vetted by risk management tool 3 (in Step Two) so the person who asks for approval will have identified several pitfalls or vulnerabilities. This is then described in this section. It assists the person or team approving and funding this activity in making a risk-sensitive decision.

Step Four: Break the plan into major action steps. These are usually connected to the plan's deliverables. Be sure that these are only the major activities and not the detailed ones.

Step Five: Describe in detail the anticipated obstacles and challenges that will be faced in carrying this plan out. Each of these could be a risk and even if a challenge or obstacle is not, it identifies work that must be done and resources that must be expended. This speeds up the approval process.

Step Six: This step is optional but helpful for the approval process. Describe some of the more important work activities or tasks that will be used to reach the goal. In an action plan that is large in scope, there will be too many to list. The intent of this step is to help the people approving this to determine if the commitment of resources is wise and the time frame realistic. Unfortunately, employees who want to do something that benefits them personally (instead of benefiting their employer) will put in very optimistic deadlines and only part of the resources required to carry the plan out.

Step Seven: Show a detailed list of all the financial resources, people and money required to carry the plan to its natural conclusion. In effect, the person proposing it provides a full-term budget for their plan. This step really jump starts the accountability inherent in this tool.

Step Eight: List all the various deliverables and their corresponding due dates.

While the due dates might be delayed or postponed, the key in this step are the deliverables. All too often work is undertaken without any hint about the work products to be produced along the way. Much later, no one can identify what was accomplished because no one included a list of deliverables. The deliverables together with the budget boost the accountability factor.

Step Nine: Detail the economic impact of this plan. In order for the person approving this to know if the investment of time and money is worth it, they need to know what improvements the work will be to the top line, bottom line, or fortunes of the business. When combined with the costs, in Step Seven, it will be easy to determine if the benefit exceeds the cost, or the cost exceeds the benefits.

Step Ten: Identify the team of employees (and maybe outsiders) who will be involved in the plan and each person's duties, role, and accountability.

I am sure you, like me, get frustrated each time a plan goes awry and when the reason is sought, the answer is: "Decisions were made." Someone made those decisions but does not want to be identified. With this step, that will never happen.

Step Eleven: For the approval process to work, the employee proposing it meets face-to-face with the approval person or team to answer questions regarding the action plan. This interactive dialog helps to foster communication and allow both parties to be heard.

Step Twelve: If the plan is not approved, the person who proposes it is allowed to amend the plan in order to resubmit it. This requires that the approving person give specific reasons why the plan was not considered to be a priority.

Step Thirteen: Assuming the original or revised plan gets approved and funded, everyone on the team is given a copy of the plan. It is used as a roadmap for the work being done. Whenever the team meets, they will use the plan as their primary agenda. Any major adjustments (except for the work activities or tasks) to the plan get reflect in an amendment to the plan and is provided to all those involved.

Outcome

This tool produces amazing results in many areas. Before your employees proceed to take on a big project, they have a clear, approved blueprint of what is being done. The team involved gets it done sooner and the organisation saves money. When combined with the next tool, the level of accountability around special projects and initiatives goes up 400% or more.

Risk Management Tool Sixteen–Formalised Action Plan Summary

To raise the visibility of the various action plans that are underway, the executive team needs a way to track them and stay informed of their current status. The action plan summary in Exhibit 8-2 is a tool that accomplishes that and more.

Quite frequently managers and others ask for resources to get something done and promise higher sales or lower costs as the rationale. Yet just as often, there is no verification if the promised financial benefits are ever achieved. This tool requires that the action plan's sponsor regularly reports on the resources expended and the financial impact achieved as of the reporting period.

Think about that. If you ask for $500,000 to accomplish something, and you must undergo a monthly face-to-face check-in with the CEO to tell him or her what has been accomplished with the money you were granted, I will bet that you'd take this endeavour seriously. As a result, tracking the financial and budgetary aspects of each action plan really enhances accountability.

Exhibit 8-2

Action Plan Reporting Tool

Action Plans Summary with Financial Results

as of April 30, 20XX

Employees Involved	Action Plan Objective	Expected Financial Results: Increased Sales $$	Expected Financial Results: (Decreased) Expenses $$	Actual Financial Results: Increased Sales $$	Actual Financial Results: (Decreased) Expenses $$
Sponsor–Junie (CEO) Advocate–Board of Directors Customers–Purchasing, Sales Champion–Roy R. Agents–Paula, Keith, Donovan	Profitably disposed of obsolete and dropped game inventory	$50,000	$27,600	$0	$17,829
Sponsor– Advocate– Customers– Champion– Agent–					
Sponsor– Advocate– Customers– Champion– Agent–					

Definitions

Sponsor–The person with ultimate accountability who has the ability to pay for the change.

Advocate–The person who drives, wants, demands the change.

Customers–The recipients who benefit from the change.

Agents–The persons responsible for facilitating the change through to the end.

Champion–The person heading up the action plan's efforts.

How to Use the Formalised Action Plan Summary

Step One: Once an action plan gets approved (as described in the previous tool) it gets added to this report and tracking tool. The master of this report need to be accessible by all the members of the project team so they can keep it updated. It works best if it is updated in real-time. If you lack that capability, the project team needs to update their contributions at least weekly.

Step Two: As milestones are met and resources are expended, the project's champion updates that on the summary. This requires your accounting team to monitor the direct spending that is associated with this plan.

Step Three: On a regular basis, at least monthly, the executive team meets with each plan's sponsor to get a status report.

The focus will be a comparison of what we proposed with what has been accomplished. Since the original plan contains all the elements necessary to measure progress—resources, deliverables, deadliness, and benefits—it will be clearly evident if the work is being done on time and on budget. These regularly scheduled meetings prevent the team champion and sponsor from saying, "I don't know what is going on."

Best of all, your senior leaders will easily spot who is being accountable to them and who is not.

Outcome

Action without follow-up and reporting leads to weak accountability. Weak accountability leads to increased risk. In ERM you will have many employees taking actions designed to reduce risk or take advantage of opportunities. This tool requires that your employees be ready and able to account for their actions and resources on a regular basis. This transparency enhancement prevents employees from wasting time and resources.

Tools for Step Five: Quickly Recover from the Negative Impacts of the Risk

Risk Management Tool Nineteen– Criteria Checkerboard

A tool called a criteria checkerboard allows you to analyse the exposure of a specific risk and then use the information to determine how to proceed. It is a key tool used by consultants for defining and matching the criteria for success with the possible alternatives. Using this information you can analyse your exposure to a risk and then use the data to decide the best solution or path to take.

Table 9-1 Criteria Checkerboard

Proposed Solution →	**Serve as manager of a planned community**
Criterion for a Best Solution:↓	
Quickly create a positive cash flow.	X
Invest in an asset that can be quickly and easily sold.	X
Manage the investment without a lot of overhead.	X
Be the primary decision maker.	X
Enhance our firm's reputation as a strategic investor.	✓
Diversify our portfolio of investments.	✓
Symbols:	
✓: Satisfies the criteria.	
X: Does not satisfy the criteria.	
?: Lacking information–more research is required.	

How to Complete the Criteria Checkerboard

Step One: Describe the risk or problem.

Step Two: Select your criteria for a best decision.

Step Three: Brainstorm alternative solutions. Every alternative is acceptable and possible, and no idea is too outrageous. You write down every idea as it is presented. You stay open to the idea no matter the source or rationale for it. Later you go back and narrow the list down to the more reasonable or realistic alternatives.

Step Four: List the criteria and alternatives on a checkerboard tool.

Step Five: Check off, using symbols, how well each solution meets your criteria.

Step Six (A): Examine the original criteria to determine their validity or reasonableness.

Step Six (B): Alter or revise the criteria and retest.

Step Seven: Add or change the scenarios (solutions) to test how well they match up with your success criteria.

Step Eight: Answer these questions:

- How will this alternative or course of action reduce our exposure to the negative consequences of this risk?
- Which of these alternatives meets our need for a best solution?
- Why is it optimal?
- Is there any other criterion or alternative we have not considered?
- What will we do with this information?

Step Nine: Make your decision based upon which solution satisfies the most criteria.

Outcome

There are probably more vulnerabilities that your organisation is subject to than time to pay attention to them. All your employees have many tasks beyond seeking out risks. So your employees need a way to decide which action to take very quickly. This tool empowers your key decision makers to act once they have thought through the risk.

Risk Management Tool Twelve–The Five Whys

This tool, known as the "Five Whys," allows you to find the root causes of risks that can lead to high exposures. The contributor to the downside of risk taking is rarely in physical things, such as bricks, mortar, technology or tools. Most of the time your operational and strategic perils are generated or caused by the way people think and act or use your assets.

How to Use the Five Whys

Step One: State the risk as a problem.

Step Two: Ask: "Why is this happening?" or "Why did this happen?"

Normally most of us would stop at the first why and react to the problem. If you only do that, however, all you have accomplished is dealing with the smoke. You failed to search for the cause of your fire. Because you are committed to risk management, you want to prevent the fire or risk from recurring. You keep drilling down into the problem.

Step Three(A): Based upon the answer you received in Step Two, ask again "Why is this happening?" or "Why did this happen?"

I will pause to review the ethical implications and risks of this situation. Assume the answer you obtain is: "the employee failed to follow policy." As someone who is concerned with the ethical attitude of your employees, you would jump up and down and demand that any employee who did not follow the rules be terminated, but how do you know if this situation is an isolated incident, a trend or a normal practice?

Step Three(B): Based upon the previous answer, ask again "Why is this happening?" or "Why did this happen?"

Step Three(C): Based upon the previous answer, ask again "Why is this happening?" or "Why did this happen?"

At this point you will start getting to the root cause. By regularly using this "Five Whys" tool, you will find that the root cause is often based around human issues, such as power, emotion, drive, greed or lust. Some human frailty is involved with lingering problems, especially those related to unwarranted risk taking and ethical breaches.

Step Three(D): Based upon the previous answer, ask again "Why is this happening?" or "Why did this happen?"

Continue to ask why until you get to a root cause that you can do something about and, when reduced or eliminated, will change the situation for the better. You do not have to stop at five whys. You can persist in asking why as many times as needed to find all the possible sources of your fire.

Step Four: Summarise your findings, and develop your recommendation for improvements that will lessen the factors that contribute to risk.

Outcome

What you will discover in using the "Five Whys" tool is that you may have split the authority with responsibility. You may have in place an incentive in the form of a bonus that did not shape the behaviour you wanted.

The lesson from this tool is that once you find the root cause for your exposures, you can take quick action to reduce the negative impacts and find solutions to prevent more exposure.

Risk Management Tool Thirteen– Establish Contingency Funds

While some leaders do not approve of this method, it is practical for unexpected risks or exposures, like emergencies or lawsuits. The funds that are set for a specific purpose have specific restrictions on their use and can only be spent when the specified conditions arise. If these funds are never used, they can either be carried over to the next budget year or fall to the bottom-line and increase the profits.

How to Use Contingency Funds

Step One: Determine if a particular risk may have a financial impact that could drain your resources, should it take place.

Example: Assume this is the deductible and co-pay on insurance that covers the construction of a new building. You have adequate financing for the building which is located in a hurricane zone. Once the building is completed, your will have adequate insurance coverage but not during the construction phase, which will take two and a half years.

Step Two: Determine the amount of financial resources that will require to quick recovery.

To protect yourself and not take money away from the business, you set aside a contingency fund equal to maximum out-of-pocket exposure.

Step Three: Set specific condition on the use of those funds you set aside.

Only when one of these conditions occurs can some of the funds be expended. This contingency fund cannot be used for any other purposes or other risk exposures.

Step Four: Re-examine the needs for the particular contingency each budget period.

If this Murphy's Law event covered by the contingency fund does not happen in the current year, then you carry the fund over to next year. Each year you can maintain or modify the conditions under which the dollars can be spent.

Step Five: If the funds are never required, decide what to do with the funds.

After a certain point of time, when the company meets all its targets related to the risk, the funds can then be returned by reversing the contingency expense, thus adding to the current year's profits because of good management.

This is how to properly handle a contingency fund.

Outcome

When you take the time to look for pitfalls and then develop contingency plans in advance, you grow in confidence in your ability to face or accept more risk. Better yet, you reduce exposure in both the short and long term.

Risk Management Tool Seventeen– Pitfall Analysis

The tool for helping you quickly recover is a pitfall analysis. You may already think in terms of pitfalls and coming up with alternative plans. It is a way of life for many, but other people do not think like this. This tool works for both methodical planners and people who normally act spontaneously. This tool forces the user to think of options. Using this decision making tool, you can create ways to lessen your risk exposure.

This tool is a complement for scenario planning of potential problems done at the employee level.

How to Conduct a Pitfall Analysis

Step One: List the possible pitfalls or obstacles of a particular course of action. Use a format like the table below.

Step Two: Create a contingency action plan for each pitfall.

Step Three: Determine what would prevent implementing the solution.

Pitfall	Contingency Plan

Outcome

When your employees believe they have no options, they feel helpless or disempowered. This tool proves the numerous ways to lessen or mitigate a pitfall or pothole. The act may seem insignificant at first, but what the tool does is instil the confidence that you always have options and that Murphy's Law is rarely fatal.

Tools for Step Five and One-Half: Learn Something, So You Can Accept Even Greater Risk with Confidence

Risk Management Tool Twenty– Plus/ Delta Analysis

The plus/delta analysis shown in Figure 9-1 is an excellent learning tool for every aspect of risk management, especially looking back to learn from the recent past. The plus/delta analysis is a summary of actions worthy of repeating and that need improving. It spawns rapid improvements, shortens learning curves and increases accountability. The plus/delta analysis gives executives, managers, employees and the risk oversight team invaluable insight on what to continue doing and what to improve. You use this tool as you plan for each risky venture, as progress reports of an on-going action plan and at the end of each opportunity taken. At every phase of your project or activity, the things that are working are identified as pluses, and the improvements, called deltas, are noted.

Figure 9-1
The Plus/Delta Tool

Pluses + (Things that worked and should be retained or repeated)	Deltas Δ (Things that need to change or be improved)

Compliance with the Sarbanes-Oxley Act of 2002 (SOX) in the US and similar legislation in Canada, Australia, Japan and the UK demands this sort of documentation because companies that got into trouble due to a high risk exposure were unable to prove the soundness of the reasons for taking the risk in the first place.

How to Use the Plus/Delta Analysis

Step One: In a normal or regular gathering of the participants, announce the purpose of the plus/delta analysis: to learn what works and gather suggestions for improvement.

Step Two: Spend adequate time gathering a list of conditions, activities and decisions that have worked well and list them on the "pluses" side.

Step Three: Spend time gathering a list of conditions, activities and decisions that people would like to see changed and list them on the "deltas" side. An idea for the delta column must be stated as an improvement, not a complaint. For example, "The room was too cold," is a complaint and not very actionable. "Someone appointed to monitor and adjust the room temperature," is a suggestion and recommends an action to be taken.

Step Four: Before the next committee meeting or stage of work, address the changes (deltas) that were recommended and accommodate those that cannot be changed. Remember there are many ways to pare an apple.

Step Five: Early in the next meeting review the most recently completed plus/delta analysis.

Step Six: Remind people in your group to continue to do what is working (pluses).

Step Seven: Inform the group of the changes that will happen as a result of their suggestions (deltas).

Step Eight: Explain those improvements that cannot be implemented, and brainstorm alternatives.

Step Nine: Continue to use the plus/delta tool at each meeting, event or gathering.

Step Ten: Notice and celebrate how quickly improvements are taking place.

Step Eleven: Retain all your plus/delta analyses because it is good documentation to prove you are being proactive in addressing risk to your boss, an insurance auditor, or your CA firm who may be checking for regulatory compliance.

Figure 9-2
Completed Plus/Delta

Pluses + (Things that worked and should be retained or repeated)	**Deltas Δ** (Things that need to change or be improved)
Giving us a workbook to take notes in.	Every employee should take this training.
Using hands-on learning of the tools.	The sessions need to be shorter and more frequent.
Using our problems and risks.	Offer more examples and suggestions for things that every employee sees in the scope of his or her job.
Making risk management simple.	I want to be able to use my cell phone during the session.
Using analogies, stories and Murphy's Law.	
Providing us with food and many breaks.	
Having us sit with the executives and managers.	
Explaining how ERM pays for itself.	

Outcome

This tool is used for both a lessons learned protocol and to demonstrate empowerment. At first employees may be reluctant to offer suggestions for improvement. But once they see that their suggestions work and are taken seriously, they buy into the process and continue to offer fresh ideas. The ideas make their jobs easier and remove many of the obstacles they see.

In addition, when used in your risk management structure, people will automatically see how easy it is to spot perils and potholes.

Appendix B

What Happened in 2007?

One day after a session was over and people were leaving, Justin invited me to dinner.

I knew he had something serious on his mind. Justin does things on his own schedule and time, so I was not surprised that during dinner he regaled me with funny stories about his adventures in New Mexico and his childhood dreams of being a cowboy. As we waited for the dishes to be cleared, Justin turned serious. "I now understand risk management thanks to you. Something has been weighing on my mind, though, and it has nothing to do with PJI. As an expert can you tell me what happened to the U.S. banking system? I know that we were on the edge of the cliff and thankfully recovered somewhat. Was it a failure of risk management?"

I responded, "In my opinion the answer is 'Yes' and 'No.'"

Poor Risk Management Did Not Foster the Great Recession

The reason I say "No" is because what happened in the United States and abroad was a failure of many different systems. An event that wasn't supposed to happen did happen. True to Murphy's law, when one institution, such as the mortgage lending system, failed, it triggered a failure of another system, and that triggered the failure of another. Soon it became like a line of dominos in which one fallen domino triggers the next domino and so on.

I refer to this economic meltdown as the Great Recession, a term made popular by media pundits. According to the "experts," this sort of fiscal collapse was not supposed to happen, yet it did happen. Douglas Hubbard, president of Hubbard Decision Research, said in a December 2009 interview in *CFO* magazine, "None of the events we've experienced was completely unforeseeable, even if it was extremely unlikely."

As a direct result of the global decline and financial meltdown, these major risks hit businesses all at once:

- A credit crunch
- Volatile commodity pricing
- The size and scope of government debt
- Lingering and high unemployment
- Lower levels of consumer spending
- Local governments' need for additional revenue
- Escalating oil prices caused in part by political instability in the Middle East

Each of these might be a negative event, yet by themselves they did not cause the Great Recession. They only weakened our economic structures that were supposed to prevent a global collapse.

I believe that, in part, risk management was not to blame for the Great Recession because perfect storms happen, and the best forecasting systems in the world could not have predicted this domino effect going global. It reminds me of a YouTube video that goes viral. No one can explain exactly what creates the feeding frenzy of people wanting to view and forward the video, but it happens anyway.

Poor Risk Management Contributed to the Great Recession

I say "Yes" because even though risk management will not prevent Murphy's Law, it will serve as an early warning system that calls out, "Danger!" Even though the red lights were on, and signals blared out "Warning! Warning!" no one seemed to be paying close attention. Developing a risk management programme alone does not decrease risk or its negative consequences. The economic crash that preceded the Great Recession was in large part caused by poor risk management. Unwarranted risk engendered by these factors caused the financial meltdown:

- Banks that made reckless bets
- Credit rating agencies that endorsed risky mortgage bonds
- Government regulators who overlooked danger signs until the signs threatened our global financial system
- Advisers and consultants who did not understand the complexity of the securities that were being packaged, bought and sold

The Financial Crisis Inquiry Report published by the Financial Crisis Inquiry Commission in January 2011 concluded that the crisis might have been prevented if banks had been more careful, and regulators had asked tougher questions. According to the report complex investments backed by risky subprime mortgages were barely understood by both regulators and bank executives. Meanwhile the Federal Reserve was the only entity that could force higher standards on lenders that would have slowed the torrent of deals that led to the crisis. The Federal Reserve failed to act quickly enough.

In some situations executives claimed they were blindsided by unknown risks, mostly because they lacked sufficient infrastructure to identify, assess and monitor emerging risks within their organisation and because they were overconfident about their ad hoc approaches to managing risk.

I do believe that if those organisations that were too big to fail and that became the first dominos to fall had honestly been applying the principles of enterprise risk management (ERM), the global economic crisis would not have been as painful and disastrous as it turned out. Notice the big *if.* They were not applying ERM, strategic risk management or even simple risk management as it was designed to be used.

To me what happened for several years leading up to 2007 was a tale of woe.

Mr Smith invests in a costly and state-of-the-art security system for his expensive and richly furnished home. Smith leaves for a month-long vacation but leaves his system turned off. Upon his return Smith is surprised to find that his house has been burglarised and vandalised. Even though he wants to blame the perpetrators, Smith needs to own his culpability. Smith told everyone about his plans. He failed to cancel his newspaper delivery. He failed to arrange for someone to cut the grass and water the lawn. Smith left all the blinds and curtains shut and did not leave on any lights, inside or out. Worst of all Smith failed to ask a trusted neighbour to watch his house.

I previously quoted Douglas Hubbard who said that much of what happened was unforeseeable and extremely unlikely. He also stated, "The data [that foretold the problem] exists, but we get lost and overwhelmed by it."

I shared with Justin 10 reasons for my opinion.

Reason One: Unreasonable Expectations

We all know that the rising prices in land and buildings were out of control well in advance of 2007. With land and buildings values growing between 4% and 10% per year, it was an unreasonable expectation that it could continue. Growth in many parts of the economy occurred mostly due to a continuing rise in valuations. Despite many experts and pundits claiming the bubble had to burst, very few people and companies changed their expectations about the future of land and buildings. When the collapses occurred at AIG, Lehman Brothers and so on, the dominos quickly fell. Washington Mutual (WaMu) was one company that had unreasonable expectations about the land and buildings market. Its collapse was unexpected, but now that the secrets are out, it can be viewed as inevitable.

In 2003 WaMu adopted a corporate slogan of "The Power of Yes." At approximately that same time, the leaders decided to heavily rely on adjustable rate mortgages because Wall Street had a ravenous appetite for them, and the accounting rules of revenue recognition allowed WaMu to book all the revenue up front without needing to be concerned, profit-wise, about the risk of bad debts. Kerry Killinger, CEO of WaMu, had a vision. He wanted his institution to be the biggest provider of financing for the American public. He envisioned WaMu being among the top five retail banks. He made acquisitions, one after the other, that helped him fulfil that dream. Some acquisitions were risky, but he believed the risks were worth it because of his role in carrying out WaMu's vision and mission.

The primary measurements that Mr. Killinger and his direct reports used to define success were

- share value (stock price).
- quantity of loans sold to Wall Street.
- balance of loans outstanding.
- revenue growth.

When "The Power of Yes" became the cultural mantra, WaMu's revenue and growth soared. WaMu grew to become the nation's sixth largest bank. To make this occur its leaders took on even greater risk, with certain decisions:

- WaMu paid large incentives in the form of commissions (as high as $10,000) to agents who brought in applicants and to brokers who steered WaMu mortgages that it could package and sell.
- WaMu's underwriting employees were pressured to fund the mortgages, but the top producers were lavished with rewards and incentives. One "sweatshop" mortgage centre in southern California produced $1 billion in loans just in 2004. The team's leader was lavished with bonuses and a perennial member of Kerry's President's Club, receiving multiple awards at the club's annual meeting. Other team leaders wanted to get the same recognition.

In the ongoing investigations of WaMu's failure, it came out that its mortgage lenders were ridiculed and chastised whenever they turned down a loan application. That was a direct result of "The Power of Yes." In hindsight the cost of these risks outweighed all the benefits. In July 2008 WaMu reported the biggest quarterly loss in its history: $3.3 billion in the second quarter. The bank added to its loss reserves at a furious pace. The losses from land and buildings mortgage financing ranged between $12m and $19m over the next few years, according to WaMu executives.

Others costs that WaMu could not afford but had to pay were

- having to immediately reduce more than $10 billion in operating expenses.
- getting out of the subprime lending business.
- having to infuse new capital, thus diluting existing shareholders' equity.

Even these actions were too little too late. The Federal Reserve took over WaMu in September 2008.

The risks WaMu undertook through its unreasonable expectations for profits and growth, focusing solely on the upside of higher than average returns and rapid growth, came back to undermine its finances and reputation. Every opportunity comes with a cost.

Reason Two: ERM Software Was Not Used Properly

It is both ironic and surprising that a majority of the financial institutions that got in trouble in the numerous events that led to the Great Recession all used ERM software. Companies that had ERM software in place were not paying attention to it or taking it seriously.

Other firms were having closed-door debates about whether their investment in ERM was worth it. Although a major investment in ERM software is required to fully implement it, many senior executives of large organisations delayed or curtailed implementation due to the required cash layout. They saw the software as a risky move for several reasons:

- They were experiencing a shortage of cash and other resources.
- They were concerned about the lengthy and challenging implementation process.
- They were not sure that the investment in the software would pay for itself.

Reason Three: Governance Was Not a Priority

Proper governance is big news in business and not for profits and is now a very popular discussion topic. As a direct result of the fallout of the ongoing economic crisis, failures associated with existing risk management processes are already generating calls for reform and increased regulatory scrutiny.

Corporate boards of public companies are under great pressure to explicitly address risk management as part of their governance responsibilities. The need has tremendously grown for boards to ensure that the management team in place is proactively managing risk and preventing fraud. The firm's management team has a great opportunity to help its board of directors build an organisation's risk management processes, so the board can focus on strategic risks. Experienced boards want ERM incorporated into their organisation's governance risk management and compliance initiatives because it requires ongoing assessments of everyday business risk.

This being said, many boards and executives only play the governance game when it is easy. The moment governance gets difficult through the examination of sacred cows, such as executive compensation, stock options and conflicts of interest, governance is pushed aside for more "important" things.

Reason Four: Excessive Demand for Profit of Share Price

In most public companies and many smaller ones, the most "important" priorities are generating profits and increasing the stock value. When the bottom line and share price are the most important key performance indicators, anything that interferes with these priorities gets ignored. Investments in ERM implementation have slowed down because executives and boards are not sure the return on investment is there. Also the implementation is long and expensive, mostly because every employee must be repeatedly trained, and ERM requires an upgrade of many systems and technology. The prevailing belief is that this effort takes employees' attention away from making sales and increasing profits. We constantly hear from executives that ERM would be nice to have but not if it costs a lot to implement and maintain. Add to that the message that Wall Street sends to public companies: more profits.

Senior leaders create expectations, which is part of their job. A leader needs an internal drive to get things done through people. Yet this drive and zeal can also cause the leader to cross the line. We see stories about CEOs, CFOs and politicians who have gotten themselves into trouble with their relentless drive to win no matter the cost. Kerry Killinger, former CEO of WaMu, is a poster child for this. His drive for ever increasing profits to satisfy Wall Street, in his mind, gave him permission to take the risks that he did, harming his company, its investors and WaMu's employees.

Reason Five: Assumption Was ERM Runs Itself

The October 2010 report from the Senior Supervisors Group (SSG), comprising financial regulators in seven countries, stated that, despite some recent progress, financial institutions (the first dominos to fall) overestimated the quality of their risk management systems. The SSG reported that despite the failure of their systems in 2007, the banks even today continue to let ERM operate without their involvement. This leads to the practice of allowing ERM to operate at a low level of the organisation without any management concern regarding the risks it uncovers. This is akin to putting your car on cruise control, so you can text while believing the system will warn you when the traffic ahead of you slows down.

Reason Six: Complexity Hid the Problems

Bundling mortgages and turning them into securities was another line of dominos. The underlying assumption of this practice was that as long as the default rate was small, there would be no problems. As soon as real estate values fell, and mortgages went into default, things began to unravel. It appears that all the financial modelling performed was solely focused on the upside of this risk, and apparently the sophisticated algorithms never considered the twin scenarios of falling values and high defaults.

A lot of the risk was hidden or undetected because these deals became more and more complex. A recent survey discussed in the article "Rethinking Risk" in the January 2009 issue of *CFO* magazine reported on the opinions of 125 CFOs who have intimate knowledge about the securitisation of mortgages and other exotic investment schemes. Sixty-two per cent of these senior executives blamed the 2007–08 financial crisis on risk management's inability to understand complex financial instruments.

Reason Seven: ERM Was Not an Executive Priority

In February 2011, Deloitte & Touche reported on the results of a survey it conducted on 1,541 executives, *Creating a Risk Intelligent infrastructure: Getting Risk Intelligence done.* It asked, "How would you rate your organization's current risk infrastructure capability?"

This is how executives described the status of their programmes:

- ERM is in the initial stage (7%).
- ERM efforts are fragmented (21%).
- ERM is top down (23%).
- ERM is fully integrated (17%).

- ERM is risk intelligent (8%).
- Don't know or not applicable (24%).

The survey also asked, "To what extent has your organization implemented 'common' risk management processes?"

The executives responded along with their reasons:

- Not at all. Have redundancy and lack a common risk language (6%).
- A little. Rationalised some control processes but still lack a common risk language (24%).
- Fair amount. Rationalised many key programmes and share common definitions (33%).
- Great deal. Eliminated most redundant processes and share a common risk language (10%).
- Don't know or not applicable (27%).

As discussed in the article "Disaster Averted?" in the April 2011 issue of *CFO* magazine, Deloitte & Touche posed this question to 131 financial institutions worldwide. These firms have an aggregated asset base of over $17 trillion. The survey showed the changes over four years.

Does your organisation have an ERM programme in place?

In 2010

- twenty-seven per cent had a programme in place.
- fifty-two per cent were currently implementing one.

In 2008

- twenty-three per cent had a programme in place.
- thirty-six per cent were currently implementing one.

In 2006

- thirty-two per cent had a programme in place.
- thirty-five per cent were currently implementing one.

Does your organisation have a chief risk officer or equivalent?

- In 2010 86% said "Yes."
- In 2008 73% said "Yes."
- In 2006 84% said "Yes."

Notice that prior to the Great Recession and after, ERM carried the same sense of urgency or importance.

Reason Eight: Black Swans

According to Nassim Nicholas Taleb who coined the term in his book *The Black Swan: The Impact of the Highly Improbable*, a black swan is an event that has high magnitude and low frequency. For an event to be considered a black swan it has three attributes:

- It is an outlier, which means it falls outside the realm of normal expectations.
- It carries an extreme impact.
- Despite its outlier status, human nature makes us concoct explanations for its occurrence after the fact, making it explainable and predictable.

In most applications of ERM, users focus their attention on normal or frequently occurring risks, even if they are improbable, such as a citywide fire or an epidemic outbreak. Yet ERM could and should be used to include scenarios when brainstorming for potential risks.

Although no one could be expected to predict Japan's 2011 earthquake, tsunami and nuclear plant explosion, any firm that outsources its entire production facilities to one location is taking on a huge risk. Many U.S. companies that did entirely rely on Japan as their only source of production, such as Toyota and Mazda, were negatively affected. This sort of vulnerability needs to be examined, so the organisation can come up with a backup or mitigation plan.

Similarly, China's recent decision to limit exports of rare earth elements hurt the automotive, energy and high-tech industries. This might be considered as beyond the realm of possibility, but when something is rare and necessary for your products, it must be discussed in a what if manner. This type of forward pessimistic thinking is what contributes to your organisation having the confidence to survive anything, including a black swan event.

Reason Nine: Attempts to Legislate Out Fraud Were Doomed

ERM, if properly applied, can prevent or at least deter fraud because of the increase in transparency. Any area that could be at risk for fraud from the inside or out will be managed and monitored. Also ERM requires that the cultural norms and attitudes towards ethical conduct be addressed and elevated.

Each time a major fraud takes place, a new law designed to stop the fraud from occurring is enacted, yet legislating fraud does not work. Despite the fraud provisions contained in the Sarbanes-Oxley Act of 2002 and the Dodd-Frank Wall Street Reform and Consumer Protection Act, it is still relatively easy for people to commit fraud, as it was during the days of Enron, WorldCom, and so on. According to the article "Where There's Smoke, There's Fraud" in the March 2011 issue of *CFO* magazine, there is a consensus amongst fraud experts that financial games and unethical practices have markedly increased. The method and ways of committing financial fraud have not significantly changed, and traditional measures of corporate governance still have limited impact on predicting fraud. With the amount of financial malfeasance that takes place, if fraud were the flu, its size and scope would qualify as a pandemic.

Fraud is not a one-time event. It is like a cancer that spreads. The risk consulting firm Kroll reported in the 2010–11 *Global Fraud Report* that business losses due to fraud increased 20% in 12 months, from $1.4m to $1.7m per billion dollars of sales. Kroll surveyed over 800 senior executives from 760 companies around the world and found that 80% of the respondents reported being victims of corporate fraud over the last 12 months.

In the March 2011 issue of *CFO* magazine, the article "Where There's Smoke, There's Fraud," states that, often, the institutions that are established to protect investors and the public are not effective. Sam E. Antar is the former CFO of the now defunct electronics chain Crazy Eddie. He and his cousin, the firm's CEO, were indicted for defrauding shareholders. He now lectures on corporate fraud. Sam, who has an insider's perspective, is pessimistic about the efforts to prevent fraud. "Nothing's changed. Wall Street analysts are just as gullible, internal controls remain weak, and the SEC is underfunded and, at best, ineffective. [Bernie] Madoff only got caught because the economy tanked. If I were out of retirement today, I'd be bigger than Bernie Madoff."

Of course we cannot forget the human element of fraud. Today many people have the attitude, "It's my turn to get rich," and they find shortcuts for getting what they believe they deserve. Steve Pedneault heads the firm Forensic Accounting Services, a company that arrives after fraud occurs to assess the damage. Steve commented in the same article, "There's a lot more employee fraud and embezzlement today than there was 10 years ago, and this past year [2010] there was much more than a year ago. People blame the economy, but much of the fraud and embezzlement that's coming to the surface now was in the works for four or five years before the recession hit."

Reason Ten: Accounting Practices Allow Game Playing

As a CPA this one concerns me. The accounting profession has yet to take a position on the enforcement of ethical accounting. This honoured profession can undermine risk management when it allows a firm's management to bend the rules in their favour. An extensive study was conducted on the failure of Lehman Brothers by the federal government, and its findings illustrate how accounting can allow unethical executives to play a shell game. The collapse of Lehman Brothers illustrates how leaders in an organisation can override efforts to practise proper risk management. This tale contains many of the reasons I cited: unreasonable expectations, governance was not a priority, demand for profit, complexity was hiding the problem, ERM was not an executive priority and existing accounting practices allowed games to be played.

Case Study– Lehman Brothers' Demise

In March 2010 the report of the bankruptcy examiner outlined the reasons for Lehman Brothers' failure and described how the firm's deteriorating financial position led to aggressive and allegedly misleading financial reporting practices. The findings of the report were summarised in the August 2010 issue of *Strategic Finance* magazine in the article "Lehman's $hell Game."

> In 2006, Lehman made a deliberate business decision to pursue a higher-growth business strategy. To do so, it switched from a low-risk brokerage model to a high-risk, capital-intensive banking model. Prior to 2006, Lehman would acquire assets primarily to "move" them to third parties, but starting in 2006, it acquired assets to "store" them as its own investments, hence internalizing the risk and returns of those investments. The mismatch between short-term debt and long-term, illiquid investments required Lehman to continuously roll over its debt, creating significant business risk. Lehman borrowed hundreds of billions of dollars on a daily basis. Since market confidence in a company's viability and debt-servicing ability is critical for accessing funds of this magnitude, it was imperative for Lehman to maintain good credit ratings.

Lehman pursued "an aggressive 13% growth rate in revenues. To support this growth, the company was targeting an even faster (15%) increase in his balance sheet and capital base."

Lehman's new strategy drastically increased its exposure to risk because its investments in long-term assets "had more uncertain prospects and were less liquid than its traditional investments. As the subprime crisis unfolded, the company doubled its holdings in illiquid investments" from $87 billion to $275 billion in less than two years. "Lehman couldn't use these assets to generate cash on short notice or as collateral to borrow funds."

> Lenders using common sense and good risk management will not accept illiquid assets as collateral because doing so increases their risk should the borrower default. There is no viable way to hedge investments in illiquid assets (commercial land and buildings, private equity, and leveraged loans) because they are difficult to value.

This practice further increased its risk of potentially large losses should Lehman's assets lose their value, which they did. "As economic conditions worsened and markets declined in 2007 and 2008, Lehman slid further into financial distress and had to reduce its exposure and leverage."

The more leveraged a company, the more important it is for the company to quickly act when market conditions turn against it. Lehman did not have that ability to swiftly act because of its real illiquidity.

"Lehman had difficulty selling its illiquid assets so was unable to reduce its leverage rapidly through typical means." It could "only offload their assets at a steep loss that would negatively impact the company in two ways. First, recognizing losses on the sale of assets would reduce equity. Second, the market's negative perceptions of the quality of Lehman's remaining assets would make it difficult for Lehman to borrow." In response to its deteriorating ability to borrow huge amounts of cash, "Lehman attempted to paint a rosy—but misleading—picture of its financial health by employing an accounting trick the company called 'Repo 105' and 'Repo 108.'"

Financial institutions commonly use sales repurchase agreements, or repos, to finance their security position. They transfer securities as collateral for short-term borrowing to obtain cash. This transaction is completed in two phases. The borrower (bank) receives cash and transfers security stock to the lender. Later the company repays the borrowed amount with interest and repossesses the securities. The security amount transferred as collateral slightly exceeds the amount borrowed by approximately 2%. This excess is the discount and is commonly called "the haircut."

"Lehman created a new type of repurchase agreement. While a typical haircut was about 2% for the period under discussion, Lehman took haircuts of 5% for fixed income securities and 8% for equity securities." For example if Lehman borrowed $100 million, it would transfer either $105 million of fixed income securities or $108 million of equity securities to its lender.

By taking this larger discount, Lehman characterised these transactions as a sale of a security, in accordance with its interpretation of Financial Accounting Standards Board Statement No. 140, *Accounting for Transfers and Servicing of Financial Assets and Extinguishment of Liabilities—a replacement of FASB Statement No. 125.* Lehman then recorded as a current asset, with an option to repurchase on a specified date, the difference between the value of the securities transferred and the cash received.

> No liability was recorded when cash was received. Instead, the Investment Securities account (an asset account) was credited. Additionally, since the difference between the amount of securities transferred and cash received was allocated to an asset account, no gain or loss was recorded on the sale of the securities. Structuring a transaction as a Repo 105 left total assets, total liabilities, equity, and income unchanged at the time of the initial borrowing. This accounting treatment contrasts with a normal repo transaction, which increases both assets and liabilities.
>
> As a separate transaction, Lehman would use the cash it borrowed to "pay down" other liabilities, reducing both assets and liabilities. At a later date, when the cash is paid back and the securities "repurchased," the journal entry to record the purchase would [recognise the discount (haircut) as an interest expense].

Again, for all intents and purposes, the transaction looked and smelled like a loan, not a sale.

> While the use of Repo 105 accounting had no material impact on the income statement, there was a significant impact on the balance sheet. Whereas accounting for ordinary repurchase agreements increases both total assets and total liabilities, Lehman's Repo 105 accounting didn't increase either assets or liabilities in the first leg of this transaction. When the cash proceeds from Repo 105 and 108 transactions were used to settle liabilities, both total assets and total liabilities were reduced, equity remained unchanged, and the leverage ratio improved.
>
> Lehman continued to receive the stream of income through coupon payments from the securities it transferred. Additionally, just as in an ordinary repo transaction, Lehman was obligated to "repurchase" the transferred securities at a specified date. "Moreover, Lehman used the same documentation to execute both Repo 105 and ordinary repo transactions, conducting these transactions with the same collateral agreements substantially with the same counterparties. Thus the two transactions were similar in substance but differed significantly with respect to their balance sheet impact.
>
> Since Repo 105 was a more expensive source of financing compared to ordinary repo agreements, its usage was timed around the end of reporting periods.

Here's how this worked. The total amount of Repo 105 transactions on February 28, 2008 (the end of the first fiscal quarter) was $49 billion. This dipped to $24.6m as of April 30, 2008. At the end of the second quarter (May 31, 2008) it jumped to $50.4 billion.

"Asset reduction and the consequent liabilities reduction were critical to Lehman because of its urgent need for short-term financing. To obtain favorable financing terms and maintain investor confidence, Lehman had to maintain its superior credit rating as well as a favorable report from financial analysts."

The leverage ratio is a widely accepted measure of a company's health and the financial sector.

> Lehman defined its leverage ratio as net assets divided by equity. Its measurement of net assets eliminated certain types of assets from total assets, including intangibles and assets held as collateral. A reduction in net assets without a corresponding change in equity reduces the leverage ratio and boosts a company's perceived health. Accounting for a transaction as a Repo 105 instead of an ordinary repurchase agreement reduced assets and improved Lehman's leverage ratio.

The use of Repo 105 improved Lehman's reported net leverage by as much as 1.9 percentage points.

> In hindsight it's clear that Lehman's reported leverage ratios misstated the company's financial position, and, arguably, the amount of the misstatement was material.
>
> The foremost concern …is Lehman's assertion that its Repo 105 transactions satisfy certain criteria in SFAS No. 140 that seem to proscribe their treatment as short-term loans and thus require accounting for them as sales. Since Lehman was apparently the only bank using Repo 105-type transactions during this time period, and since apparently no U.S. law firm

> would support Lehman's accounting treatment, the conclusion that Lehman's interpretation of SFAS No. 140 had "general acceptance" seems tenuous.

As for disclosure of its risk and deviation from generally accepted accounting principles (GAAP),

> a review of Lehman's 10-K and 10-Q forms won't reveal Lehman's use of Repo 105 transactions ... Since the only apparent purpose of executing Repo 105 transactions in lieu of ordinary repo transactions was to manage Lehman's leverage ratios in its financial statements, Lehman's management must have known Repo 105 activity would affect users' judgments."

> Lehman was entitled to collect interest and dividends from the "sold" securities. Additionally, Lehman used identical contract agreements and paperwork to document both normal repurchase agreements and Repo 105 transactions, implicitly acknowledging that the transactions were similar in substance.

In its conclusion the bankruptcy examiner's report stated, "Lehman Brothers failed to adhere to the principles contained in [other accounting profession guidelines]." Its management unwisely acted and failed to implement an ethical culture within the organisation. In using its Repo 105 and 108 transactions, Lehman may have complied with the letter of existing financial reporting rules but definitely not the spirit. The actions it took were certainly unethical and intentionally misleading in order to cover a serious problem. Top management at Lehman failed to reinforce the system of internal controls. They were intent on reporting favourable leverage ratios and structured transactions to hide the substance and incredible risks without regard for the ethical implications of their actions.

Lehman Brothers, like WaMu, claimed to have formal risk management programmes in place prior to its demise.

The Moral of the Case Study

GAAP is guidelines established by the accounting profession to advise public companies on the proper way to account for turnover, expenses and so on. These principles are not rules or laws, only guidelines, so a company can choose to apply a principle in a way that makes it look good, as Lehman's management did.

GAAP is often criticised as being rules based and as serving as a poor model for reporting profits because it permits the recording of transactions in a way that emphasises form over substance. Management accountants and auditors, however, violate professional standards whenever they allow their employers or clients to apply GAAP in a manner that deliberately obscures the economic substance of the transaction. A core objective of proper financial reporting is that the form of an accounting practice is irrelevant. What's relevant is its economic substance. Even though Lehman claimed the Repos 105 and 108 were a sale by the way the transaction was recorded (the form), they were actually loans (the substance). Lehman used this form over substance approach for two years before it imploded.

Although one could argue that Lehman's external auditors are at fault for failing to detect and report shortcomings in their financial reporting process, the ultimate responsibility lies with Lehman's management for developing and using Repo 105 for the purpose of managing its balance sheet.

The final key lesson from Lehman's and WaMu's implosions is that corporate governance must apply to all organisations. The need for an ethical culture is perhaps greatest when an unplanned event occurs. Without a policy to refer to, employees will develop a course of action they believe represents the official policy of the organisation. Their actions will be based on what they believe are the organisation's values or moral code, but that may not be the case.

Sign of the Future?

Ernst & Young issued a report, *The multi-billion dollar black hole: Is your governance, risk and compliance investment being sucked in?*, on governance in the financial sector, the industry whose actions caused the first dominos to fall.

> Now, in the aftermath of the most severe economic crisis in a generation, they [financial and investment institutions] are acutely conscious of the need to demonstrate sound risk management. They believe that their reputations, customer loyalty and even their credit rating and access to capital depend on it. Some reports suggest that financial institutions alone will spend about US $100 billion globally on mitigating risk in 2010; others indicate that US companies alone will invest US $29.8 billion over the same period.

Ernst & Young also reported that "69% of companies believe that investors and shareholders increasingly look to [risk management] as a measure of their corporate stability. Companies are unwilling to tolerate and unable to afford lapses in risk management and, as a result, they spend even more shoring up their [ERM] capabilities as a defence against failure."

Appendix C
Enterprise Risk Management

Tracy, Grace and several other managers asked if I could provide them with more technical information about enterprise risk management (ERM). Tracy said, "I know that you simplified much of the details, and I appreciate that. Can you provide information for us to obtain a deeper understanding of this emerging best practice?"

For Tracy, Grace and anyone who would like a little more information about ERM, enjoy this appendix, starting at its overall purpose and inception. Based upon a career spent analysing risk and leadership's impacts, I offer the following view, especially for auditors and CFOs.

Purpose of ERM

ERM enables an organisation's leaders to deal with any uncertainty that harms a firm's value, which are aspects of the entity that shareholders and other stakeholders are interested in protecting.

The Committee of Sponsoring Organizations of the Treadway Commission and ERM's Inception

ERM represents a fundamental shift in the way businesses must approach everyday risk. As our economy becomes more service and technology driven and globally oriented, businesses cannot afford to let new, unforeseen areas of risk remain unidentified or ignored. We now have more guidance on the implementation of a consistent ERM structure from the Commission of Sponsoring Organizations of the Treadway Commission's (COSO's) ERM framework. The framework defines and describes ERM and provides a standard against which businesses can assess their ERM programme and determine how to improve it. This effort began in 1984 when COSO first addressed the issue of internal controls and inherent risks to respond to excessive frauds, scandals and audit failures.

In 2004 COSO crafted this definition of global and holistic risk management: "Enterprise risk management is a process effected by an entity's board of directors, management and other personnel, applied in strategy setting and across the enterprise, designed to identify potential events that may affect the entity, and manage risk to be with his risk appetite, to provide reasonable assurance regarding the achievement of entity objectives."

In 2009 COSO then issued the framework *Enterprise Risk Management—Integrated Framework*. This framework builds upon the 1992 report that addressed auditing internal control. The updated ERM framework was written by PricewaterhouseCoopers on behalf of COSO. This guideline contains key concepts and components of effective risk management, such as philosophy, risk appetite and looking at risk as a portfolio.

COSO more recently issued a white paper, *Strengthening Enterprise Risk Management for Strategic Advantage*, that it believed would be a helpful resource and that articulates the strategic value of effective ERM. A second white paper, *Effective Enterprise Risk Oversight: The Role of the Board of Directors*, discusses four core responsibilities of boards in the oversight of their organisation's processes.

Lessons from M&M Candy

M&M candy is one thing universally loved and enjoy. Their catchphrase years ago was, "Melts in your mouth, not in your hands." The concept was that the protective shell insured that the inner chocolate would not bleed out in the warmth of your hands.

ERM applies a protective cover at multiple levels that works to detect, deflect and defend against all pesky perils that move towards your firm. Firm value is the vulnerable centre you want to protect most of all.

The entire organisation is moving towards some sort of reward, usually in the form of capturing opportunities that turn into revenue and growth or another important result. However, in addition to the costs associated with opportunity, risks are all around you. All sorts of risks, represented by the lightning bolts in Figure C-1, occur from many sources, such as

Figure C-1
Risk Is All Around You

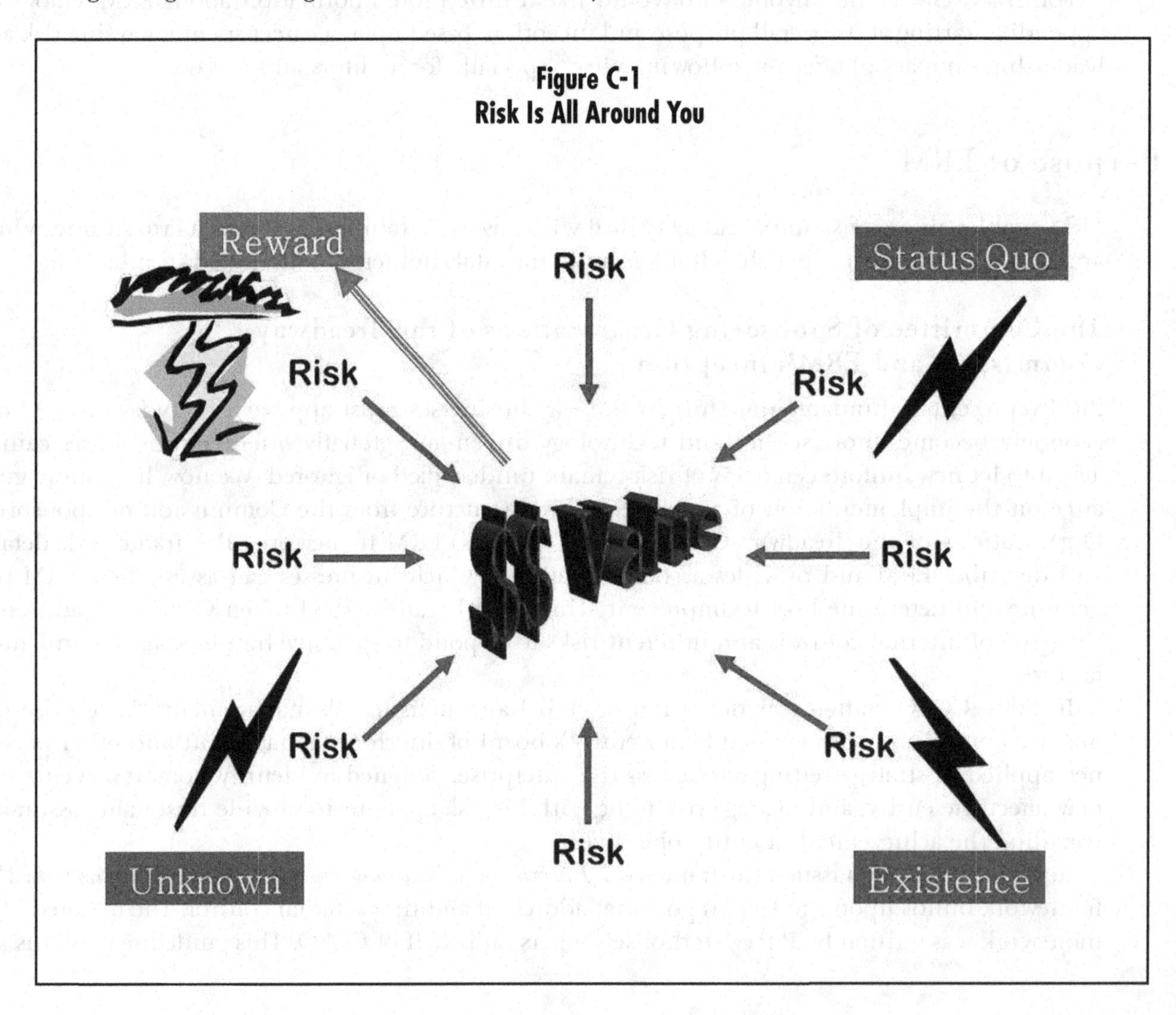

- the status quo.
- the unknown.
- just being in existence.

Your risks could harm firm value. Your ERM culture and methodology work to deflect, defer and minimise most of the risks. Although some of the risks will break through this protective shell, your organisation is strong enough to deal with those few risks that get past the ERM structure, as shown in Figure C-1.

ERM is designed to be just like an M&M with the hard shell. As shown in Figure C-2 ERM provides a protective coating to the core, which is your firm's value.

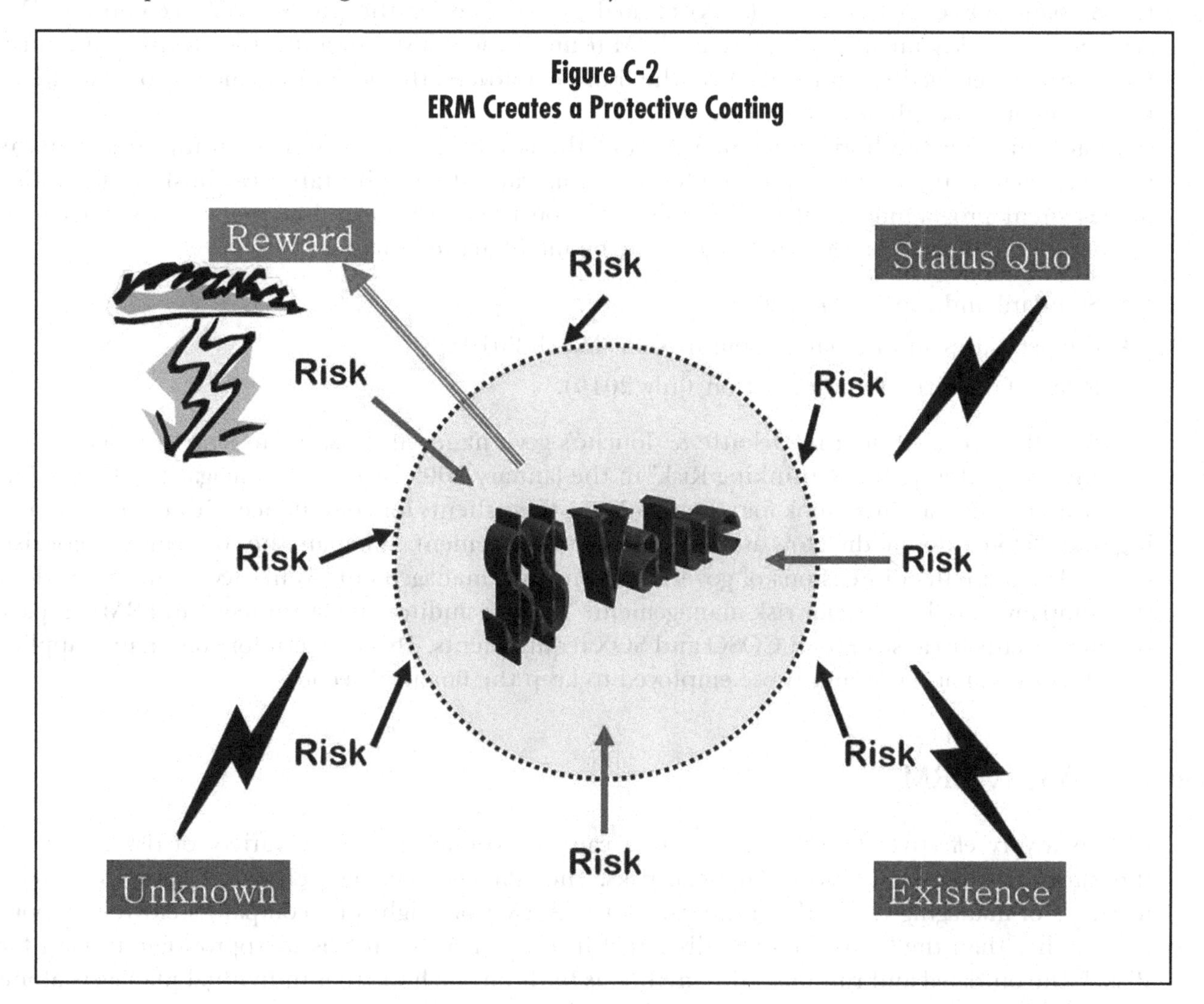

Success Requires ERM

Effective risk management is a critical component of any winning management strategy. Properly designed, a risk management programme allows an organisation to actually take on additional risk while more securely growing. Options for treatment of exposure to loss include avoidance, reduction, contractual transfer, insurance transfer and retention. The most effective treatment of risk usually involves the application of more than one of these methods. Experienced coordination of the selected methods of treatment is essential to effect real change and accurately monitor results.

Because no one organisation can house the broad scope of expertise needed to address the full spectrum of risk faced in an evolving economy and marketplace, it is essential to enrol and engage employees in your organisation to be part of the risk management programme. This works to bring about success through a holistic firm wide awareness.

Finance's Role in ERM

Finance managers and auditors must recognise that their role includes providing assurance that controls are in place for detecting and monitoring problems. Both COSO's recent framework and the Sarbanes-Oxley Act of 2002 (SOX) created a new role for the professional accountant. The accountant is a key member of the firm's ERM team. Becasue a significant business risk could arise from nearly every action undertaken by the firm's employees, the accountant needs to be aware of the causes and contributors to costly risk.

Changes are on the horizon for members of the accounting profession regarding risk management, as well as their clients and employers. Firms can either voluntarily establish a viable risk management programme, or it will be mandated on them. The organisations and laws that now require a formal risk management programme be implemented include

- Standard and Poor's (May 2008).
- the Securities and Exchange Commission (March 2010).
- federal financial reform legislation (July 2010).

Henry Ristuccia, a leader in Deloitte & Touche's governance and risk management practice, was interviewed in the article "Rethinking Risk" in the January 2009 issue of *CFO* magazine about what public accountant auditors look for when auditing their clients for compliance with the rule regarding risks. "More external directors are asking senior management: What are the company's major risk issues? What are the dimensions of governance and risk management? What levers and tools does the company have in place for risk management?" Today's auditors must understand ERM's impact on their clients because of both COSO and SOX requirements. This concern for compliance applies to both internal auditors and those employed to keep the financial records.

How to Apply ERM

ERM is a very effective strategy that any firm can use to manage a wide variety of risks, running the gamut from strategic risks to financial risks. The difference between ERM and more traditional methods of managing risk is that ERM calls for high-level oversight of a company's entire risk portfolio, rather than the "silo" approach discussed in chapter 5, "WHEN Is It Appropriate to Plan for Risk?" The outdated and ruinous "silo" method is built on the hope that individual managers alone will identify and oversee specific risks.

These are a few of the key decisions your firm's leader must make early on when implementing a risk management programme:

- Who leads it?
- What sorts of risk are included in the analysis?
- What happens after a risk is assessed?
- How is the risk reported?
- How will the risk be followed up?

- What is the tipping point between accepting a risk and doing something?
- What are the employees' roles in assessing and monitoring risk?

ERM centralises all risk management under a chief risk officer (CRO) position or a risk committee that supports the individual risk owners to help each one of them identify how much risk the entire entity can tolerate, formulate mitigation strategies and otherwise capture advantages of risk opportunities.

Meanwhile some large firms have created a CRO position to monitor and manage risk. Other firms have opted for a decentralised approach. Some CFOs embrace the holistic approach of risk management so much that they tell the senior leaders that appointing a CRO is not necessary. Virgin Mobile chose to decentralise that function. CFO John Feehan said in the same *CFO* magazine article previously mentioned that his firm's relatively small size of 400 employees allows it to take a hands-on approach to risk by "perceiving risk management as part of our daily life. We don't separate it out as a separate function; it's just a part of how we manage every aspect of the business."

A growing number of risk management experts are urging their companies and clients to shift away from risk management specialists and move towards having a broader base of employees involved in managing risk. Proper risk management is done by gathering information from the various people overseeing risk areas and using the combined knowledge to determine the threats to the organisation, their financial impact and the effectiveness of the firm to handle such risk. The goal, of course, is to determine the appropriate amount of capital you need to protect yourself from risk. The risk committee is the champion for the information gathering efforts.

Risk requires absorbing, hedging or transferring risk and applying capital to it, which is money that could be spent in other parts of the business. This view of throwing dollars at risk or the cost of ERM, in effect, helps the organisation's leaders determine the right amount of capital that should be directed towards risk.

ERM's Global Risk Plan

Within the ERM structure or framework, the firm establishes a risk definition and the tolerance levels (the cost you cannot afford), as well as the policies and procedures required to assess and measure the risk and create systems for monitoring. While implementing ERM your leaders need to conduct a regular check-in to determine the easiest, best and cost effective ways to answer these questions for risk.

For risk strategy

- What is our organisation's ERM strategy?
- How is the ERM strategy communicated and executed throughout our company?

For risk ownership

- How does each division, unit or team contribute to meeting our goals of the ERM strategy?
- How are our teams and the individuals involved held accountable for success?

For risk identification

- What is our organisation's definition of risk?
- What are our organisation's top five risks?

For risk ranking

- What is the estimated probability for the top five risks?
- What are the financial consequences to our company?

- Which risks are material?
- How should our identified risks be prioritised?

For risk treatment (mitigation and abatement)

- How are these risks currently managed?
- Is the approach effective, or is there an alternate approach?

For risk solutions

- What risk management processes are appropriate based upon the findings of the preceding elements?
- What risk-addressing action plans should be in place?
- How are risks to be monitored?

ERM– Self-Sustaining Evergreen Process

Effective risk management has gone from an attitude of, "I would like to do," to a frame of mind of, "We must do this." It is something you want employees to think about. This requires making it a self-perpetuating system. You accomplish this by emphasising that ERM is a continuum.

Figure C-3 is a visual view of the ERM continuum. It starts with defining risk then moves to providing employees with tools to identify risk. From there ERM requires using tools to do risk scoring and cost valuation while ensuring that someone owns the responsibility for the many people managing the risk. The next two steps include employing a protocol for risk recovery and defining specific action plans for learning from the risks taken. Notice this continuum follows the continuous six steps that we will be following in this book's main content to create a risk and balanced culture.

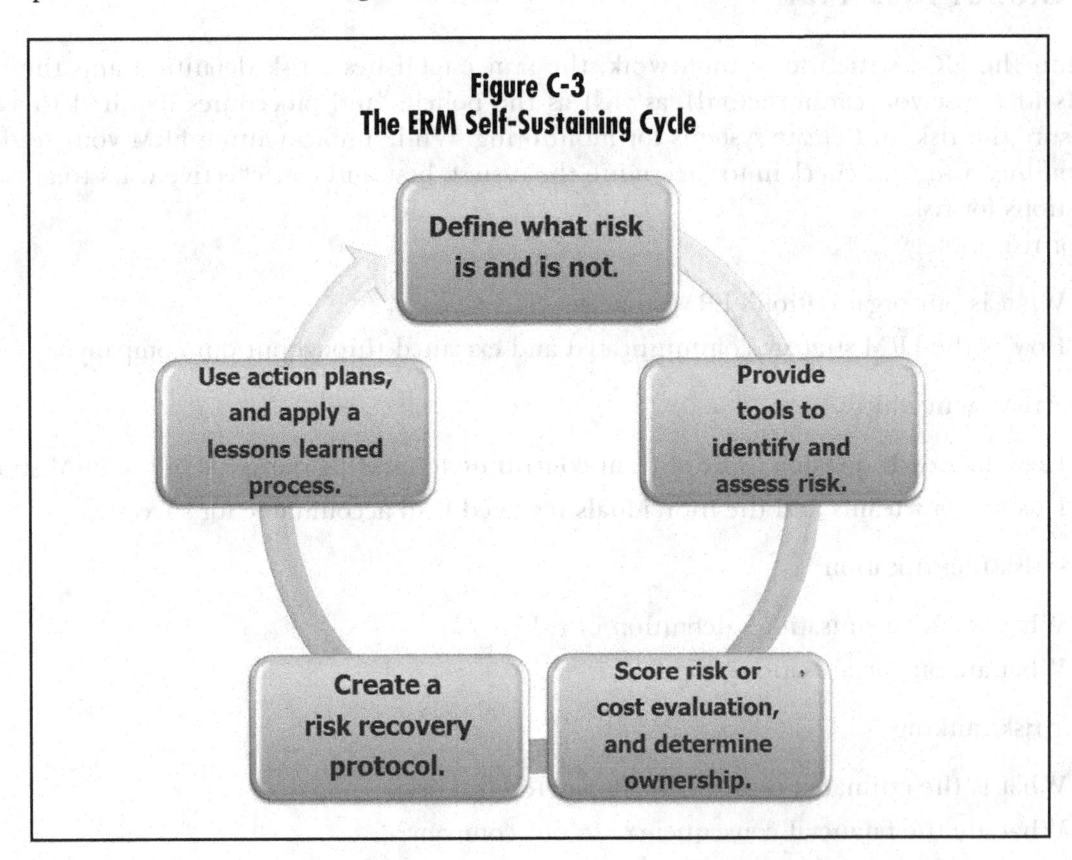
Define what risk is and is not.
Provide tools to identify and assess risk.
Score risk or cost evaluation, and determine ownership.
Create a risk recovery protocol.
Use action plans, and apply a lessons learned process.

Figure C-3
The ERM Self-Sustaining Cycle

ERM and Controls

Your firm must implement sufficient controls within each process to ensure that the risk will likely be detected. An effective risk process

- gathers and compares actual and forecast information.
- measures the potential risk.
- calculates the cost.
- suggests alternatives or options to minimise the risk.

Risk controls should be integrated into your firm's operational and financial controls because the two systems overlap. An effective control process

- runs on a transparent and an auditable platform.
- forces a clear separation of roles and responsibilities.
- incorporates business processes that enforce compliance for both external regulatory issues and internal policy compliance.

ERM and People

Studies have shown that successful managers have a propensity for taking risk. At the same time the driving force behind risky and rash decisions is risk aversion. This occurs because when making decisions, people in both business and life tend to focus more on what they could lose rather than what they could gain.

This drive for success and risk clashes with your internal cultural structures. Pressures that arise from financial accountability often block or send messages to managers to not take risks. As a direct result only a crisis forces most managers to take anything more than an ordinary risk.

Bureaucratic corporate cultures in larger organisations discourage risk taking. Managers in big companies take fewer risks than managers in smaller companies. When making a risky decision many managers have trouble figuring out how much data is sufficient and how much is overkill. Greed and jealousy cloud rational judgement and can lead to risky behaviours that have nothing to do with taking a risk.

In the end how often you have successfully risked and "won" in the past affects your ability to take a risk in the future.

Strategic Risk Management

The strategic management of risk taking is the latest twist on ERM. Strategic risk management is a process of identifying, assessing, and managing risks and uncertainties that are affected by internal and external events that could inhibit an organisation's ability to achieve its strategy and strategic objectives. Its ultimate intent is to create and protect shareholder and stakeholder value, and it is a primary component and necessary foundation of ERM. In risk management you must understand the risks that shape your firm's corporate strategy and the chosen tactics to implement that strategy.

Companies are adopting strategic risk management because they recognise that a great strategy will lead to sustainable success. The primary function of the board of directors is to oversee the development of strategy and its ethical execution. As risk management becomes a key agenda item for boards, connecting the strategy to the risk management effort is a natural progression. In strategic risk management an organisation must define and assess those key risks that can prevent it from achieving those strategic plans. This is accomplished by establishing key performance indicators, along with key risk indicators.

The steps of strategic risk management generally match those of ERM

- *Step One.* Assess the maturity of the organisation to achieve a deep understanding of the strategy and related risks.
- *Step Two.* Gather views and data on strategic risks.
- *Step Three.* Review the process for identifying risks in the strategy setting process.
- *Step Four.* Review the process for measuring and monitoring the organisation's performance.
- *Step Five.* Develop an ongoing process to periodically update the assessments of strategic risks.

ERM and Growth

One strategic goal common to numerous organisations is growth. Although not a strategy by itself, the other global strategies embarked on by the executive team will hopefully lead to sustainable and ethical growth. However, as you realise, growth carries costs you may not be able to afford.

Risk in Emerging Markets

According to the Multilateral Investment Guarantee Agency's report, *World Investment and Political Risk 2010,* over the next three years the most commonly cited political risks while doing business in developing nations include

- breach of contract (51%).
- regulatory changes (43%).
- transfer and convertibility restrictions (41%).
- not honouring sovereign guarantees (32%).
- civil disturbance (31%).
- expropriation (22%).
- terrorism (19%).
- war (10%).

Onward

As a direct result of the damage to the U.S. financial systems, boards and executives are taking risk management seriously. However implementation of risk management is in a very immature stage, particularly in small and mid-sized organisations.

Companies are just starting to become aware and proactive in revisiting risk management, but the transformations are slow in coming. At long last corporate directors in some industries have elevated risk awareness as something that must be on the executive team's continuing agenda. Risk management has taken many forms: simple awareness, informal programmes and corporatewide ERM.

A survey sponsored by *CFO* magazine and conducted by Towers Perrin found that companies are more interested in systematic solutions to risk management than they have been in the past. Nearly half the respondents expect to implement broad changes to their risk management policies and practices that will affect both the shop floor and board. The jury is still out on whether ERM will be part of every organisation's culture.

Printed in the United States
By Bookmasters